POPULAR DIPLOMACY AND WAR

By

SISLEY HUDDLESTON

RICHARD R. SMITH PUBLISHER, INC.

Rindge, New Hampshire

1954

Set up, printed and bound in
the United States of America by
The Colonial Press Inc.

Sisley Huddleston

CONTENTS

CONTENTS

i

.

FOREWORD

By Harry Elmer Barnes

THIS BOOK grew out of a visit that I paid to Sisley Huddleston at his home in Normandy early in September, 1951. For years, I had been an admirer of his wide knowledge of world affairs, his honesty, integrity, and intelligence. I had many years before contributed a Foreword to the American edition of one of his books on French history, but I had never met him personally, and I was delighted at this opportunity to visit him.

In the light of the conditions then prevailing, it was most natural that our conversation would turn to world affairs, and Mr. Huddleston was especially concerned with the sad state of diplomacy. This seemed to him to be the key problem in international affairs, based on the reasoning that unless diplomacy can avert a third World War, what remains of civilization faces destruction by atomic bombs, guided missiles, and bacterial and gas warfare. He discussed at length the many, impressive, and distressing contrasts between the old and the new diplomacy, and stressed the grave menace of the latter, while not denying that the older diplomacy had many defects and had been superseded by the newer or Popular Diplomacy mainly because it proved inadequate to the crisis of 1914.

His observations on this matter seemed so intelligent and cogent that I urged him to write a book on the subject. He consented and, lamentably, it proved to be his swan song, for he died on the very day that he finished the revision of the manuscript, Bastille Day, July 14, 1952.

Those professionally familiar with journalistic comments on world affairs between 1914 and 1938 need no introduction to Sisley Huddleston; not even Americans, for he was a frequent visitor to the United States and a contributor to leading American, as well as English, newspapers and liberal periodicals of the day. In the space available we can list only the more important of these.

Mr. Huddleston began his coverage of foreign news in 1915 when he took over the editorship of an army newspaper for British soldiers in the first World War. Later on, he served as the Paris Correspondent of the London *Times*, and European Correspondent of the London *Observer*, the *Westminster Gazeett, John O'London's Weekly*, and the *Christian Science Monitor*. He contributed extensively to the *Fortnightly Review*, the *Contemporary Review*, the *New Statesman, Blackwood's Magazine*, the *Atlantic Monthly*, the *New Republic, The Nation*, and the New York *Times*.

It was rather generally conceded that Mr. Huddleston was the ablest journalist who concentrated on international affairs between the two World Wars. His experiences and his main observations in this period are set forth in what may be regarded as his professional autobiography, *In My Time* (1938).

During these years Mr. Huddleston covered the Paris Peace Conference, the series of international conferences at San Remo, Spa, Stresa, Rappallo, and Locarno, the several Disarmament Conferences, and all important meetings of the League of Nations. Perhaps his most sensational feat was the scoop of a candid personal interview with Lloyd George when the latter finally became disillusioned about the probable outcome of the Paris Peace Conference. He was at one time President of the Anglo-American Press Association.

Mr. Huddleston was more than a journalist; he was a prolific and informed author, having some thirty books to his credit, eight of which were of a directly political and diplomatic nature. Probably the most illuminating of these prior to 1939 was *In My Time*, mentioned above. This was a trenchant firsthand review of the tragic succession of diplomatic blunders which led straight to the second World War. Although international affairs were his main interest, he also wrote with charm and insight on travel, topography, art and literature. He travelled and lectured extensively in the United States between 1920 and 1938, among other things amiably analyzing our culture and traits.

As was the case with many other honest observers, Mr. Huddleston's popularity and his former following faded away with the approach of the second World War; indeed his journalistic career virtually came to an end in the 1930's. The decline began with his honest and intelligent comments on the later days of the League of Nations and on the Spanish Civil War.

The non-totalitarian world was not prepared gracefully to receive his account of how Litvinov converted the League to the view that the only menace of totalitarianism resided in the threat from the Right. Had he been listened to then, the world would not now be tottering on the verge of total destruction. While, as a lifelong liberal and lover of peace, he appraised General Franco for what he was and still is, he discerned from afar the truth about the Spanish Civil War which even so astute an observer as George Orwell nearly gave his life to discover by personal participation in the conflict. Such honesty and intelligence were as distasteful amidst the welter of Communist and pseudo-liberal propaganda as his views on the pro-Communist tenor of League opinion in its twilight period.

Mr. Huddleston was too honest and realistic to sell his soul to the service of war-mongering propaganda after 1937, or the far worse propaganda of wartime, for any monetary reward or professional prestige, however great. He refused to participate in the journalistic debauch which catapulted so many reporters, especially American writers, from penury and obscurity into opulence and world fame. He retired to his charming home in a converted mill at St. Pierre d'Autils in Normandy, where he lived until the German invasion forced him to leave. Then he went to the neutral area of Monaco where he resided until the Allied counter-invasion of France. Thereupon, he returned to his devastated home in Normandy which he rebuilt and occupied until his death in 1952, although he spent his winters in Switzerland. After the War, he wrote the one honest book that I have read dealing with France during wartime and its aftermath. This will soon be published and will enable Americans to learn the vital and startling facts which have hitherto remained obscure or entirely hidden from public view. Since Mr. Huddleston made his home in France for most of the period after 1915 and married a French lady, it is not surprising that he became a French citizen in 1943.

Whatever view one takes of Sisley Huddleston's opinions on the theme of diplomacy, no informed person can well deny the vital importance of the subject itself. Only through effective diplomacy can a third World War be averted and, if the war comes, it will surely result in unparalleled devastation and world chaos. This was apparent enough in 1951 when I was discussing the matter with Mr. Huddleston. It is more certain today, and the devastation potential of warfare will increase with every passing year. In a Foreword it is not fitting to do more than outline the essentials of the argument. The full story is to be found in the book in the author's relentless logic and absorbing style.

As Mr. Huddleston described the situation to me and details it in this book, the older diplomacy was characterized by certain definite traits and policies which differentiate it sharply from the Popular Diplomacy which has prevailed since 1918, brought on the second World War, and seems to be hastening us toward a third world conflict and the terminal stage of human experience on the planet.

In the first place, the men who operated the diplomacy of earlier days, while they may not always have been experts in international law, or "career" diplomats, in the superficial sense of our day, were experts in that they were men of distinction with seasoned experience in public affairs. The names of Choiseul, Talleyrand, Metternich, Castlereagh, Beaconsfield, Bismarck and Salisbury will suffice to illustrate this point.

As such, the older diplomats were men of courtesy and good manners who observed the customary etiquette and protocol, however sharply their policies and objectives might conflict. They did not indulge in the billingsgate and personal abuse which is fitting only for political campaigns in democracies and the exchange of propaganda between totalitarian leaders—between a Goebbels and *Pravda.*

The older diplomats were able to conduct their negotiations in more or less complete secrecy, confident that they could bring a conference to its conclusion without pressure from an ignorant and explosive populace whipped to hysteria by public and private propagandists. They did not have to operate in a gold fish bowl harassed by kibitzers and smear artists representing sordid public and private interests.

While there were rare exceptions, such as the dramatic meeting of the monarchs on the Field of the Cloth of Gold, the heads of states and their foreign ministers usually remained in their offices in the capitals, entrusting diplomatic negotiations to trained emissaries, while devoting their own time and energies to digesting the reports of their representatives and formulating thoughtfully, on the basis of such information, what appeared to be wise policies which might decide the fate of mankind.

The older diplomats sought to limit wars so far as possible; they did not endeavor to convert every distant "dogfight" into a world war. The dangerous Muscovite myth of "collective security" and the mischievous doctrine that "peace is indivisible" were as yet unborn and did not plague and upset their labors. At the end of a war, the diplomats contented themselves with what was possible and practical and there was always a peace treaty which sought to resolve the existing problems and assure at least a decent period of peace after a major war.

Finally, the older diplomacy was really *diplomatic*. It rested upon the principle of "give-and-take," each emissary recognizing that it was unlikely that any absolute demands would be conceded. To compromise and conciliate was not regarded as wicked "appeasement," but was held to be the very foundation of all true diplomacy and international negotiations. There was no demand for "unconditional surrender" on the part of a defeated state, not even of France after Napoleon had been overthrown following years of bloody warfare and endless devastation.

Yet the older diplomacy broke down in 1914. It failed to prevent the first World War. This was due in large measure to the emergence of a new factor in the international scene, the power of the popular press which, to get news, sell papers, and make profits, blew up trivial diplomatic disputes into the proportions of major international crises and carried on campaigns of vilification against opposing nations. How this operated has been described in detail in the works of Oron J. Hale and Jonathan French Scott, to mention only books by American writers. Comparable exposures were written by men like Georges Demartial in France and Sidney Rogerson and Arthur Ponsonby in England. In short, the older diplomacy collapsed under the impact of what was to become the chief instrument of the new diplomacy, irresponsible publicity which sought political triumph or monetary profits rather than the peace of mankind.

This rise of the popular press to a position of dominance in the determination of world trends was the development that transformed what Gabriel Tarde described as "the public" into what Gustave Le Bon depicted as the hysterical and irrational crowd. Its progress was hastened by the indignant reaction, especially American reaction, to the Secret Treaties which gave the lie to American and British war propaganda during the first World War. Woodrow Wilson thought he had found the answer to such mendacity and calamity in "open covenants openly arrived at." The liberals of the world hailed this announcement, and the writer of this Foreword was one of those who believed that it meant a new and better era in world affairs but, alas, this was not to be.

The Franco-Prussian War of 1870 was followed by over forty years of freedom from any major war; President Wilson's proclamation has been followed by nearly forty years of incomparable and unprecedented world chaos, violence and devastation, and the worst is apparently yet to come. The Treaty of Versailles and allied pacts after the first World War, all negotiated after Mr. Wilson's bold words about "open covenants," were far more malicious and menacing than the Secret Treaties—indeed, than any outstanding peace treaties ever enacted in the previous history of mankind, and most of the treaties of 1918–1919 were actually negotiated in an atmosphere of secrecy equal to that which attended the Berlin Conference of 1878, despite the presence in Paris of a veritable army of reporters. These treaties after 1918 brought on the second World War and set the pattern for the arrival of the third.

A new and miscellaneous breed of men have appeared to operate the new or Popular Diplomacy. Some are trained career diplomats, but they usually find their hands tied by amateurs who hold the superior posts to which they have been appointed as a reward for social or political services. Men who have piled up great fortunes instructing private business interests how most safely and successfully to skirt or defy local, national or international law have been put in charge of State Departments and Foreign Offices. Military men—generals, admirals and air corps commanders—have forged to the front seeking to dictate foreign policies, a practice hitherto unknown in political experience on any such scale as now, and exacerbated by the vast and favorable ballyhoo accorded these professional military men in the public prints. Legislators have assumed almost daily to instruct secretaries of state and lesser diplomats. Demagogues of the Left and Right have sought to intimidate diplomats formerly subject only to the directives of the executive department of the government. That incompetence, indecision and chaos have resulted has been inevitable, and this is uniquely ominous in an era in which incitement to war means an invitation to planetary destruction.

Public abuse, boorishness, and arrogance, have replaced courtesy and traditional etiquette in the handling of international negotiations. Opposing blocs of nations hurl defiance and abuse at each other openly, often as much for domestic political consumption as for the shaping of world trends. Ambassadors arriving to present their credentials to the head of a state are abused and lectured before they have had an opportunity to lay aside their coats and canes.

There is no longer any opportunity for diplomats to conduct their business in privacy or secrecy until they have arrived at some decent settlement of their problems. There is incessant and pitiless publicity which impels diplomats to seek immediate partisan advantage and personal prestige rather than to arrive at the same solution of basic issues. The ablest diplomats are paralyzed by such surroundings and pressures. It is alleged that this goldfish-bowl diplomacy is necessary in democracies and among free peoples. But there is no logical reason why the more fundamental operations of top diplomats should not be as much safeguarded by secrecy as the top-secret plans of the General Staff of any army. The future of mankind, today, if there is to be any future, reposes more in the hands of the diplomats than in those of the military. The latter is only equipped to destroy.

The new agencies of publicity, the press, radio and television, the ease and speed of travel, and the zest for personal notice and acclaim have all encouraged diplomats, even foreign secretaries, to scurry about over the planet, holding frequent and invariably futile conferences which usually increase world tensions. They have little time left to be in their offices digesting basic facts and formulating sound policies.

The very core of the older diplomacy, the making of concessions and the principle of give-and-take, has been discredited and branded as wicked and futile appeasement. Opponents are expected to make a more or less unconditional surrender of their demands and ideology, or the international impasse must continue unresolved.

With the rise and perfection of modern methods of propaganda the publics of the past have been transformed into hysterical, vindictive and impatient crowds, in the process of which passive ignorance has been transmuted into sheer mass pathology. And diplomats cannot afford to ignore even pressures on this low level. Self-seeking politicians and publicity agents see to this.

Despite all the public talk to the contrary, there appears to be little real interest in promoting world peace. In fact, we are approaching the point where even sincere peace sentiments have become suspect and somewhat contemptible in the eyes of the conditioned public. Although the treaties after the first World War were fatally bad, at least treaties were negotiated. But there has been no general peace treaty after the second World War. Opposing groups of powers hurl at each other charges of plots for world conquest. The traditional policy of live-and-let-live and the coëxistence of opposing political and economic ideologies, which was the very basis of foreign policy until 1918, and especially of American foreign policy, has been abandoned. It is arrogantly assumed that one ideology or the other must conquer the world, even if nothing is left after the dubious conquest.

Opponents of democracy allege that all these defects of the new or Popular Diplomacy are the price of democracy and are limited to democratic countries. But no honest observer, however skeptical of the new diplomatic trends, can concede the truth of any such charge. The same methods and attitudes dominate the totalitarian states, even if their mode of operation is colored and modified somewhat by the techniques of despotic government.

Although Mr. Huddleston is pessimistic about the likely outcome of present trends, he does offer suggestions which might recover the best from the older diplomacy and merge it with the more commendable trends of free government.

The obstacles to success are, however, formidable. Publicity, representing an investment of many billions of dollars and carried to almost obscene excesses, has become a vested interest which even the vista of impending world destruction does not seem able to curb decisively. Alarming progress has been made toward entry into the essentials of the Orwellian era in which the masses are deliberately stirred to irrational fears and hatreds and the economies and political policies of the world are linked to perpetual cold or phony war, with the ever present danger that this may be let loose any day into a hot war of unlimited destructiveness.

While the Free World is avowedly combatting the menace of Communism with the most extreme thoroughness at home and abroad, it conducts its foreign policy under the slavish domination of, and in complete conformity with, the most sinister and dangerous Communist dogma which has thus far gained general acceptance—the myth of collective security which, following the Geneva Protocol and the Briand-Kellogg policy, Litvinov sold to the League of Nations liberals in the 1930's. As such great international lawyers as John Bassett Moore and Edwin M. Borchard have made clear, this can produce only that strange and menacing paradox of "perpetual war for perpetual peace." It is, perhaps, the most striking and alarming example of subservience to the "doublethinking" of an Orwellian system that the United States and the "Free Nations" should be conducting a world crusade against Communism in the very name and wholly within the framework of a shrewd Communist ruse.

Whatever the outcome, the publication of Mr. Huddleston's book means that the world will have been cogently warned of what may lie ahead unless a rational and responsible diplomacy can once more be placed in control of foreign affairs. That the author does not stand alone in recognizing the dangers of the newer diplomacy can be seen in recent and comparable warnings by such veteran and realistic authorities on diplomacy as Harold Nicolson in England and George F. Kennan in the United States, and such leading publicists as Walter Lippmann.

1
THE CLAMOR BOYS
ENTER DIPLOMACY

COMMONPLACES are the staple of conversation—and of most writing—and, therefore, nobody was astonished when an American professor, who had come with a party of students to Europe, remarked that all too many of the inventions and discoveries of the twentieth century had been turned to the destruction of mankind. The assertion is banal, and is neither to be confirmed nor refuted.

But in that Normandy orchard on the hillside, above the ancient mill that has survived the drums and tramplings of four centuries, we were startled to attention when he went on:

"Take the airplane: I do not deny that it has brought many benefits and, properly used, ought to have brought many more. But it has also, alas, been employed in the dropping of atom-bombs and the transport of the Clamor Boys."

The Clamor Boys! That is to say, the "pin-up" diplomats who fly from country to country, perpetually occupying public attention, keeping us in jitters as they publicly discuss the most delicate problems of international policy, parading on a hundred platforms, making our flesh creep by their prophecies of imminent war, or trying to soothe us occasionally with their Browningian declarations that

X . . .'s in the Kremlin (or the White House)

All's well with the world! (or, in the alternative, "all's wrong.")

For forty years I had watched the diplomats at work: I had

seen the deterioration of the diplomatic methods which, in my youth, were characterized by sobriety, discretion, dignity, decorum. They had become increasingly feverish and spectacular and, finally, they consisted of an unceasing hurrying to and fro, of brief but theatrical meetings, of endless debates, of agitation, of objurgation, of loud challenge. But it had not occurred to me to bracket the atom-bomb and the Clamor Boys as twin evils. Yet, at once, I saw that the professor was right. Not a day passes without large headlines in the newspapers that set our nerves on edge: one of the "stars" or "starlets" of diplomacy has made a statement meant to be sensational; we are bidden to be righteously wrathful or pleasantly confident; we are informed of the strength of the "enemy" or of our own—or, on the other hand, of our own weakness or the weakness of the "enemy"; we are gorged with atrocities (always on the other side), and regaled with blood-and-thunder stories of incredible misdeeds—which might be true, for nothing is too bad for the new kind of Dark Age into which we have entered.

The handshakes of the "top-of-the-bills" or the "bottom-of-the-bills," and of all the minor tableaux between, are photographed, interviews are accorded, speculation runs rife, mysteries are hinted at, there is a flourish of pens over heavily sealed documents, and the next day the show starts all over again. Or a rostrum is erected in the market-place, and delegates of all nations are given a glorious (or inglorious) opportunity for indulging in much-publicized insults; they all take their stand on preconceived positions; they do their best to frighten the public, to exacerbate its sentiments, to arouse scorn and hatred, and, generally, to produce a poisonous atmosphere from which, sooner or later, but inevitably, war must come.

To this sorry level has diplomacy, which was once the art of lubricating the wheels of international relations, fallen in our time! I have observed the decline, and I am not witnessing the downfall of popular diplomacy. Downfall it is, however long the performance may be continued before it is hissed off the stage—or the stage collapses beneath it. All men who have eyes to see how different is the current spectacle from that which, even in a single short lifetime, we have known, must turn away sadly in disgust.

At the outset, I must make it clear that my purpose is not to attack democracy as such. I criticize only a specious conception of democracy which insists that the public, as well as the players, should crowd on to the field. Certainly, the public has a right to decide, in the ultimate stage, on the issues of war and peace since, after all, it is the public which pays in both money and blood. But its business is to choose the players whom it trusts, not to interfere with their game. What is inadmissible is that the players should constantly call on the crowd to descend into the arena, or that the crowd should expect to be able to order the plays in accordance with its emotions. It is not un-democratic to suggest that there are certain subjects which are entirely outside the scope of mass intelligence; and to enlist their support for every move is to make defeat, in the long or the short run, certain.

Since I began my study of diplomacy, I have been aware of the growing influence of the crowd on statesmen, and of statesmen on the crowd, ever leading to disaster after disaster. It should have been apparent almost from the beginning that the "new diplomacy"—definitely adopted as the only proper kind of diplomacy after the first World War—was a ghastly error. But it has been so easy for the statesmen to float with the stream and obtain personal advantages from acquiescence in popular outcries, that it soon became sheer blasphemy to point out its defects.

That excellent and perspicacious diplomatic correspondent, Paul Scott Mowrer, had, like myself, misgivings as early as 1924, but he wrote, in *Our Foreign Affairs*, "the experiment is begun, and it must be seen through, and diplomacy must adjust itself accordingly." This, in spite of the fact that he recognized that "it is by no means certain that democratic peoples are going to be able to live up to their supervisory ambitions, for those who are public-spirited enough to be willing to devote a part of their leisure to the problems of statecraft are few."

He might have added that, among those few capable of understanding, there would certainly be found some with sinister intentions of misleading the public and, if they could obtain control of the machinery for manufacturing public opinion—i.e., the press, the radio, the cinema, etc.—then "democratically-controlled" diplomacy would be the negation of true diplomacy. He might also have added that the temptation for statesmen to curry popularity by appealing to mass emotions might prove irresistible.

Well, the "experiment" has been "seen through," in more senses than one. It has been carried to the point of world suicide. That is seeing it through to the bitter end. It has, likewise, been seen through, in that it has been detected for what it is, and I am quite sure that no genuinely diplomatically-minded man—as distinct from the demagogic vote-catcher —has any doubts whatever about its failure. But how is such a diplomatically-minded man to denounce the fatal mistake? It is certain that he will lose both place and power. Perhaps it is too late to oppose the current, but I, who have no place or power to lose, may make the attempt.

It is necessary—and more than time—to ask why the twentieth century, which opened so promisingly and has seen such an unprecedented development of our material resources, has become a political and moral shambles.

Science should have brought prosperity to mankind. It has brought, to nine-tenths of the world, mainly ruin. The education of the masses should have made for peace. It has apparently made—in spite of our hope of a more orderly world governed by law and reason—for the diffusion of that half-knowledge which is "a dangerous thing." Democratic control should have made for the discomfiture of the warring propensities of ambitious rulers. It has, on the contrary, twice forced on us "the wrong war in the wrong place at the wrong time," and it has been unable sanely to conclude its wars— which is even more important than to wage them success- fully. I believe in the untutored common sense of the average individual, but I do not believe in the common sense of the crowd, which absorbs and transforms the individual. The crowd has no intelligence; it has only sentiments. It has no clearly defined objectives; it has only blind antipathies. So we have had, instead of a "better world," constant upheavals, civil wars, revolutions, oppression, misery, widespread devas- tation, concentration camps, "displaced persons," immense massacres, and insensate destructions. After a dismal series of international conflicts without remission or mercy, we tremble at the dark prospect of a greater Armageddon in which our civilization, if not the globe itself, will be irremediably shat- tered.

If there is not by now a realization that something is wrong with the "new diplomacy," which has given us such results, I should like to know what fresh catastrophe will finally awaken us to realities.

Various causes have been urged and argued to explain the vast difference between the wars of the past forty years—the wars of the twentieth century—and the wars of preceding centuries. True, there have been Hundred Years' Wars and Thirty Years' Wars, which have left Europe exhausted; true, there have been periods of barbaric invasions. But, in modern times, which are supposed to be times of reason, there have been no wars which, for their intensity and ruthlessness, for their capacity of inflicting suffering, for their universality, can be compared with those which many of us have experi- enced in the past four decades. In their quality and kind, there are no wars in any age to be compared with ours. With the most effective weapons for destruction we have gone back to a primitive pitilessness. One could regard the French Revolutionary and Napoleonic wars as the precursors and pre-figuration of those that have afflicted our generation; and they, too, arose from mass movements and emotions. But even these wars, despite their reach and duration, were relatively localized. They were not planetary; they were internecine quarrels.

These new world-wide wars of our day, in which whole countries (Korea, for example) are completely wiped out without compunction, without special regret, nobody knows why, in a casual episodic manner; these world-wide wars which stretch from Germany to Japan, which involve great territories of two hundred million inhabitants like Russia, or still greater territories, of nearly five hundred million inhabitants like China, and the tiniest remote islands lost in the Pacific Ocean; these world-wide wars whose capitals are London and Washington, Moscow, Berlin and Tokyo, in which men, women, and children are slain by tens of millions, in which homes are shattered by hundreds of millions, in which nations are swallowed up, in which famine adds to the terrors of fire and slaughter, in which, when a mere hundred thousand soldiers fall, the incident is regarded as negligible, a minor item in an interlude euphemistically called a "cold" war; these world-wide wars which, in one form or another, have never ceased since 1914, and are not likely to cease while there are combatants left—these are a hitherto unknown phenomenon, the outcome of mass civilization—save the mark!—and of a system of popular diplomacy which, for forty years, we have held to be sacrosanct.

Will anyone dare to indict me for challenging the organizations and methods which were adopted not long ago, according to the measure of our lives, and have co-existed with an era of unprecedented havoc? Will anyone regard me as reactionary because I inquire into the relation of these organizations and methods to the patent fact of our impotence to check the process of ravaging and brutalizing our world? The bitter irony, the gigantic paradox, is that all the scurryings of ministers, the institution of Leagues of Nations, of U.N.'s, of conferences, of congresses, of commissions, of committees, the ballyhoo of Barnum in international affairs, were ostensibly designed to prevent such holocausts; they were designed, no doubt sincerely, to give us peace. At the best, we must acknowledge that they have failed. At the worst, we may wonder whether they are not actually the cause—or at least one of the causes—of the ills they were designed to cure.

The latter conclusion, should we reach it, may well appear stupendous. What! mankind is so feeble of intellect, is so lacking in self-restraint, is so much the prey of its own foolish impulses, that its best intentions turn inexorably to its damage? It is, of course, far too disingenuous to put the blame on a section of mankind. It is far too naïve to assume that we would have succeeded had everybody been like us. The first truth is that everybody *is* like ourselves, and that, if we have failed, it is not because half of mankind is good and the other half bad, but because we have all gone wrong somewhere. Unless we are profoundly penetrated with the consciousness of our essential sameness, it is altogether useless to begin our inquiry. It is our fault—or the fault of our leaders—that we have fallen into a mode of life that we all feel to be intolerable and senseless. It is plain that our institutions are not made to the measure of mankind, and that our limbs are being stretched on a Procrustean bed that is too long for us, or that we are too long for the Procrustean bed and are cutting off our limbs. The bed must be made to fit us, and not we the bed.

If I do not at present go the whole length of the conclusion that our institutions and methods are the root cause of our ills, they are at any rate the symptoms of the disease that has entered the body politic, and, in their turn, by our stimulation of the symptoms, they intensify the malady. The root cause of our sickness is the false belief that our foreign affairs should or can be conducted by the whole community, informed or ignorant, wise or foolish, in a state of excitement, in which we must all participate, instead of by trained specialists of the highest integrity and intelligence, who are not obliged to solicit the frenzied support of the public at every moment in order to obtain and maintain the functions to which they are called.

Who has not, in his secret heart, deplored the limelighted stage on which are compelled to strut the mannequins of diplomacy, amid the clatter of the press and the plaudits of the public? Who has not seen—though unable, because of the overwhelming weight of the new doctrine of diplomacy, to express his thought—that the incessant propaganda of the reporters, the movie news, the radio interviewers, can only render general accords—as distinct from accords antagonistic in their very nature, coalitions directed against other groups, and founded on animosity or fear—virtually impossible? And yet the protagonists of such methods on the world stage, who must be aware of the impossible handicap they carry, have come to expect and demand the agitation created around them. They look for a swarm of witnesses to their acts and movements. Self-advertisement has become the breath of their nostrils. Whether they are merely figureheads, the multifarious throng from the ends of the earth strutting their little hour, or are the leading personages in the drama, whose lightest words are recorded, whose vestments are described, whose menus are set out for our admiration, they have all learned to live in a whirl of comment, of adulation, or of criticism. Their performance would, indeed, be flat, and their existence stale and unprofitable, were they not borne up by a tornado of hullabaloo.

Not what they are but what they may be made to appear to the hungry multitude, not what they accomplish but how much noise they can provoke, have become their *raison d'être*. One has sometimes a certain pity for them when one thinks of the turmoil in which they work. Are they ever really alone? Do they have time to think? Are they not—and I do not exclude the highest and most belauded statesmen—by virtue of this treatment, pure automata, puppets pulled by the strings of public opinion, marionettes dancing for the pleasure of their audience?

Such is their condition, which has been made, at first slowly, and then with increasing swiftness, and they cannot, however able they may be, extract themselves from the swirl. They accept their servitude willingly enough, and that is surely a sign of their inferiority. I do not assert that they are always without talent or perception, but in so far as they do not rebel against the artificiality of their office they are insufficient for their functions.

In reality, I have known, in the course of my career, scores —indeed hundreds—of men whose business it was to conduct, or be conducted by, foreign affairs, and the majority have been as mediocre as are the majority of other professional men. Three or four of them were of outstanding ability and might have been real leaders had they not been compelled to pander to the wishes of the greatest number. Others have been modest and undemonstrative, efficient in their sphere, but to them did not go the prizes reserved for the "clever" politicians. Nobody who, like myself, has been brought into daily contact—sometimes intimate contact—with public men for many years would honestly venture to pass a more favorable judgment than mine.

In passing, I will recall a conversation I had with one of the advisers of a great American party some time before the nomination of presidential candidates. He told me that X. . . would probably be selected, and he predicted unhappy results on account of the notorious flippancy of his character. "Why then choose him?" I asked. He explained that so-and-so was a Catholic, that another was a League of Nations man, that a third (and he the best) was not a good mixer. By a process of elimination, X. . . was left; but X. . . , who frequently changed his mind, was at once easily influenced and domineering, would be a dreadful liability for the party. No matter: he would win the election. I never forgot that conversation; and the fulfillment of the prophecy was not long in coming. The candidate—afterwards President—was built up by the press and other publicizing agencies into a "great man" and, in due course, led the world to unprecedented disaster.

Most reputations resemble that of X. . . . They are ephemeral and false, but while the reputation lasts it may do infinite harm. Statesmen vie with movie favorites; they must cultivate the picturesque, they must be surprising, sensational on occasion; and, above all, they must reflect the mode of thinking—if thinking be not a misnomer—of the masses. They must aim at popularity. Now, in foreign affairs, such an attitude is fatal. Renan rightly said that the truth lies in nuances. But nuances cannot be "put over." Diplomacy is a difficult and delicate art, demanding moderation, prudence, and patience. There should be no *éclat*, no showmanship. But that is what our age will not admit or permit.

"By their fruits shall ye know them." It would seem that, when presidents and prime ministers have been grossly mistaken, when they bid us to reverse the roles, and (for example) regard ex-enemies as our friends and ex-allies as our foes, even the dullest intelligence would find them out. Yet, as we know, nobody asks awkward questions about such matters. Nobody cares to remember even the immediate past. Nobody blames presidents and prime ministers for their lack of elementary foresight. Today, nobody inquires "how we got like this." "The fault, dear Brutus, is not in our stars" . . . but *we* ascribe past errors to fatality. Each day, in the words of the hymn, is a fresh beginning; and if the statesman in his utterances corresponds to the mood of the moment, all is well.

The public does not remind itself of cause and effect, of

how yesterday affects today and today tomorrow; and the same statesman who is the putative author of our woes is cheered when he proposes to remedy them by a diametrically opposite policy. Nobody troubles to remark that he is disqualified. The French have a saying for such a situation: *"Pas ça, ou pas vous!"* (Not that, or not you!) If, to take a specific case, Churchill and Roosevelt, and Truman, the continuator of Roosevelt, were wrong in their policy of "unconditional surrender" for Germany and Japan, and of permission and encouragement to Russia to occupy large areas of Europe and of Asia, it is certainly not for them, when the pernicious results of their policy are revealed, to take the lead blithely in the bolstering up of Germany and Japan in resistance to Russian greed. Unless, indeed, they first confess their egregious mistake that has cost us so dearly and may cost us much more, and penitently beg to be allowed to undo the evil they have done! They should not have it both ways, and expect (and often receive) praise for contradictory policies.

I am no iconoclast, but we must have at least a minimum of logic in foreign affairs if we are not to fall into confusion, as in fact we have.

It is obvious that no policy is thought through to its end. The leaders follow the masses and the masses follow the leaders in their most spontaneous and least sensible manifestations. Their effect on each other is reciprocal. Statesmen identify themselves with the lowest common denominator. He who would sway the masses must be swayed by the masses. It need not be assumed that their emotions are necessarily always base or selfish. They are often ready to make great sacrifices. It is only the superficial politician who invariably promises tangible benefits. The superior politician may exalt the people at times by promising ruin and death. The most striking example is that of Churchill who became—and remained—the national hero because he told Englishmen that he had nothing to offer them but tears, toil, blood and sweat. It was a stroke of inspiration that enabled him to conquer the public mind. Plenty of other examples could be had for the searching in the history of the French Revolution, when an orator could inflame the crowd by arousing its masochistic instincts. It is so that heroes are made in wartime, and it is thus that martyrs are happy to suffer for their faith.

We talk today as never before of internationalism, but every nation is now becoming more nationalist—is more resentful of foreign interference or influence. It would be a mistake to imagine, for example, that the movement for a European federation, or confederation, has any extensive foundation in popular opinion. Every informed person knows that, whether in France or England or elsewhere in Europe, there is a deep sentiment of anti-Americanism—sometimes expressed openly in slogans such as "Go home!"—but perhaps deeper when it is most concealed. Whatever profit Europe has received from association with the United States, the armies of the liberation, the money of the Marshall Plan, the organizations of Eisenhower or Ridgway, she cannot be grateful, for national pride is hurt. Every nation believes it is different—that is to say, better, braver, stronger, wittier, than the rest of the world. Only the credulous or the hypocritical can pretend that there is a genuine desire for union and surrender of sovereignty. Of course, we give opprobrious names to the nationalism of other countries; our own brand is the only true and proper patriotism.

Now this pride in our own nation, and contempt (not unmixed with fear) of other nations, make up a complex that can easily be touched off into bellicosity. There is always a latent war between nations that have rival interests, painful historical memories, or competing social or religious creeds. It follows that there is always a place of honor for the "diplomat" who seems to incarnate the instinctive hostility of his country for another. At certain moments there is no place for the peacemaker, the "appeaser" (a current derogatory epithet), the kind-hearted, the farsighted.

So it was after Munich, in 1938, when Chamberlain was despised by "patriots" for not leaping into war against Hitler, whether England or France were ready or not, and was actually driven into war a year later, when neither France nor England was a match for Germany. I need hardly point out that Russia has since done much more evil than Germany ever did, but today the *anti-Munichois*, the anti-appeasers, of 1938, are—for how long?—themselves *Munichois* and appeasers. In 1914, as I well remember, the few men in the British Government who were opposed to war were ignominiously sent into obscurity and were considered to be pro-Germans and almost traitors. The same story may be told of France, where statesmen like Caillaux were put on trial on various pretexts, but, in reality, in the case of Caillaux, chiefly because he had, a few years before, averted war. What happened in the United States in both the first and second World Wars is too well known to need recalling here.

These then are the undeniable facts, and all the false pacifism which cannot stand the test of moments of popular excitement (for nearly all the preachers of good-will suddenly became ardent patriots, and haters of other nations, as soon as the war-drums are tapped and the trumpet blown), cannot change them. I have learned, in a long experience, to beware of the rhetorical pacifist more than the patriot for, once aroused, his belligerency usually exceeds all bounds.

Now the sound conclusion to be drawn—as I shall try to show in this book—is precisely the opposite of that which it is the fashion, since 1914, to draw. Popular diplomacy pretends, against all reason, that we should perpetually discuss the possible causes of a new world conflagration, that we should indulge in loud threats, that we should ostentatiously arm, that we should sign scores of pacts against the eventual "aggressor" that the Clamor Boys should never cease their antics before high heaven and low minds. My contention is that the new diplomacy supplies the predestined provocation of wars, inasmuch as it arouses the ready antagonism of the masses, bringing every dispute into prominence, exacerbating passions, playing on fears, lighting the torch of public opinion in the powder-magazines of the world. And it is particularly dangerous to protest that we are peaceful while others are preparing war. Assuming the statement—which can only increase our distrust—to be true, would it not be better to proceed with silence and discretion? Consider the thousands of books, articles and speeches before 1939 which described Germany and Japan as war-mongers, while we were peace lovers! Could they have any other effect than to bring war nearer and make it more certain? And now the thousands of utterances which represent Russia as the potential warmaker (has she not taken what our statesmen offered her in 1943 and later?) while we are wholly innocent!

It is a stupid and unfounded affirmation that there are two kinds of nations, peace lovers and war-mongers. Human nature is more or less the same the world over, and the circumstances in which peoples find themselves determine the display of a bellicosity always near the surface. The fundamental fact about human nature—in spite of the pacific philosophy of our time (refuted by the history of forty years) —is its periodic disposition to pugnacity. Fear of the foreigner, envy, jealousy, economic rivalry, revenge and (let it be added to our credit) a crusading desire to right wrongs (though this may be the most deadly impulse of all) are all part of our intense sense of nationality, which is, a priori, antagonistic to other nations, despising them, detesting them, afraid of them and yet eager to measure up to them. I have myself, in the course of my career, seen the latent xenophobia—normally restrained by the necessities of interdependence—directed against practically very nation in turn: against England, against the United States, against France, against Germany, against Russia, against Japan, against China, and so on and so forth; and I have seen friends converted into foes, and foes into friends, until the friends become foes once more.

In short, the materials for war, and the occasions, are always at hand. In the past, it was not the people, or the peoples' representatives, who decided. Kings and emperors made and unmade wars; they made and unmade them far too often; and we cannot revert to such a system. But at least they had definite objectives. At least, they usually took care to limit the danger and the damage. At least, they knew how to conclude their wars by more or less equitable arrangements that were not certain to lead to new wars at an early date. Now we have wars on a world-wide scale, the implacable wars to a finish —the finish of what? Of civilization?—the wars whose objective, if such a vague generality can be regarded as an objective, is no less than the total destruction of the "enemy" (whose help we may need a few years later). These wars began with the new diplomacy, popular diplomacy, open diplomacy.

I cannot regard this synchronization as a mere coincidence. I consider the new diplomacy to have a large responsibility for our recent wars. It certainly does not cure us of war. The old rulers—right up to our own century—kept cool heads and a tight rein. Our new rulers—who are, in reality the masses—can no longer control the forces they set in motion. There are "leaders" who are eager to make their political fortunes in stimulating the masses to wrath; there are unprecedented methods of propaganda; there are our talking-shops, like the League and the U.N., which never cease to air grievances; and, above all, there are the Clamor Boys of diplomacy who flit from capital to capital carrying their messages of fear and distrust, forming unstable coalitions, making foolish speeches, giving absurd interviews, keeping up the agitation, basking in the limelight that beats upon them. Wars will become more embittered, more frequent, more catastrophic, unless we decide to limit our diplomacy to restricted circles, in which the diplomats will no longer enjoy the incense of popular acclaim, in which they may work quietly and, let us hope, effectively, at their highly specialized trade of oiling the wheels of international relations.

Only at the price of scrapping our diplomatic machinery of 1914–1952 can we expect to have a relatively orderly world. I shall, in making this assertion, have against me all the hosts who are interested, for various reasons, in the present system. But I trust I shall have with me all those who are able to see where our new diplomacy, now bankrupt, has led us, and who genuinely want peace—not eternal peace, as we are lightly promised by the Clamor Boys—but relative peace in which there will be fewer rumors of war.

The leading menace of today is not so much the atom-bomb, bad as this invention of the peace lovers may be; the chief menace of today is the sorry blood-laden performance the Clamor Boys put on under the arc-lights of the international circus.

2

DIPLOMACY BEFORE THE RISE
OF THE CLAMOR BOYS

WOULD it not be possible, asks a learned friend who has
read my notes, to introduce here a brief account of earlier
European diplomacy, in order to show the contrast between
diplomatic methods then and now? This friend, a well-known
American historian, recalled Sir Henry Wotton's famous
seventeenth-century definition of a diplomat as "an honest
man who is sent to lie abroad for the good of his country."
He observed that "at least an ambassador in the seventeenth
century lied for the good of *his own* country." Of recent
American diplomats, he said, it would all too often be more
accurate to describe them as dishonest men sent abroad to lie
to Americans in the interest of one or more foreign countries.

I must first make it clear that it is not my purpose to
defend the old diplomacy. It belonged to its time, and
developed certain traditional features which we have
foolishly abandoned; but it, too, had grave defects, and I
would not wish to appear as its apologist. Condemnation of
the new does not in the least imply unreserved admiration for
the old.

Nor, in the space that I can spare, can any adequate indication be given of the incredible complexity of European problems. America started, as it were, with a clean slate; Europe,
after the collapse of the Roman Empire and the re-groupings
that followed the Middle Ages, could not escape a series of
conflicts that were neither, as is generally supposed, personal

enterprises of monarchs and their mistresses, nor senseless struggles for national prestige and power. They arose out of circumstances and, for the most part, had some logical meaning. Unhappily, war has been a vast preoccupation of mankind throughout history, and in all ages has been accompanied by cruelty. But never has there been such universal cruelty as today, and never have wars been engaged on so great a scale, with such deadly instruments, with such passion, with such disregard of reasonable objectives—in short, with such absence of diplomacy—as in our century of popular government.

"There are two things," said Diodorus, the Athenian, "contrary to wise deliberation—precipitation and anger," and the truth is that precipitation and anger are the attributes of present-day diplomacy which depends on the support of the people.

As a lifetime student of history, and especially of the memoirs of the men who were associated with the events of history, I affirm that diplomacy, whether in the hands of kings, ministers or ambassadors, from the time of Francis I of France—from which date we may note the rise of modern diplomacy—to around 1900 was generally served by shrewd, far-seeing, persuasive, instructed, dignified and courteous men, not subjected to the ignorant criticism of demagogues, and not animated by unreasoning hatred of the "enemy." They were often high dignitaries of the Church, which had not lost its universal outlook; they were highly skilled legists; they were of aristocratic rank; they were often of outstanding ability, and devoted their lives to the study of international relations. They had a comprehensive knowledge of men and things, were acquainted with the customs of courts and countries, and had military and financial experience and judgment. They were men of the world, participating in the life of arts and letters, the amusements and the refinements, of their age. They had tact, charm, subtlety, wit and, even in

Anthony Eden

Dean G. Acheson

the turmoil of warfare, they kept definite aims in view and were usually careful not to overshoot the mark. And I repeat —as I shall repeat throughout this book—they were not swayed by the vagaries of irresponsible public opinion.

I think it is Motley who writes of a war caused by the bad temper of an ambassador provoked by the refusal of a gatekeeper to open to him and his concubine. I will not inquire whether such an absurd story is true; for in any case it cannot be the whole truth, any more than the pretense that our last war was for Danzig and the "salvation" of Poland. There were always greater issues at stake.

In the centuries that succeeded the Middle Ages, the struggle was between the conception of a united Europe, under a single (or dual) domination—that of the Pope and the Emperor—and the spontaneous reaction of an awakening national consciousness. The United States of Europe were once a reality, and the overlordship of the spiritual and temporal chiefs (both, be it remarked, elected) was for a long time not disputed. The virtue has gone out of Empire, as it must go out of all old institutions, but to ignore the services that Pope and Emperor rendered to Europe is to betray a parochial mind. To condemn nationalism as it gradually developed in France and elsewhere, is to confess a complete absence of all historical sense. France, by her natural conformation, at the extremity of the Empire, between the Rhine, the Alps and the Pyrenees, by the division of Charlemagne, by a certain independence of character, opposed the idea of universal monarchy. The rest of Europe was under the suzerainty of the House of Habsburg (or Austria) and the shadow of the Papacy. Charles V extended his domain to Spain, to the Indies, to America, to Italy, to the Low Countries (Belgium, Holland, etc.), and his brother Ferdinand was the heir to Bohemia and Hungary. France was thus surrounded by the Empire, except on the Atlantic, but between the Atlantic and the Empire she was a barrier.

At the same time that the spirit of nationalism was born, there was also born the spirit of Protestantism, which was to make headway in Germany and England. It is proper to state, without excessive simplification, that France stood for the principle of nationalism, while Central Europe stood for the principle of imperialism. These two conceptions, equally respectable in their time, were not deliberately invented to create strife, but strife they did create, and all European diplomacy for some centuries turned upon them.

Rarely has France forgotten her essential mission. Francis I himself did, indeed, put forward his candidature for the post of Emperor: had he won the votes of the Electors, European history would have been very different. But the rôle had become virtually hereditary and Germanic. Napoleon, who was more Italian than French, and therefore in the imperial tradition, broke with the sounder instincts of the French, with disastrous results to himself and France. I should add that England, by her island position, has always been hostile to European unity—hegemony, imperialism, call it what you like—as a menace to her own existence.

Now even in the schematic form in which I am compelled to cast this exposition, it will be seen what a vast field for shifting alliances, intrigues, combinations of all kinds, was afforded to the princes and diplomats. Though France remained, for the most part, Catholic, she joined hands with German Protestant princes against the Empire. Though England was Protestant, she joined hands with the Empire against France. To maintain an equilibrium of force, bargains had to be struck between seemingly irreconcilable elements. Europe has no double dose of original sin; no particular country is worse than the others; and the diplomats were not fiendishly bent on war. On the contrary, they were usually intent on limiting the damage and of keeping antagonisms within bounds.

Let us note, in passing, that a Treaty of Perpetual Peace

was concluded at Freiburg in November, 1516. Briand-Kellogg pacts are no innovation, but the flow of history cannot be stemmed by King (or President) Canute, and paper barriers, to which we attach so much importance today, are quite ineffective against realities. In this treaty of 1516, the machinery of arbitration was proposed, if I am not mistaken, for the first—but not the last—time.

In the constant search for a delicately poised balance of power ("negotiations from strength") there was not, as in our day, a desire to annihilate each other. Charles V specifically advised his son not to try to smash the French, though they interfered with the communications between the distant parts of his Empire. Henry VIII of England did not ask for complete victory—"unconditional surrender." The rapid dislocation of the Empire would have brought confusion to Europe. The crushing of France would have been to nobody's advantage. Whole nations were not whipped to fury with the cry: "*Delenda est Carthago.*" Wiser counsels always prevailed, the door was kept open to equitable arrangements and, while fighting proceeded, diplomacy continued and negotiations proceeded. Terrible as were many European wars, the purpose was not mutual obliteration. Nor was there any prejudice against "ideologies." Though France had signed a concordat with the Vatican, Francis I did not hesitate to conclude an alliance with the Sultan. Sometimes the powerful Ottoman Empire advanced far into Europe and had to be repulsed, but, when the occasion was favorable, Christianity and Mohammedanism clasped hands. The Pope recognized the services rendered to Christianity by the Treaty of Constantinople (La Forest, 1536) by which France obtained privileges and protection in the Near East. The aim was to prevent either the East or the West from becoming undisputed "master of the world."

Opinions and policies differed: the Constable Montmorency, under Henry II, would have preferred an alliance with Philip

of Spain against the Turks and the Protestant princes, while
the Cardinal of Lorraine saw in the presence of the Habsburgs
on the Somme, the Pyrenees, in Alsace, in Italy, and in England (when Philip II of Spain espoused Mary Tudor) a mortal
peril for France. The Hohenzollerns, the rising royal family
in Prussia, signed a treaty with France against the Empire in
1552 at Friedwald (Hesse)—a document of capital importance. Seven years later, the Duke of Alba came, on behalf of
Spain, to an arrangement with France at Cateau-Cambrésis.
There were fluctuations, contradictions, variations, but something could be said for each treaty in its time, and the diplomats were not influenced by violent expressions of politicians,
demagogues, the press, or emotional and uninformed public
opinion. Long before Einstein, they had learned the meaning
of relativity in foreign affairs: every nation could be a friend
or a foe in particular circumstances, and nothing could have
been regarded as more unstatesmanlike than to humiliate
each other unnecessarily or to exalt each other inconsider-
ately.

Among the great names in European diplomacy is that of
Richelieu, from which that of his disciple, Mazarin, is inseparable. In the seventeenth century, the House of Austria was
still the main "enemy" of France. The principle of imperialism was still opposed to the principle of nationality. Richelieu
was faced with great difficulties. The Protestants were now a
state within the state; peace with Spain threatened war with
England; alliance with the Protestant princes meant the alien-
ation of Catholicism. For twenty-five uneasy years Richelieu
avoided a "showdown," and in that lay his skill. The Emperor Ferdinand still aimed at the unification of Europe. He
was worsted by Gustavus Adolphus, the Swedish King, and
it was only after the death of Gustavus Adolphus that Richelieu deemed the time had come to strike a blow. Patience is
surely one of the highest qualities of the diplomat—not
"anger" and "precipitation." "He was a great statesman,"

writes Jacques Bainville, "not so much by his calculations and plans, as by his exact appreciation of the means necessary to reach his ends." Happily, he had not needed to seek public approval. When the Cardinal died there was a sigh of relief, for he had committed the unpardonable sin of seeing a little farther than the masses.

Mazarin, the astute Italian, was still more unpopular, yet, he concluded at Westphalia, in 1648, a treaty which, for a hundred and fifty years, was regarded as the Charter of Europe. France and Austria were in agreement on "Germanic liberties"—i.e., the "self-determination" later so dear to Woodrow Wilson. Each Germanic state (there were more than three hundred of them) was master of its movements, free to make whatever alliances it pleased. The Germanic states were content, France was content, and the Empire could make the concession without great loss, since the House of Habsburg could always command the preponderant vote in the election of the Emperor, and, in fact, it was Leopold of Austria who succeeded Ferdinand.

Spain was now separated from Austria and, in 1659, the Pyrenees Treaty was signed. France had reached her peak of power. But to maintain the European order required no less diplomacy than had gone into its establishment. The communal memory, and even the diplomatic memory, more lasting than the individual memory, persisted in regarding the Empire—that is, Austria—as its principal "enemy," overlooking or encouraging, the rise of the Hohenzollerns in Prussia. This anachronism operated as late as 1919, when the men of Versailles took a political sledge-hammer to break up the decaying Austro-Hungarian Empire.

And yet, by a curious confusion—one of those falsifications of history, those legends which democratic propaganda is capable of creating—Germany, in the shape of the German Empire after the unification of 1871, was represented as the "hereditary" enemy of France. If the term "hereditary" is not ill-applied in such a connection—if it simply implies a certain continuance of conditions which range country against country—then it is true that the Empire, that is the House of Austria, might be regarded as the "hereditary" enemy of France. In reality, however, the Germanic states might properly be described as the "hereditary" allies (when they were not the victims) of France. On the other hand, England, the inspirer and the leader for many centuries of continental coalitions against France, her most implacable adversary on the seas, her successful rival in the colonies, must be placed by any impartial historian who looks a little further back than the twentieth century, as the true hereditary enemy of France. Spain, too, must take a foremost place among the redoubtable opponents of France whose chief preoccupation was to "round off" her territory, to place herself on defensive lines against possible invaders.

What America, free to expand in every direction without encountering any formidable opposition except the forces of nature, is inclined to overlook, when considering the checkered and complicated history of Europe, is the normal process of growth and decay, the ebb and flow of national power, when once the central unifying and universal conception of Empire began to crumble, and the ethnic groups, each with its laws and language, were compelled to struggle for their existence, continually faced by obstacles, constantly menaced by competing expansion. Nor must it be forgotten that, alien in spirit to the Europe which had its roots in Rome —what we may properly call Western Europe—two Eastern peoples, Russian and Ottoman, Slav and Turk, non-European civilizations, pressed heavily on the borders of this divided Europe. Any comparison of Europe and America is utterly fallacious, and the best-informed American diplomat should beware of intervention in the terribly tangled business of "sorting-out" Europe which followed the Middle Ages and is as yet far from finished.

As an example of the give-and-take character of European diplomacy, so different from the "no-compromise" character of recent diplomacy, we may take the Treaty of Nimwegen (Nijmwegen in Flemish). There, after the war with Spain for the Low Countries, Louis XIV concluded a series of accords in 1678. Spain obtained the restitution of Ghent, Charleroi and Courtrai while France, for the security of her frontier, retained Valenciennes, Cambrai, Saint-Omer, and Maubeuge. Maestricht was restored to Holland, and William of Orange received back his principality. The Emperor Leopold retained certain places he had taken, and ceded others. A satisfactory arrangement was likewise made with Sweden. There were commercial agreements. In short, there were no clear-cut victors and vanquished, as we would have it today, when we are told that all the wrong is on one side and all the right on the other, that there must be an unconditional surrender, and that punishment must be inflicted by the victors.

The same lesson may be drawn from the treaties signed at Ryswick in 1697. William of Orange, who became King of England, had formed the League of Augsburg against France to preserve his interests in Holland. Virtually all the European countries entered, and it is worth remarking that so greatly had the former conception of "universal monarchy"—that is, the Empire—fallen into disrepute that it was on the false charge that Louis XIV aimed at such "universal monarchy"—more than ever an anachronism and grotesquely impossible of attainment—that William succeeded in rallying the opponents of imperialism, the champions of nationality.

The costly and futile war was brought to an end by the mediation of Sweden. William of Orange, satisfied with his recognition as King of England, agreed to mutual restitution of countries, islands, fortresses, and colonies, as they were before hostilities began. Between France and the Low Countries there was similar restitution. France yielded up to Spain everything in the provinces she had taken—notably in Luxembourg, Namur, Brabant, Flanders, Hainaut, which today we would imagine as having more French affiliations than Spanish. As for the Empire, it obtained Kehl and Freiburg. Lorraine was restored to its Duke; but France kept Strassburg.

Now the point to be emphasized is that all parties compromised, and the peace was regarded as "advantageous and honorable." On this occasion, the French king was accused by some of timidity in yielding and by others he was accused of audacity in taking. The criticisms cancel each other out, and seem to me to justify Louis in his refusing to listen to popular outcry.

We may glance at the Treaty of Utrecht (1713) which ended the unhappy war of the Spanish Succession, since it was a milestone in English policy on the seas and in colonial expansion. This treaty (together with that of Rastadt and Baden, 1714) was also a compromise. The English, who had developed a fixed idea about the Low Countries, were tired; Austria was concerned with the threat of an attack by the Turks; and the French had suffered considerably. Spain gave up the Low Countries, but Philip V kept his crown. France retained her frontiers. Now Belgium (whose ports were "a pistol pointed at the heart of England"), was, strangely enough, conceded to the Emperor, who also received compensation in Lombardy, Tuscany, and Naples. The centre of the Empire was thus shifted to Italy and away from the Germanic body. Holland was treated as a sort of annex of England, which William of Orange could be trusted to keep out of French hands. England demanded the demolition of the fortifications of Dunkirk, and obtained Gibraltar and Minorca. She installed herself in Newfoundland and Acadia (the old French name of Nova Scotia and New Brunswick), commanding the Gulf of St. Lawrence, thus menacing the French in Canada. The bases of British colonial and sea-power were established, although the implications of British policy were not then apparent to the French.

The Secretary for Foreign Affairs in the reign of Louis XV, Choiseul, on whom the most contradictory judgments have been passed, perceived the danger too late. He finally regarded England as the "tyrant of the seas," and, in fact, France lost most of her colonial possessions, Canada, India, Senegal to England, and ceded Louisiana to Spain in compensation for Florida, which Spain ceded to England in the disastrous Treaty of Paris of 1763. But it must be confessed that France, though a marvellous pioneer, cared little for her colonies until the nineteenth century—if then—and threw them away lightly. Choiseul turned for aid to Austria and Spain. The marriage of the Dauphin of France (afterwards the unfortunate Louis XVI) to Marie-Antoinette of Austria, eventually reviving the long traditional hostility of the French towards the Empire, was, indirectly, a contributing cause of the Great Revolution.[1]

It was in the same year, and almost at the same time, that the Treaty of Paris was signed, that one of the most momentous diplomatic acts of modern times was concluded at Hubertsburg. King Frederick the Great of Prussia had struggled for seven long years against the most powerful forces of Europe, including France, Russia, and Austria. His position often seemed hopeless, but he fought on desperately against the coalition, and he had the good fortune to be aided by various unexpected events, until at last Russia and Sweden grew weary of the attempt to force him to restore Silesia to Austria. Finally, Maria-Teresa of Austria gave way; she renounced all claims on the territories of the Hohenzollerns, until then the comparatively insignificant rulers of a somewhat mixed population who were, in the end, to become the German Emperors. There is no more astonishing story

---

[1] To me the study of history is chiefly interesting in showing the inexorable sequence of causes and consequences, which often appear unrelated. No event is without its influence on all future events. How far ahead can the ordinary man look?

than the rise of the Hohenzollerns to commanding power in Europe.

Summary as are these references to the diplomatic history of centuries crowded with incident, they and the peace which followed Waterloo, indicate the general desire of European diplomats, in view of the inextricable perplexity and complexity of the problems, to refrain from any action that would push the adversary into his last trenches. They made innumerable mistakes, some of them with the most serious consequences, but at least they understood that history cannot be made to stand still and that some thought must be taken for the uncertain tomorrow, when the help of a former "enemy" might be needed. There was none of the fanaticism, the frantic popular hatred, that belief in a millennium of future peace engenders. There was often insufficient foresight—for human vision is limited—but there was no willful blindness brought on by unreasoning wrath, clamorous propaganda, deliberate appeals to ignorance.

I will conclude this survey with a succinct account of the negotiations which resulted in the Berlin Congress of July, 1878, for although they terminated in a spectacular assembly, they were conducted in secrecy, and it was precisely this secrecy that averted a European war. Russia was joined by Germany and Austria in a protest against Turkish atrocities in Bulgaria, then under the domination of the Sultan. Gladstone violently took the same side and wrote a fiery pamphlet which Beaconsfield wittily described as the worst Bulgarian atrocity of all since, in effect, it was a cry for war. However unpardonable the Turkish behavior in Bulgaria, should the proper reply be a general European butchery? To encourage Russia was to allow her to enter the Mediterranean, to push into Asia Minor on the road to India, to give her control of the Suez Canal. She must, in English interests, never reach Constantinople. But public opinion was already beginning to be a force with which to reckon, and English public opinion was inflamed against Turkey.

Only the coolness of the Prime Minister, Lord Beaconsfield, averted a conflict that would have been, whatever the outcome, disastrous to England. He was helped by Bismarck, who saw an advantage in opposing Russian ambitions and in offering his services as an "honest broker." He proposed a Congress at Berlin when the Russians, after hard fighting, were already approaching Constantinople, and Russia reluctantly agreed. But the terms suggested by Gortchakov were declared unacceptable by Beaconsfield. In direct negotiations with Russia, and with the ultimate threat of force, he compelled Gortchekov to abandon the project of a Russian-dominated greater Bulgaria and a Russian Armenia. At the same time, by promises of British support, Beaconsfield obtained Cyprus from the Sultan as a base against Russian pretensions. Thus, before the Congress opened, England already had an accord with Russia, and had made a bargain—a "secret bargain"—with Turkey; Austria was promised Bosnia and Herzegovina; France was assured that the question of Egypt would be left outside the discussions. It was all very cynical, perhaps, but everybody was, in the end, satisfied, except Russia which had spent money and men in an abortive military effort.

There were a few unrehearsed incidents in the Congress, but the proceedings, conducted shrewdly by Bismarck, followed a pattern agreed upon in advance. Bulgaria was cut in two, and other Balkan territories received semi-independence. It is worthy of mention that Beaconsfield was sufficiently grateful to Germany to hint that it was in the Balkans that Bismarck might begin the work of German "colonization" —just as Bismarck hinted to France, after 1871, that her field of colonization was overseas.

Thus was "Peace with Honor," against the long odds of

hostile public opinion, first aroused against Turkey by atrocities in Bulgaria, and afterwards by Russian designs on the Dardanelles, achieved by statesmen who chose to ignore irresponsible (and even highly responsible) outbursts of popular indignation. Perhaps it would be as well not to insist too much on "honor" in politics, but "honor" is more entitled to a high place in diplomacy than "morality," which is the hypocritical term we employ today. I have never exalted the "old diplomacy" as against the "new diplomacy" for its virtue. All international relations depend not so much on good faith as on the threat of force intelligently applied. To pretend otherwise is to betray naiveté or insincerity.

One basic fault of diplomacy since Woodrow Wilson, is the postulate of I-am-holier-than-thou. It is a postulate that is utterly false. Every nation in Europe—and in America—has lived and thrived by giving and taking knocks. Perhaps the Empire was a little better than the others, because it started with some sort of inherited right as well as might. Spain became the most powerful and richest nation of the Continent by sheer ferocity and greed. France succeeded her by calculated ruthlessness. England built up her empire partly by piracy and brigandage. Germany started late in the race, and, by a mixture of disciplined industrialism and militarism, began to outstrip her rivals. When Italy tried to develop in Africa, we might reprove her ambition, but assuredly we could not pretend that she was exceptionally guilty. I will not extend the list; except to say that Russia, much as we dislike the conquests she has lately made with our unthinking permission, is no worse than other nations who have taken advantage of the weakness of neighbors.

I should be grossly misunderstood were I thought to be condoning double-dealing, cunning, treachery, in diplomacy. What I am urging is that there is now, as ever, a perpetual attempt on the part of statesmen to get the better of other nations, by diplomacy, by force, or by threats, and that they are only kept in check by the balance of interests and forces. The difference lies in the hypocritical assertion that today we are acting on strictly "moral" grounds. That is the mendacious "justification" which appeals to the masses, and saves us much thinking. We prepare (as I personally learned in 1939) enough poison gas to asphyxiate a great part of Europe, we employ phosphorus bombs on great civilian agglomerations, we use napalm to burn up towns and their inhabitants, we release atom-bombs on defenseless cities, authorize the "displacement" of millions of peaceful citizens, we commit many other "Bulgarian atrocities," but we still claim to be the messengers of morality, while our adversaries are linked with Satan.

Now it is this glib assumption of righteousness which is a new note in popular diplomacy, allowing us to behave with a total lack of intelligence and foresight and, in the end, with far more brutality than under the *Ancien Régime*. I am not so foolish as to claim that earlier generations were better than ours—although they could hardly be worse—and nothing could be more absurd than to praise the past at the expense of the present. We have countless amenities that our fathers did not possess; could we choose between living in the sixteenth or seventeenth or eighteenth century and living in our own, none of us would hesitate for a second in spite of the military massacres that disgrace our vaunted progress. Yet human nature remains much the same, whatever our inventions and discoveries and social triumphs. On some points we can surely learn from those who have gone before us, and I propose to sum up, without condoning the vices of the old diplomacy, what I take to be its virtues, negative though some of them may be.

First, then, the old diplomacy was not based on uninformed popular opinion. It was not conceived in view of the potential appeal to the mob or crowd. It excluded electoral considerations. It was relatively innocent of political posturings. This does not mean that uninformed opinion has failed to express itself in all ages. It has always had some influence on diplomacy, for rulers, whether hereditary or elected, whether appointed by monarchs or masses, cannot entirely detach themselves from the spirit of the time, with its false beliefs, prejudices, ambitions, and emotions. But it does mean that the few men who were consecrated to public affairs were peculiarly conscious of their duty and responsibility; they did not seek an alibi for personal stupidity by appealing to public opinion; they knew that they alone would be blamed for their failures.

They were aware that they and their adversaries were each playing a game that required skill and prudence. They, therefore, kept a courteous tone; they did not vituperate each other; they would never have dreamed, as we do today, of inviting the spectators to invade the playing-field, vociferating, gesticulating, exchanging fisticuffs, reducing diplomacy to a free-for-all fight. Each had a calm and shrewd sense of the openings to be made, the advantages to be taken, the goals to be aimed at; and each could maneuver freely, feinting, retreating, yielding whenever advisable, without incurring the hostility of the onlookers.

It was possible for a superior statesman to weigh carefully the consequences of his acts. He might, of course, be wrong —they have all been wrong, for consequences are often unforeseeable—but at least he could exercise his judgment and not be stampeded into rash courses. There was no "presidential year" or "general election" which compelled him to commit himself to ruinous policies.

The future was hidden from him, as from all of us, but at least it was his job to peer into the darkness. It is true that a French king cried: "After us, the deluge!" But in thus crying he was false to his office and, in general, wise rulers thought not only of immediate interests but of more remote concerns. Have we not seen in our own day rulers who, to win an immediate war, sacrificed everything, and were compelled to repudiate (though trying to hide the repudiation from the public, which, happily for them, has a short memory) their own policy or the policy of their predecessor one, two, or three years later? Can any honest person suppose that our present policy towards Japan, Germany, and Russia, to mention only three countries, is not the exact opposite of our policy of a few years ago?

The men who practiced the old diplomacy were persons of culture and good manners who heeded the admonition of the great Swiss jurist, Emeric de Vattel, that they should avoid "offensive expressions indicating sentiments of hatred, animosity and bitterness" which were likely to promote war, increase its ferocity, and make more difficult a lasting peace settlement. They treated their fellow diplomats with ostensible courtesy even in wartime. Vattel had counselled against using offensive language even in wartime. Today, under popular diplomacy, the only limit to offensive and violent language used against enemies in wartime is its ability to get into print. Indeed, there is much which is said that cannot be printed.

But popular diplomacy today goes much further. Rival nations, their leaders, and their propagandists use the most violent and offensive expressions of hatred and contempt even in the time of peace. Examples are the denunciations handed out between Nazi Germany and Soviet Russia for nearly a decade before June 22, 1941, Churchill's vehement attacks on Lenin, Trotsky and Stalin and his belated fury against Hitler and the Nazis, President Roosevelt's reference to the Nazis in his public addresses before December, 1941, as "rattlesnakes," and the like. Popular diplomacy has even renounced the formal courtesies of diplomatic ritual: witness President Truman's reception of the Czechoslovak envoy by immediately lecturing him on the wickedness of the government he represented. The international conferences and the

United Nations' meetings have provided a great stage, wired for sound to the world at large, on which the representatives of rival groups of nations can hurl the most harsh epithets at their opponents. Such procedure and such language lends its powerful aid to the disruption, if not the total destruction, of orderly diplomatic give-and-take.

Again, the old diplomacy was not hampered by its own propaganda. Today, we build up lies, create legends, give them the widest possible circulation, and then discover that we have thereby tied our own hands. We can—and do—build up other lies, create counter-legends, but for these to be effective there must be a time-lag wherein lies perhaps a mortal peril; and, in any case, we involve ourselves in contradictions, lose face, and destroy our prestige in lands where it is important to maintain our reputation for honesty and sincerity.

Further, our system, unlike the earlier system, is essentially one of false pretenses, of fakery, of unreality. We pretend that this or that pact which we have signed in a hurry (perhaps because it will help our candidature) assures our safety, the safety of Europe and America, when we well know that it is worthless, and that there is no real agreement. I can imagine nothing more dangerous than these mock accords. But, indeed, when are we told the truth? One day, for political purposes, we are told that there will be no war; the next day, for another political purpose, we are told that there will be war next year or in two years' time, or in 1960 or any other date that has been pulled out of a bag. We are told that we will be kept out of war—and are rushed into one after the election. We are told that the atom-bomb is a protective "umbrella" held over our heads. A queer sort of "umbrella" which looks more like a sword of Damocles! Then, a few years later, we are warned that it is a mortal peril to the nation, threatening the extinction of the whole population. In short, we are told anything that may suit the particular audience at a particular moment, until the wise man refuses to believe any official statement.

But the "moral" argument is still the ace in the card pack of popular diplomacy. We are willing to be highly "moral" in respect of other nations when it pleases us; and this self-complacent morality is the parent of immorality in ourselves. It is a convenient excuse to behave like "the other fellow." The mote in his eye blinds us to the beam in our own. If he bombs civilians, for example, we will bomb more civilians, we will bomb harder. "Oh, wad the gods the giftie gi'e us to see oursel's as others see us!" Every people thinks it is uniquely virtuous. "Dost thou think because thou art virtuous there shall be no more cakes and ale?" But what if we are not virtuous?

We have seen that had Lord Beaconsfield succumbed to public feeling, stirred up by Gladstone, England would have had to fight the Turks, and then the Russians—for by smashing the Ottoman Empire at that moment he would have opened the way to the Mediterranean and to India for Russia. I wonder whether a Beaconsfield in 1939–1945 would have seen that the crushing of Germany would fling open the door to Pan-Slavism? The analogy is interesting. I wonder whether he would have seen that the "sanctions" against Italy in 1936 would lead to a world war? I wonder whether a little "secret bargaining," immoral though it may be, with the perpetrators of "atrocities," is not preferable to the "new diplomacy," stirring up "moral" indignation, and provoking universal "immorality," carrying us all on the torrent of popular passion over cataract after cataract until we are dashed to pieces amid the wreckage of the world?

Finally, the new or popular diplomacy has, through its propagandists, all but ruled out the possibility of any real diplomacy in international relations. Diplomacy in the past. has meant a process of give-and-take between nations, some conceding this and others that point or policy. Since Munich, the propagandists serving popular diplomacy have smeared all concessions and diplomatic adjustments as "appeasement," perhaps the most opprobrious word in the vocabulary of the exponents of popular diplomacy today. Enemy proposals for peaceful negotiations are speedily and contemptuously rejected as requiring the "appeasement" of a rival state. Hence, when rivals become strong enough and the rivalry bitter enough to threaten war, the only public relations and attitude between the rivals must be a condition of cold or hot warfare. We must not negotiate with our rivals; we must seek to "contain" them—until warfare bursts the bonds of the containment.

3

THE FAILURE OF THE OLD
DIPLOMACY IN 1914

LIKE THE false report of Mark Twain's death, the American apprehension of European diplomatic duplicity has been "greatly exaggerated." What was true was that European problems were to Americans inconceivably complex and criss-crossed. History, tradition, frequent changes in the status of territories, racial rivalries, hatreds, jealousies, differing languages, ethnic peculiarities, shadowy claims to which some force could be given by the revival of forgotten legends, economic considerations, incipient revolts against old yokes, political agitation, and many other things created a political complex puzzling to the cleverest diplomats, even of the Old World.

G. H. Perris, in his *War and Peace*, admits that a territorial settlement is essential to any stable civilization and, although I am far from agreeing with his conclusion, it is true that in the sixteenth, seventeenth, and eighteenth centuries, only a fair balance of national powers could guarantee peace and progress. There could be no general European authority after the breakdown of the older imperialism; and all efforts to re-establish such imperialism on the Continent were bound to fail. The Central European Empire increasingly faltered, though at one time it was supreme; the Reformation shattered the fiat of the Pope; the bid of Francis I had no chance of success; the conquests of Louis XIV, insofar as they were extended outside the real France, could not endure; the Revolutionary and Napoleonic armies were doomed to even-

49

tual defeat. In short, in spite of ingenious speculation and innocent idealism, the peace of Europe depended on an equilibrium of forces.

Let me make a personal observation: I was born in England, of families which I understand came originally from Scandinavia and from Western (i.e., Celtic) France. I worked twenty years and more for America. I lived in France, Switzerland, Italy, Spain, and (for a very short time) Germany. I am acquainted with most of the European countries. I may like or like less this or that way of life: but whenever I have written of international politics I have sought to cast aside any prepossessions. I am neither pro-this nor anti-that. Such an attitude would be completely destructive of all useful study or observation. I trust, therefore, that no trace of partiality will be detected—or exist—in the following brief explanation of the origin of the first World War.

We must, however, go back to the Franco-Prussian war of 1870, about which so many lies have been told. Bismarck was by far the ablest statesman of the nineteenth century. His fist was strong, but his astuteness was a more important factor in his success in making a first-class power of a German state. He knew the value of moderation. He was aware that nothing is gained by unduly humiliating a beaten foe. He studied the other German states when he was a member of the Diet of Frankfort. He studied European states when he was Ambassador in St. Petersburg, and, later, in Paris. When the struggle with the decaying Austro-Hungarian Empire came, his first step was to expel the Empire from the German Confederation. But he joined with Austria in the Schleswig-Holstein dispute. He obtained the neutrality of Russia by promises of aid against Poland—essentially the affair of Russia, as it is today. He obtained the neutrality of France when he felt obliged to attack the Empire—and indeed France, anti-imperialist, was delighted with the Prussian victory of Sadowa or, more correctly, Königgrätz

(July, 1866). It was not until some time afterwards that France realized that a new power, far stronger than the sprawling Empire, had come into being. A cartoon by Daumier in my study shows a French bourgeois contemplating rather sadly a shield surmounted by flags in commemoration of the anniversary of the battle, and remarking: "The laurels have begun to fade since last year." In his triumph, Bismarck took care not to push Austria too hard. She would be a useful ally of Prussia. Instead of forcing into the North German Federation the German states which had helped Austria, he conciliated them.

France was becoming alarmed. The Second Empire had no statesman perspicacious enough to avoid the snare that Bismarck set. A Hohenzollern prince was proposed for the throne of Spain. France protested. His name was thereupon withdrawn by Bismarck. The incident ought to have closed there. But France was not satisfied. She insisted that Prussia should give guarantees for the future. An absurd demand! But the French people were already taking a hand in diplomacy and, sure of their force, were shouting: "To Berlin!" The Prussian monarch's reply to the French representations was polite enough, although it is true that it reads more peremptorily in the abridged version of Bismarck known as the telegram of Ems. Yet nobody in his senses who has compared the two versions can pretend that the Ems message was "faked." Nor can anybody pretend that France was justified in declaring war on Germany. I do not doubt that Bismarck, knowing the French temperament, intended to be provocative, that he wanted war. So much more foolish of France to give him his chance—his chance of defeating the country that had declared war, of establishing the German Reich, and of proclaiming the Prussian monarch Emperor of Germany in the *Galerie des Glaces* at Versailles.

Now it is probable that the 1914–1918 war would never have been fought had not the Ministers of Napoleon III made their light-hearted blunder in 1870. The memory of the defeat, the loss of Alsace-Lorraine, the rise of a new first-class power in Europe, haunted the minds of Frenchmen. Germany became the "hereditary enemy." I knew many Frenchmen of that generation, such as Raymond Poincaré, who lived for the *revanche*. But this does not mean that many of them ever deliberately plotted war. It merely means that, in 1914, France was still obsessed by the German menace, that the French people, who were taking a still more active part in diplomacy, were again ready to march to Berlin.

The dismissal of the old statesman who had served his country so well, by the young Emperor William II, in 1890, was an event of ill omen. For democracy had now made great headway, both Liberal democracy and Tory democracy, in France, in Germany, and in England. The personality of the new German Emperor was dangerous. However much he might have believed in his "divine right," he too identified himself with the people. He made strenuous bids for popularity. His glorification of the "flaming sword," his impulsive gestures such as his telegram to Kruger, the landing in Tangiers, the dispatch of the gun-boat to Morocco, his interview in the *Daily Telegraph*, his "Mailed Fist" speech, and so on, not only aroused misgivings in France, Russia, and England, but stirred the German masses. His flamboyant utterances, his histrionic poses fired the German democracy. Foreign affairs had broken out of the Cabinet, they were flaunted in the streets of the city, they were discussed in the homes of the countryside. How different was all this posturing from the cold and careful calculation of Bismarck and Beaconsfield! Paradoxical as it may seem, the Kaiser was a demagogue and his eloquence was a boomerang. It is highly probable that he had no intention whatever of making war, but he had—when the time came in 1914—to maintain his reputation.

In England public life was taking fresh forms. I consider the sweeping victory of the Liberals in 1906 to be a revolution. It brought into office men with new ideals, fresh vigor, a keen sympathy for the humble. I knew Lloyd George, the most outstanding figure, well, and I could but admire his downrightness, his capacity for fiery and picturesque speech, his unsparing denunciation of class selfishness. He was the champion of the common people. If ever a man believed in the force of democracy, it was Lloyd George. He embarrassed many of his fellow-ministers. I do not think he deliberately deserted his colors, but in the career of a politician changes seem to be inescapable. He copied and introduced into England the system of state insurance which was in operation in Germany, then by far the most advanced country in Europe in respect of social security. He had opposed the Boer War. He stood for peace with all the continental nations. Yet, by an irony of fate, it was he who was delegated to repulse the ambition of the Kaiser to sea-power. When, England being in the war, Prime Minister Asquith was seen to be a feeble leader in the hour of crisis, Lloyd George was cast, contrary to his convictions, in the role of war chief.

The Kaiser's prediction that the destiny of Germany was on the sea vastly disturbed England. She could brook no rivals in a domain where she had long been supreme. Her communications with the British Empire, her commerce, her ability to feed the millions crowded on a comparatively unproductive island where industry had relegated agriculture to the position of a poor relation, her very existence seemed to depend on sea-power, on sea-supremacy. The people as well as the politicians were convinced of the necessity of maintaining at all costs England's primacy on the oceans of the world. Besides, that other British axiom—the axiom that had caused her to lead coalition after coalition against Napoleon—that no land power on the Continent should hold

Europe at its mercy, had, a short time before, induced England to make an *Entente Cordiale* with France, although France had just before clashed seriously with England at Fashoda (in Africa). As France, in her turn, had entered into an alliance with Czarist Russia—the most barbarous of Great Powers—it was clear that Germany was being hemmed in and threatened on all sides. She was feared, and she feared.

From a diplomatic viewpoint the association of France—and in a lesser degree, England—with autocratic Russia, can doubtless be justified. Had not Francis I made a pact with the Turks? Had not Richelieu joined hands with the Protestants? Yet vividly do I remember the horror we in Europe felt for that great sprawling Eastern country of absolutism, in which only an arbitrary bureaucracy stood between the revolutionaries and the small "governing" class, in which the great landholders—the nobility—oppressed the peasants, in which European culture thinly covered Asiatic misery, in which the knout and the prison and the icy exile of Siberia maintained order, in which the "intellectuals" were conspirators, and the poor were resigned to their dismal lot. There have been immense changes in Russia since 1917, but the essential Russia is to be found in the works of the Russian novelists before the Revolution. Even the novel of Conrad *Under Western Eyes* will teach us more about the essential Russia than many books of travellers and newspaper reporters. Then, as now, Russia aimed at the domination of the Slav countries of Eastern Europe; she aimed at the possession of Constantinople, the control of the Straits, the freedom of the Eastern Mediterranean—all objectives which England violently opposed, and must, while she has an overseas Empire, continue to oppose.

It is, therefore, both remarkable and peculiar that France, where the principles of her own Revolution were not forgotten, and England, which regarded Russian ambitions as fatal, if fulfilled, to her own settled position, should, in their opposition to the growth of Germany, have chosen as an eventual ally a country which was utterly alien to them, in ideals, in customs, and in designs. Russia had been modeled by the long and cruel sway of the Mongols; she had escaped most of the Greco-Roman influences of the classical world, and the Christian teaching (for the Russo-Greek Church with its splendid ritual, its fixed dogma, its rejection of intellectual freedom, represents something that is quite different from Western Christianity) which have set the pattern for Western Europe. Moreover, the régime was honeycombed with sedition, it was obviously incompetent, and its collapse, in the event of war, was to be foreseen. I cannot help thinking, now as then, that Franco-British diplomacy was not so much aggressive as mistaken. While the Czar, like the Kaiser, recoiled from the idea of war in the crisis of 1914, Russia was the chief "aggressor" in that fatal moment. Izvolski felt that the Straits could only be obtained by war and Sazanov, inflamed by the Austrian threat to Serbia, pushed the Czar into war.

I suppose I saw more French statesmen, and saw them more intimately, than any other foreigner of my time—Raymond Poincaré I knew particularly well, and I confess to a feeling of compassion for this sad and lonely man, haunted by a sense of guilt which he constantly endeavored to exorcise. As he, himself, has told us, he was from his youth obsessed by the desire to recover Alsace-Lorraine. By 1914, Izvolski had convinced him that this was most likely to be attained by a joint Franco-Russian war on Germany. In assuring Russia of France's support in a war with the Central Powers and approving the fatal Russian mobilization, a large measure of responsibility must fall on Poincaré and on the French Ambassador to Russia, Paléologue.

As for Sir Edward Grey, in England, surely any impartial survey of the facts and of the man will discern his fatal weakness. It was his hesitancy that was, at the last moment, the decisive factor in producing war in July, 1914. There were two courses open to him, as I saw things in my youth, and as I see them now. He could have warned Germany and Austria in time that, in the event of war, England would range herself on the side of France and Russia against Germany and Austria. Or he could have told France—and Russia—that, in the coming war, England would remain neutral. Either of these attitudes would almost certainly have averted a war that everybody dreaded, a war whose political results were unpredictable, whose economic results were incalculable. Grey waited until the die was cast, and then took false and hypocritical refuge in the poor pretext of a German violation of Belgian neutrality. I do not condone the violation, but, once the war began, Germany, assailed on two sides, could not, from a military viewpoint, have failed to demand—and enforce if refused—the passage of her troops through Belgium in order to gain time, to dispose of one enemy before facing the immense Russian hordes. The violations of neutrality in the 1939–1945 war (Churchill, I remember, declared neutrality was not possible in such a struggle) were far greater, and this excuse brought forth by Grey against the great background of the European (and afterwards the world) war, seems extraordinarily trivial. Moreover, as John Morley and John Burns have revealed, the British Cabinet had decided on war in 1914 before the matter of the invasion of Belgium had ever been brought up for discussion.

Indeed, tragic as were the final results, the incidents which started the conflagration in 1914 were all trivial. Serbia naturally desired national unity for all Serbians, those who were under the rule of Austria as well as those who had been under the rule of Turkey, but she risked much in adopting the method of assassination and war. It is highly probable that she would have attained her purpose far more certainly in peace. The assassination of the Austrian Archduke Franz

Ferdinand, the heir to the Austrian throne, who was not unfavorable to the cause of the Serbians, on Serbian soil, should have been regretted and apologized for without delay. But Serbia was backed up by Russia, and Austria, whose power was waning, felt that she had to check nationalistic tendencies (expressed by such bloody means) in her Empire, and could hardly be expected to refrain from acting in what she conceived to be self-defense by issuing an ultimatum to Serbia. At the worst, she imagined, there would be only a local war. So there would have been, had not the rival alliances come into play. Europe would have been none the worse if Austria had insisted on the punishment of the murderers and the other Great Powers had remained aloof. There would have been another deplorable but relatively insignificant incident to add to European military annals. But Russia encouraged Serbia in her intransigence; Germany supported Austria in her demand for compensation for an outrage; France rushed to the aid of Russia; and England plumped at the last minute for France.

In all this there seemed some kind of fatality; and deeply as I feel the inadequacy of the diplomats of 1914, profoundly as I am convinced of the criminal failure of the old diplomacy in this crisis, I consider that the responsibility for war in 1914 was divided. Everybody was responsible in some degree. Nobody, unless it was Izvolski, willed the war deliberately. It was not presided over by a cunning Machiavelli, but rather by a group of bungling and terrified statesmen and diplomats. Documents may well pin the blame for this or that imprudent move on this or that person; and it is not necessary to spare our censure of the foolish and provocative game played by all the parties by whom a war more terrible and irrevocable in its calamitous consequences than the wars of a hundred years before, did not seem to have been seriously envisaged. But the final upshot was due to a series of blunders in diplomacy; and I, like Wilson, looked upon the diplomats of that time as little better than a pack of idiots, rather than a gang of criminals.

The difference between myself and Wilson—if I indulge in a moment of immodesty—is that Wilson later joined the sorry pack of idiots, and then invented—or at least gave shape to—a worse kind of diplomacy—namely, popular diplomacy, or the "new diplomacy," which has brought us to our present sorry pass in world affairs.

The failure of the old diplomacy may have been brought to a head and exposed in all its naked obsolescence by the outbreak of war in the summer of 1914, but what really undermined its dominion and tenure was the increasing public interest in diplomatic doings and the growing pressure of public opinion on diplomats and leading statesmen to take violent action in the case of diplomatic crises. So long as these crises, whether necessary or not, were provoked and handled in relative secrecy by trained and astute diplomats, there was less danger of their leading to a major war. When, however, they came to be played up by the press they created great public excitement and the politicians in an increasingly democratic society had to take heed of this public clamor for bombast, action, or both. The new diplomacy was displacing the old, and the traditional diplomatic game was no longer safe. What once would have only stimulated a Talleyrand or a Beaconsfield to greater subtlety behind closed doors, could now stir a world to armed fury. This epoch-making and fatal transformation of diplomacy produced by the growing influence of the press and its propaganda, combined with the increasing sensitivity of politicians to the temper of the voting populace, has been well described by the English jurist, F. J. P. Veale, in the greatly expanded American edition of his striking book, *Advance to Barbarism:*

> The peace of Europe rested on nothing more substantial than the political life of one old man. So long as

Bismarck remained Chancellor, the German Empire served as a mighty makeweight for a stable equilibrium. Once he had gone, his successors were free to join with zest in the time-honored game of European diplomacy. . . . In the circumstances then existing this was not a difficult game in which to take part. . . .

If the diplomatist in charge played his cards so well that the other power felt compelled to give way, he was held to have scored a diplomatic triumph and his grateful sovereign would reward him with titles and honors. On the other hand, if he played his cards so badly that the other power felt itself strong enough to reject his claim, his country was held to have suffered a diplomatic rebuff. In that case, he would probably be dismissed, and his successor would be entrusted with the task of vindicating the national honor, it being an inflexible rule of the game that the losing side must take immediate steps to avenge a diplomatic rebuff, a rule which ensured that the game went on *ad infinitum*. . . .

No one seems to have realized that conditions had changed markedly since the eighteenth century or suspected that new and potent forces had been released.

The power of one of these new forces, namely the power of the press, should at least have been foreseen, since in peace time it had already developed a disastrous influence over international relations. By the rules of the old diplomatic game, double-dealing and sharp practice were permissible within certain ill-defined limits. If these limits were exceeded, a formal "sharp note of protest" was sent to the offending party. Such notes, couched in stereotyped, diplomatic language, gave no offense. It was a recognized move in the game to profess indignation on occasion at the doings of the other side. But to the press they possessed news value: they served as a means of arousing public interest and, if well handled, of increasing sales. The offending power was, therefore, roundly denounced for trickery and perfidy and, needless to say, its press retorted in the same strain. The language employed, although moderate compared with the language now habitually employed by the press on such occasions, served to accustom the publics of the various European countries to regard certain groups of foreigners as gallant allies and certain other groups of foreigners as treacherous enemies. . . .

No other explanation [of the failure of the old diplomacy and the outbreak of war in 1914] is tenable on the facts except on the assumption that a sudden wave of insanity had swept over the governments of Europe.

If, therefore, the old diplomacy failed, because its practitioners in the years preceding 1914 were—one and all—far below the task assigned them, it also failed because it was already in process of transformation into the new diplomacy. It was already swayed by popular emotion. No one who lived as an alert observer through those days can doubt that, in most countries, the idea of war was enthusiastically received in 1914. The "leaders" had played up—or down—to the public. They had not kept clear and cool heads. They were all practicing the baneful art of demagogy. They had recognized the "advent of the masses in history"—to use a phrase coined by politico-philosophers—and they did not perform their duty, which is to hold in check, and certainly not stimulate, the nationalistic and warlike sentiments of the unthinking crowd. In his important book, *Five Weeks,* the American historian Dr. Jonathan French Scott has shown how the European press (radio was then unknown) whipped popular opinion into a war frenzy.

It is impossible to deny the paramount reason for the first World War, though it will be found in no document, namely, the "advent of the masses in history." That is why I do not attribute the new diplomacy to Wilson alone: under the guise of the old diplomacy it had begun to manifest itself before Wilson was elected in 1912, although it was not to be openly avowed until a few years later. There were clamorous cries for war, which carried away the diplomats. The war was "popular," and therefore it came. This invasion of diplomacy by the masses has gone on, with ever-increasing vigor and volume since 1914; it has been recognized and regularized; it has been given status; it is blasphemous to oppose it. The result is that history has accelerated its pace; it rushes us headlong into an unknown abyss, from which it is nobody's business to save us.

That is the supreme lesson of 1914 for anyone who can stand aside from the tumult. The date marks an epoch. We had come to be at the mercy of stampeding herds, and diplomacy, which has nothing to do with popular passions, which should calmly appraise the results of action, which should prevent war that defeats its own ends, or stop war before it reaches disastrous extremes, is now no more, whatever fraud it uses to obscure its unfortunate demise.

Nothing in the way of sane counsel could halt the war of 1914–1918—when once it had begun—because it was a people's war, and not a diplomat's war. In 1914–1918, it was the fashion of propaganda—which precedes as well as follows the crowd, or rather which follows as well as precedes the crowd—to describe the Germans as "Huns." It was an opprobrious name, well calculated to gratify popular passion. Do I need to remind my readers that the Huns were a wild Asiatic race which swept over Europe in the fifth century, routing the Goths and forcing the Romans to pay tribute? Nobody would seriously pretend that the Germans are their descendants. In the interest of historical fairness, it is also desirable to remind the reader that the Kaiser had furnished his enemies after 1914 with the suggestion of the "Hun" epithet. When, in 1900, he dispatched a German force to help quell the Boxer Revolt in China, he had said: "Let all who fall into your hands be at your mercy. Just as the Huns a thousand years ago, under the leadership of Attila, gained a reputation by virtue of which they still live in historical tradition, so may the name of Germany become known in such a manner in China, that no Chinese will ever again even dare to look askance at a German."

Nevertheless, if the "Hun" epithet was accurately to be fastened on anyone, it should have been fastened on *all* the countries that flung themselves unanimously into the conflict. None of us were guided by reason; we were all, with our virtues and our vices, fighting for we knew not what, unless it was the destruction of the "enemy," boastful of our superiority, enraged and vindictive, lost to all sense of proportion, masses of men in homicidal collision with each other in a struggle without commensurate meaning.

Diplomacy, statesmanship, were denied any part in the conflict. Politicians and demagogues took over, cheering on the troops, inventing slogans, seeking to put into understandable words "causes," chiefly "moral" (for there was no material "cause" important enough), which would seem to lend some sort of justification for the huge expenditure of resources and the immense massacre of men.

Diplomacy, I repeat, insofar as it is the servant of statecraft, is the art of doing just enough and no more than is necessary to achieve possible national objectives, that must, in the nature of the case, be limited. Diplomacy was dethroned after 1914. "We will not sheathe the sword. . . ." cried Asquith. "We will hang the Kaiser," promised Lloyd George, his instinct telling him that sanguinary expectations of vengeance are a sure way to the hearts of excited men. "We will squeeze them till the pips squeak," affirmed an "economist" ignorant of economic laws. "Germany will pay," assured the French "leaders," when doubts were awakened in more reasonable minds. American catch-cries tried to strike a higher note. The war was "a war to end war"—as if anything can end war but peace. Or, "we are making the world safe for democracy!" Out of the war would spring "homes for heroes"—though homes were being demolished, and heroes were being killed.

When I look back to the unimaginably crazy nonsense that was diffused during the war, I am distressed at the low intelligence of humanity. The sad and humiliating story of propaganda excesses during the first World War has been told for England by Irene Cooper Willis, Sidney Rogerson, and Sir Arthur Ponsonby; for the United States by H. C. Peterson, James R. Mock and Cedric Larson, and for France by Georges Demartial. Even men as normally wise as H. G. Wells completely lost their heads. Now we are bidden to laugh at Germany's claim that God was on her side! In England, Archdeacon William D. D. Cunningham even repudiated the right of pacifists to invoke the Mosaic Code or the Sermon on the Mount as any restraint upon the Christian duty to kill Germans. Was he not on ours? Did not every church proclaim the joyful news? You know the absurd story of the lunatic who thought himself sane, and who was greatly amused at his fellow-inmate's belief that he was Jesus Christ. "Of course he is mad," he chuckled, "he does not know that I am Jesus Christ!"

When Austria offered to capitulate, the offer was spurned. She must first be broken up and the Balkans brought to the doorstep of Western Europe. No responsible "diplomat" dared to negotiate, although one of the precepts of the old diplomacy was to keep open every door to a satisfactory arrangement. A few unofficial statesmen such as Joseph Caillaux and Lord Lansdowne, who had more common sense and more courage than the official leaders of the mobs, were rebuked as "traitors" and were hounded out of public life, tried for treason, or driven into obscurity. What we needed in 1914–1918 was not a "new" diplomacy, but any sort of decent diplomacy.

And yet it is true that there had been secret pacts, both

before and during the war. But they were secret pacts not to end the fighting but to divide the anticipated spoils. Russia could have the Dardanelles. Italy would have territorial compensations if she joined us. These pacts were never fulfilled. I wonder what would have happened had Bolshevism not produced the Revolution in Russia before Versailles? Would we have given her the Dardanelles? Or would we have cheated her? Italy we could afford to bilk, for she was not a really first-class power. I, too, castigate these feeble falterings of a senile diplomacy—the point is that there was no diplomacy at all. I wish there had been more secret diplomacy —of the right kind—for the essence of diplomacy is secrecy or, at least, discretion.

What we had was "mass madness"—that is, the negation of diplomacy. Politicians sacrificed every other consideration to their popularity: that is to say, they cared nothing for their country, they cared nothing for the world (democratic or undemocratic), they cared nothing for the lives blasted, the riches shattered, the future of humanity (about which they used such lofty language) darkened. If they were not as ignorant and blind as the mob, then they betrayed their trust; if they were as blind and ignorant then they were, one and all, unfitted for their posts.

Why do I relate these things? It is assuredly not for the vain pleasure of raking up dead embers, or of showing that I was wiser than those, who, in accepting popular diplomacy led us to ruin. It is because the past cannot be separated from the present, it is because we shall not understand what is happening today unless we try to understand, not as the official records would have us understand, the tragic events of nearly forty years ago when the old diplomacy abdicated its rights and responsibilities into the hands of the masses— where they still remain.

Some of the responsible men had misgivings—more than

justified. The Kaiser sorrowfully sighed: "I did not will this."
Sir Edward Grey sadly dropped a tear on the tomb of traditional diplomacy: "The lamps are going out all over Europe;
we shall not see them lit again in our time." Nor have we.

4.

FROM MACHIAVELLI TO PRESIDENT
MONROE AND AFTER

It would be unfair to regard President Wilson as the sole author and begetter of the doctrine of "open covenants openly arrived at," which implies a constant appeal to the masses. The thing was in the air long before 1919. It had become the habit of statesmen in Europe to count on the emotions of the mob. I myself am old enough to remember the frenzied support in England for the war with the Boers, which most outside observers and a few men in England, who afterwards overcame their unpopular defense of Kruger, deemed iniquitous. But, strangely mixed up with popular excitement, were underhand dealings.

The combination of secret bargaining, tortuous intrigue, bribery and corruption of the press (especially by Czarist Russia), and of mass diplomacy, quite understandably disgusted Wilson. He came to Europe with a mind filled with prejudice, no doubt deserved, against the hidden causes and the hidden designs of the 1914–1918 war, for which the full responsibility was wrongly attributed at the time to the German Kaiser and his advisers. I recall a conversation which I had long afterwards with Colonel Edward M. House, once the most intimate friend of Wilson, in his New York home. Still rankling in House's mind was the duplicity of European countries during the war decade. He told me—I do not know whether it was ever written down, but I vouch for the fact— that, when America reluctantly felt that she must come into the war, she begged for a clear exposition of England's aims, but was unable to obtain a satisfactory answer. Indeed, the English and French leaders became wroth and indignant at such "effrontery."

From the beginning to the end of the war, there was the gravest suspicion among some in the highest political circles, not only about the origin of the war, but also concerning the motives which dictated its prolongation, and the unacceptable conditions that the Allies sought to impose. Unhappily, the mistakes of Wilson made confusion worse confounded, and (as we shall see later) the peace that ensued was a lamentably interlaced tissue of the principles of the old diplomacy and the new diplomacy.

For the moment, I would like to consider the traditional distrust by America of European diplomacy. Rightly or wrongly, the President and many persons in the United States believed Europe to be guided by the spirit of Machiavelli. They believed they could establish a new order in international relations. It is this "experiment" which has since been in operation. It has not succeeded in casting out the old devil. It has merely added a new devil—mob spirit—to diplomacy, and the partnership of old and new has been doubly disastrous.

Machiavelli bears a name that, as Macaulay, with his customary exaggeration, remarks, is held to be synonymous with that of Satan. "Old Nick" has, indeed, been adopted from his Christian name, Niccolo. He is the arch-perjurer, the supreme hypocrite, the ultra-traitor, stopping at no convenient crime. For more than four centuries he has been taken as the prototype of the diplomat. The obloquy, unfair in part, which is his has fallen on his descendants in the profession.

Now this odium, whether merited or not, fails to take into account the age in which he lived. We are at the very beginning of the sixteenth century, when the Florentine monk Savonarola, the forerunner of Luther, was preaching against a corrupt Church, and was cheered in the pulpit before being burned in the market-place. The young Machiavelli was already secretary of State in the Republic of Florence, and was sent to persuade Caesar Borgia, Duke of Romagna, the brilliant but dissolute son of the terrible Pope Alexander, to help Florence. The Pope was poisoned a year later, while Caesar was stripped of everything and cast into prison. In the meantime, Caesar was rejoicing in his power, a vital personality without any sort of scruple, fighting, stealing, torturing, betraying, pressing the last drop of the juice out of the grapes of life. Soon, the return of the Medicis to Florence as rulers, after their exile, brought disgrace, imprisonment and torture, to Machiavelli. It was not until he was in his fifties that he was again allowed to serve, but in 1524 we find him employed on a mission to Rome. Then the old quarrel between the Pope and the Emperor was renewed, and Florence was endangered by both sides, as well as by the neighboring city-states of Italy. The troops of the Empire entered Rome; there was a rising in Florence and the Medicis were again expelled. The new Republic had no use for a man who, after opposing, had helped the Medicis.

It was rich with these harsh but illuminating experiences, and instructed by his reading of Plutarch, that Machiavelli composed his works which many have thought to be cynical: besides his *Florentine History*, *The Prince*, *Discourses on the First Ten Books of Titus Livy*, and *The Art of War*. That he should conclude that man is both evil and foolish, that it is better to be feared than loved, that a single strong man may determine the fate of nations, that all means are admissible for the protection of the state, that it may be wrong to keep one's word when circumstances alter, that it may be fatal to be honest though an advantage to appear virtuous, are precepts which were forced upon him by a troubled epoch. Meek resignation, as taught by Christianity, meant destruction in those days. It would be disingenuous to pretend that statesmen actually repudiate these precepts today. They do not forget, either, the maxim of Machiavelli which would base power, once achieved, on the support of the people.

Yet *The Prince* has never, in our day, been deliberately taken as a manual for diplomats. Machiavelli was the child of his age—a particularly intelligent child—and his book is a reflection of the manners and morals of his time. It is not a permanent guide to international conduct; it possesses no universality. It is not a universal model but a local text-book; and we find a man like Frederick the Great, in his youth, writing an anti-Machiavellian treatise.

The city-states that sprang up in Italy after the downfall of the Roman Empire, depended for their safety on "diplomacy." They were opulent, they were artistic, but they were not warriors. They called in mercenary troops, who might change sides during a war; their campaigns were more like maneuvers, battles of chessmen. The political leaders developed a capacity for fraud, falsehood, and rhetoric; they duped those who would dupe them. So we have a code of diplomatic conduct, as intricate as some intellectual game, in which courtesy has its political purpose, thoughts are concealed, sentiments are disciplined, moves premeditated. There is here no place for petty provocations, blustering arrogance, useless brutality. I trust that I shall not be misunderstood if I say that there is a sense in which such diplomacy was much more civilized and far less dangerous than much of the popular diplomacy of today.

Macaulay bids us contrast our own reception of Shakespeare's personages, Othello and Iago, with their probable reception in the Italy of the early sixteenth century. We admire, though we pity, the brave but simple-minded Moor, so easily deceived, and we are contemptuous of the sly, insinuating, revengeful Iago who tricked the dull-witted general into murder and suicide. But in a state of society in which intellectual dexterity, detached from morality, is among the qualities most necessary for survival, the courageous but credulous Othello would be despised for his stupidity, and the cunning Iago found not unworthy of sympathy. I sometimes wonder whether we are not, in some countries, again becoming Iago "fans." At least, we tend to excuse crime if it is successful.

My own main complaint against present-day diplomacy is not that it is secret and treacherous (though it often is just that), but rather that much of it is too loud and frank. Both we and our late enemies—in spite of our protestations of peaceful intentions which are belied by our acts—talk too much and too blatantly, and think and plan far too little. Our public manners are atrocious and exhibitionist. Sound and fury, fist-shaking, boasting, are now part of the technique of diplomacy, because they correspond to popular instincts. Not only do we behave like this towards our potential enemies, but when, for example, England and America are not in agreement about Korean strategy, the matter is at once made the subject of angry public debate, to the delight of the adversary. Or, to take another example, should France and the United States have different views on policy in North Africa and Indo-China, there are voices in the United States raised against French imperialism, and voices in France raised against American interference with national sovereignty—sometimes, indeed, accusing the United States of being an accomplice of the Communists or the Germans. To this extreme have we swung, and if the diplomacy of Machiavelli deserves our condemnation, the diplomacy of democracy is equally to be deprecated. The rise of the diplomacy of democracy constitutes, indeed, the downfall of genuine diplomacy.

The most curious feature of the change-over in diplomatic methods and manners, is that, until about forty years ago, the whole trend of American policy was against direct involvement in the subtleties of little-understood foreign problems, particularly those of Europe; while, today, no issue is too disputed, no question is too entangled, no contingency is too remote, for American intervention. America will all too often jump in with both feet, and think afterwards —if at all. And when I say America, I mean not only American statesmen, but the whole American public; and woe betide the daring few Americans who venture to observe that American intervention will, perhaps, hopelessly snarl up foreign situations which might otherwise straighten themselves out. America wonders why Europe and Asia are not grateful for the gigantic material efforts of the United States to assist them. Alas, ingratitude is a human failing, and it occasionally happens that Europe and Asia feel that, without the new diplomacy exported from America—though immediately endorsed and belauded by large sections of Europeans and Asiatics—the world would not be in an Augean mess in which Hercules himself would feel helpless.

In my reading of American history I have been greatly struck by the comparative smoothness and simplicity of the international dealings of the United States from the time of Washington to the advent of Wilson. America was independent of the Old World in more senses than one. Her foreign policy was limited to a few sane and moderate objectives. The ingenious interpretations and rationalizations we have lately heard or read cannot abolish the original meaning of the Monroe doctrine. Washington and Jefferson, indeed, had laid down the principle of non-interference either by America in Europe or Europe in America, before the fifth president did so.

I am not, be it observed, suggesting "isolationism." That stage is passed. One can never go back to a starting-point in history. What has been done is done; and it would be monstrous for America to withdraw entirely from an imbroglio that she has helped to create. She is in, and must stay in.

For better or worse, the die is cast. I believe, ultimately, each nation must work out its own salvation and, if it cannot stand on its own feet, it cannot stand at all. I believe that no amount of American or other aid will preserve any country that does not want to be preserved and will not strive for self-preservation. Neither money nor munitions nor armies will permanently bolster up a people that abandons itself—on the contrary, foreign help, too much and too long, will weaken the fibres of the assisted nation, and will make its end as a free nation all the more certain and rapid. But I hasten to add that I also believe that it is the duty of America, in large part responsible for the disasters which have lately taken place in Europe and Asia, to continue to lend a helping hand, as long as necessary, to the countries it has "saved" or "liberated," on the strict condition that those countries are trying with all their might to help themselves. You do not pull a drowning man out of the water to leave him to die of asphyxiation or exposure on the bank; it would have been better to let him drown, if drown he must.

The proclamation of 1823 clearly forbids "colonization" by any non-American power on the American continent; and it surely postulates non-intervention of the United States in the network of European affairs.[1] American diplomacy has, of course, encountered difficulties: disputes with England, with Spain, with France, with Russia. But, on the whole, until the decision to participate on the side of France, England and Russia in the 1914–1918 war, no overwhelming problems, no problems that have baffled European statesmen for many centuries, presented themselves to the United States. It was surely presumptuous to imagine that American participation would automatically provide the solutions, and that American statesmen knew, by inspiration, by a natural gift,

---

[1] "In the wars of the European powers in matters relating to themselves we have never taken part, nor does it comport with our policy to do so."

much more about the problems of the Old World than the Europeans—or, for that matter, the Asiatics.

The United States might well be envied their own freedom from alliances. Alliances, if they are seriously meant, imply a framing of policies not solely in accordance with national needs, aspirations, and interests, but also in harmony with the needs, aspirations and interests of the associates. Sometimes national needs will be incompatible with the national needs of others, aspirations in opposition, ways of thought vastly different. What is then to be done? Should America endeavor to impose her will on reluctant allies? Plenty of instances will occur to the enlightened reader who has followed recent events when such divergences have manifested themselves. That is the inescapable snag of alliances; it is their weakness when opposed to a homogeneous foe, and no amount of plastering labels of "Unity" on disparate elements will make them one.

It would be superfluous for me to trace the development of a doctrine adumbrated by Secretary of State John Quincy Adams and incorporated by Monroe in his Presidential address: it can be found in any school book. I will only note that there was a real danger that European countries might seek to conquer territories in Central and South America, and thus bring their quarrels to the doorstep of the United States. I will merely refer to the fear of British Foreign Minister George Canning, that England would lose valuable markets in Latin America; and the formal resolve of the United States to remain outside European diplomacy and to view with displeasure any attempt of the European nations to subject the nations of the New World to their political systems. The doctrine was re-stated in 1845 and 1848 by President Polk, and shortly thereafter by John M. Clayton as Secretary of State. President Grant likewise insisted that there should be no transfer of American territories to non-Europeans or from one power to another.

Now this doctrine was so deeply embedded in American policy that it was actually referred to in the Covenant of the League of Nations in 1919 (Article 21). But the doctrine was not defined, and I will confess that, as a diplomatic correspondent at the Versailles Conference, it seemed to me somewhat ambiguous, if not altogether illogical, for the United States to stand on the Monroe Doctrine at the very moment when, if previous interpretations were correct, she was, in fact, engaged in settling the affairs of Europe, imposing stern obligations on certain countries; re-drawing the map, fixing to all eternity (or at least as far as statesmen can pronounce for eternity) the conditions in which should live a continent from which America had, under the identical doctrine, excluded herself. These inconsistencies, however, seem to be inherent in the new diplomacy, and no doubt can be brushed aside by a fresh interpretation of preceding pronouncements and resolves.

In any case, the American Senate refused to ratify the Covenant or to enter the League of Nations. The drowning man had been pulled from the water but he was left on the bank. In this metaphor, I am assuming that the League could have provided artificial respiration for Europe—and, therefore, I immediately withdraw the assumption and the metaphor.

With such a relatively simple program, how could America produce minor Machiavellis? She usually had a horror of anything that was not plain dealing. Benjamin Franklin, in the days when America was struggling towards independence, was certainly not without great acumen. He found sympathy in France where the ideas of revolution were stirring; he contrived to obtain, at a later date, understanding and loans in Great Britain. He laid with painstaking care the foundations of friendly relations. But it would be ludicrous to set side by side as diplomats the honest, plain-dealing, common-sensible Franklin with the crafty, shifty Florentine.

Two totally different types, in two totally different eras, were exemplified in their persons. And it may properly be said that, so far as America is concerned, down to 1937, there has never been the smallest justification for the charge of her practicing diplomacy of the Renaissance kind. The charge may well be made that America has been too candid—in the French sense of the word, which has connotations of naïveté. It may even be said that, when Roosevelt tried to go behind the back of his partners at Yalta and elsewhere, he betrayed his amateurishness in adopting Machiavellian techniques.

I, myself, find evidence of American friendliness, her desire to think well of European nations, in her choice of ambassadors. There were among them, of course, many remarkable men, but they were often remarkable more for their literary gifts than their purely diplomatic vocation. They cultivated courtly qualities. They were eager to disprove the suggestion that the America of the earlier days lacked culture. They were, then, men of letters. Washington Irving was perhaps the first notable American littérateur, and he served his country on the staff of the United States Legation in Madrid from 1826 to 1829. He afterwards went to the Court of St. James. He returned to Spain. I could not say off-hand what work he accomplished as Minister between 1842–1846, though I am sure he was competent. But I am aware, as we are all aware, of his delightful sketches of English life and his interesting studies of Spanish subjects. John Lothrop Motley was sent as a young man to St. Petersburg (now Leningrad), later to Austria, and finally to London. I imagine that it is as a writer of vigorous and sometimes noble prose, such as his *History of the Rise of the Dutch Republic* and also his *History of the United Netherlands,* that he is best remembered rather than as minister. Whether Nathaniel Hawthorne was an outstanding American consul in England does not much matter: what matters is the admirable series of novels and stories that flowed from his graceful pen. James Russell Lowell was U. S. Minister in Madrid and in England, but it is as the dignified representative of the New England intelligentsia that his fame endures. The Adamses definitely belong to a diplomatic family, but we cannot forget their literary activities—particularly the historical work of Henry Adams, and his autobiography— one of the most marked-up books in my library. Nearer to our own time, Walter Hines Page was a journalist and publisher before going as emissary to London; but, in his case, it may be that his diplomatic work, as an advocate of war on the side of the British when Wilson was still unpersuaded, is doubtless more important than his contribution to literature.

It would be easy to extend the list, but my purpose is to suggest that the functions of an ambassador were regarded in America as those of an apostle of good-will, a delegate of culture, rather than those of a secret intriguer or a manipulator of political opinion. It was more important to make a good social impression, to smooth out international relations, than to intervene in high and mighty matters of European politics. And that is, after all, the best rôle that an ambassador can fill.

Another aspect of American thought cannot be overlooked when we examine the new diplomacy. The people of the United States, nourished on the Declaration of Independence, and on the eloquent orations of Abraham Lincoln, remembering their own history, were hostile to any form of political domination. They were anti-colonialists; while the greater European nations, with the possible exception of Russia,[1] were all colonialists. And Russia had her Pan-Slavism.

England was, in fact, the greatest overlord of overseas peoples. She had snatched the scepter from Spain which had been the pioneer and exploiter of colonialism. England had,

[1] Russian "colonization" consisted of englobing European and Asiatic countries in a single expanse of territory.

even in the negotiations of 1713 (Utrecht), obtained the monopoly of the infamous slave trade with Spanish America. For England, colonialism signified trading monopolies, and the exploitation of natural resources. However humane might be her actual treatment of the natives, whatever form was given to labor contracts then or now, British colonialism appeared to mean a kind of slavery. France, though generally indifferent to colonization, instinctively standing for nationalism and not imperialism, throwing away "possessions" as of no value (Voltaire described Canada, which the French lost to British settlers, as "a few miles of snow"), had nevertheless been pushed into colonialism by the remarkable sailors and explorers, the devoted missionaries, the enterprising engineers and businessmen, who make such a strange contrast with the average stay-at-home Frenchman. She had, moreover, been "oriented," as the French say, towards colonialism by Bismarck after 1871, for Bismarck (not unapprehensive of the spirit of *revanche*) thought colonialism a safe outlet for French energies.

Germany herself realized, too late, the advantages of colonialism—though she was always half-hearted in her African ambitions. At the height of Hitler's power in Germany, I had a long talk with Heinrich Schnee, the chief German exponent of colonialism, in which he complained bitterly that Hitler could not be moved to a serious demand for the return of the German "possessions" in Africa taken from her at Versailles. Germany herself had, nevertheless, begun, long before 1914, to follow the lead of the other European powers. I do not, of course, regard Germany's relative freedom from colonialism in the accepted sense, as a virtue. We have seen that Beaconsfield had indicated Eastern Europe as a fertile field for German cultivation; and, with sharply defined frontiers, her general design was to extend eastward.

Italy had begun colonial expansion too late, and her resources were insufficient, although her workers were incomparably laborious, for her to play a leading role outside the peninsula. That is why, moral grounds apart—and moral grounds surely could not fairly be urged by the greater colonial powers—I considered Mussolini's attack on Ethiopia to be a blunder. Still, Italy had joined the colonial movement. Of Holland and Belgium, small countries, but greatly enriched by their colonies, I will do no more than indicate that, as we have lately seen, America regards their privileged position in overseas territories as an anachronism.

There is a case for colonialism, which I do not propose to argue in this place. It is a case founded on the presumption, true or false—though it seems to me partly true—that the colonizing countries, while wresting from the soil riches that would otherwise be wasted for mankind—for mankind in general, and not solely for the colonizing countries—do raise the conditions of life of the subject peoples, and have an ultimate desire to bring to these peoples, in return, civilization and independence. Sometimes the methods have been brutal and quite inexcusable, but it is certain that the world would have been poorer had there not been this organized search for new lands, new materials of industry, and new markets for commerce.

However this may be, there was in the American mind until about 1900 an ingrained antipathy to colonialism not shared by the majority of Europeans. America, North and South, had once been colonies, British, French, Spanish, Portuguese. The United States, on that memorable day, July 4, 1776, when they repudiated the status of subordination to George III, repudiated by implication, the status of subordination for all peoples. They appealed to the principle of natural rights, derived from British philosophers, such as Locke, and French writers, such as Rousseau. They proclaimed the right of every man to life, liberty, and the pursuit of happiness. A few years later—in 1789—the French drew up a similar Declaration of the Rights of Man, asserting that all men are equal and noble, and that civilization had often been a perverting force.

It is not my business to examine whether these ideas are strictly sound, nor how well they have been put into practice. It is not my business to examine the objective behavior of America, since, subjectively, she has always been faithful to the fundamental beliefs on which the Republic was based. It has been urged—not by me—that economic domination may be more oppressive than political oppression, and that it does not matter whose flag flies over a territory if the money power rules. What is certain is that America, when she is most respectful to Europe, cannot exclude from her consciousness a condemnation of a system rooted in colonialism, and that this condemnation is inextricably involved in the American view of European diplomacy.

This view is strengthened by the successive waves of immigrants who have brought to America an unfavorable impression of their native land. They may have a nostalgia for home scenes, yet they would not have left them had they not imagined that their lives would be freer in the New World. I think that immigrants, whether settled for generations or of recent date, bring in their baggage, not a love of Europe and of European ways of life, but rather a multitude of converging prejudices.

For these and other reasons it was inevitable that the participation of the United States in the war of 1914–1918 in Europe would mark a turning-point in international relations. Gone was the simplicity of American diplomacy. The problems were new and strange. America was now veritably governed by public opinion, which had, however, hitherto little occasion to express itself in the domain of foreign affairs.

Inexperienced, the American statesmen were ready to emit snap judgments, looking with suspicion—not unfounded—on subtle and cautious European diplomacy. Foreign diplomats were, to the American mind, all disciples of Machiavelli. They were lurking in ambush to trick the American emissaries. Until then, Americans in Europe had been complacent observers, penning their pleasant accounts of the contemporary scene, or delving at leisure in the archives of foreign lands in order to find the substance of their admirable histories, or discovering (like Longfellow) inspiration for their romances and poems in exotic conditions. Now they came in contact with grim realities, rivalries arising out of a thousand years of war and intrigue. They thought they could bring quick and simple solutions to age-old problems.

That there was need of a new diplomacy was evident. But the mistake of Wilson was that he thought national questions could be safely discussed in international assemblies, that quiet negotiations could properly be replaced by public debates, that for trained diplomats there could be substituted well-meaning amateurs, that the whole mass of mankind could engage in the pursuit of peace without plunging the world into universal war.

If things did not turn out so well, whose was the fault? The answer came easily. It was the scoundrelly Florentine who had contaminated Europe. American statesmen had fallen into a den of cut-throat Machiavellians.

5

THE TRAGEDY OF VERSAILLES

I$_T$ is desirable, before I comment on the Versailles Conference, which was actually conducted not by statesmen but by the peoples, to glance at the Congress of Vienna (together with the Paris negotiations) of 1815. We shall find the comparison most instructive.

Writers on historical events have a curious habit of following each other, of repeating the hackneyed praise or the stereotyped criticism of an era. Only rarely do they pause to inquire whether the accepted opinion is correct or not. Thus we are told, in these democratic days, that the treaties after the Napoleonic wars were made by diplomats—as though that alone were sufficient to condemn them. We are told that they adopted the principle of legitimacy—as though any other principle could, at the time, have been adopted if Europe was to be saved from anarchy. We are told that there were compromises on territorial distribution—as though the allies ought to have started fighting among themselves. We are told that there was dancing in Vienna. Now I would not, myself, think it proper to dance in celebration, even of the end of a great European tragedy. But I happened to see the whole of Europe and America dancing-mad in 1919—and the sort of dancing was such that it drew from Clemenceau the remark: "In my day we used to go to a *chambre d'hotel*."

The truth is, of course, that after "revolutionary" wars there could not fail to be a "reactionary" peace. The chief consideration is whether a lasting peace was made by the "reactionaries." Did it work? It did. For a hundred years there was no major war in Europe. I apply the term "major" to wars like those of Napoleon and like those of 1914–1918 and 1939–1945, and not to local wars like those between Austria and Prussia, the Crimean war, the Franco-Prussian war, and the wars in Eastern Europe, which indeed cannot be compared in their extent or consequences with the earlier or the later wars. Local wars there had to be in an evolving Europe but at least for many decades relative peace was assured.

In his badly entitled book, *How Europe Made Peace without America*—for alas, Europe was not allowed to make peace without America in 1919—Frank H. Simonds, writing of the settlement of 1814–1815, made by Wellington, Castlereagh, Talleyrand, Metternich, and the delegates of the Czar Alexander, remarks:

> It was made by men who were the fine and finished product of a system which had long endured and, with the passing of the centuries, had acquired a technique in dealing with precisely the questions which constituted the task of Paris (and Vienna) after the Napoleonic wars. Sovereigns had learned to associate with themselves those of their subjects whose brains, knowledge and character permitted them to become great foreign ministers or successful captains. There was nothing approaching public opinion in any of the continental countries which had fought France. Nor was there anything remotely suggesting representative parliaments through which public opinion could make itself felt.

Certainly there can be no question of reverting to these conditions; but I would ask the critics of the Congress of Vienna whether France would have fared so well had the voice of the peoples, instead of the voice of trained diplomats, been heard. France had behaved much worse than Germany did in 1914–1918, or even in 1939–1945. For nearly a quarter of a century she had ravaged Europe. She had humiliated many countries. She had made many conquests. She had drawn boundaries as she pleased without considering the feelings of her adversaries. She had thoroughly scared the great powers. She had cost them untold treasure, immense losses in men. She had plundered on the largest possible scale; she had left few art galleries of Europe untouched. Imagine the resentment and fury of the masses, had all this happened in our own day.

The allies had every reason to be incensed. But, although Napoleon had, after the era of the revolutionaries, been the chief author of Europe's woes, it was not proposed to hang him, as the Kaiser was to be hung and as, in fact, the generals and statesmen of Hitler's Reich were hung. We are bidden to shed tears over the harsh treatment of Napoleon, exiled on the island of St. Helena, and doubtless he suffered greatly; but was it possible to allow him to roam at large? Today, we may regret that the Bourbons were recalled, but even the most democratic politicians today would surely not suggest that there should have been "general elections" in France, and the revolutionary struggle renewed under conditions of complete disorder. Legitimacy, the reversion to the *status quo ante*—was the the only conceivable policy in the situation of 1814–1815 unless, indeed, the allies had chosen, as we chose in 1919 in respect to Austria, and in 1945 in respect to Germany, to break up France, to reduce her to a subordinate country.

By the Treaty of Paris (May, 1814) the utmost politic moderation was observed. There was to be no indemnity. There was to be no foreign occupation. There was to be no restoration of the booty which had enriched France after years of systematic looting. France's foreign conquests were, naturally, to be surrendered, but the territory of Louis XVIII, the brother of the guillotined king, was slightly larger than France before 1789. There was to be no Carthaginian peace, such as Stalin and Henry Morgenthau proposed for Germany a few years ago and, in fact, by the willful destruction of the German industrial plant that had survived the war, was undertaken by the Russians, the Americans and the English in a devastated country. On the whole, I would describe the peacemakers of 1814 as far more civilized and much more astute diplomats than the champions of popular diplomacy today.

At the Congress of Vienna, in the following November, the final settlement was worked out. The Revolution and Napoleon had caused upheavals throughout Europe that can only be compared to the upheavals of Russian Bolshevism since 1917, and the problem was to restore order. On the eastern borders of France, a series of buffer States were designed to protect the tender body of Europe. On the northern side, the Netherlands (i.e., Calvinist Holland and Catholic Belgium) were united to save them from France. They were separated in 1830. In the south, the Sardinian Kingdom was united to Genoa and Savoy, and thus were laid the foundations of modern Italy. On the other hand, Austria, under the skillful conduct of Metternich, obtained (as seemed natural then) control in Lombardy, Venetia, Trieste, and on the Dalmatian littoral, with an Archduke in Florence and an Archduchess in Parma. Prussia, which had played no small part in the downfall of Napoleon, was given the "watch on the Rhine." On all these arrangements which, in spite of modern sneers, seemed essentially fair, there was practically no controversy—or at any rate no public controversy.

But there were two problems that were more prickly. One was the Grand Duchy of Warsaw, which Napoleon had carved from the Polish provinces of Prussia, and the second was that of Saxony. Russia demanded the whole of Poland. Prussia wanted Saxony, in which claim she was opposed by Austria. In the end, it was decided to make a Polish kingdom under the Czar of Russia, and to place two-thirds of Saxony and the Rhine provinces within the Prussian sphere. On the whole, although we are told that the peoples were not consulted, I do not think any substantial criticism can be made of the compromise. I will point out that Saxony and the Rhine provinces have since voluntarily become part of Germany and, although we have fought two wars for Polish independence, Poland is now virtually part of the Russian Union.

Compare these achievements of trained diplomats, "reactionary" as they may have been in the sense of opposing the disintegrating forces of the French Revolution, as we oppose the disintegrating forces of the Russian Revolution which has absorbed many satellite states today, with the work of 1919, with its creation of new republics that could not possibly endure but were bound to provoke strife, the drawing of new and disputable frontiers that could not fail to promote contention, the dissolution of Austria-Hungary that necessarily brought anarchy to Central Europe, and the promulgation of the mischievous creed of self-determination which encouraged any little ethnic group to break away from the country in which it was placed. I will only mention that Croatia at once agitated for its separation from Yugoslavia, and that Slovakia claimed detachment from the impossibly artificial state of Czechoslovakia, not to speak of the resentment of the Sudeten Germans in a country of which the Czechs formed a minority.

In March, 1815, Napoleon returned to France, and struck out for Brussels, for Belgium was the dearest of French possessions. There was alarm in Vienna. In June, Napoleon was beaten at Waterloo. After these Hundred Days, which might well have hardened the hearts of the exponents of popular diplomacy, the diplomats remained moderate. Wellington and Castlereagh opposed the taking of Alsace-Lorraine from France—although the history of its annexation and the character of its people undoubtedly were open to discussion; the statesmen realized that to give a truncated France to Louis XVIII would render his authority precarious. They

gave a few concessions to the Netherlands, and the forts of
Saarlouis and Landau to Germany; they imposed a fine of
700 million francs on France; they now asked for a partial
restoration of stolen art treasures; and they considered that a
three to five years' occupation had become necessary. Surely,
they could hardly have done less. Again, I say, compare the
peace terms imposed on France—at least as great a culprit as
Germany a hundred years later—by men skilled in statecraft,
with the peace dictated to Germany in 1919, and the unde-
fined application of "unconditional surrender" in 1943.

I must add that England would have nothing to do with
the mystical Holy Alliance of Alexander I—a vague forerunner of the League of Nations, designed to stereotype a
still growing Europe—but she did join the more practical
Concert of Europe which barred the Bonapartes from power
for many years. There was no deliberate generosity shown
by the statesmen; they considered what would be most profit-
able to themselves and Europe. Their ideas differed from ours,
and we may condemn them; but at least they were ideas and
not emotions. They were not acting in the spirit of popular
diplomacy—and I, for one, do not hold that as a reproach
against them. Therefore, they were not seeking vengeance
for the sake of vengeance, they were not inflicting punishment such as mass "morality" would have inflicted, they were
not exploiting victory by placing burdens on the vanquished
too heavy to be borne and infallibly producing fresh upheavals; they were simply behaving like sensible international
technicians who had no political axe to grind and no elections
to fear.

Should we admire Talleyrand-Perigord, Prince of Bene-
vento, renegade priest and married bishop, whose skilful negotiations saved France? As a man, no; as a statesman, who
served his country (and incidentally himself) well, yes. He
had received honors under the *Ancien Régime*, rich benefices
from the Court. He was a revolutionary, when the wind set

in that quarter, and undertook diplomatic missions. Under the reign of Robespierre he thought it advisable to emigrate. He came back to become minister under the Directory. He continued in office under the Consulate. We find him serving at Erfurt. He managed (happily for France) to be appointed Minister of Foreign Affairs under the Bourbon restoration. In the Congress of Vienna he shifted sides on the Polish and Saxony questions. He persuaded Alexander and he cajoled Metternich, he was with England, and he was with Prussia. He flitted lightly from position to position, without fettering himself by principles. He had an acute sense of opportunity, of expediency. For my part, I hold loyalty to be among the greatest of virtues. Talleyrand was completely lacking in loyalty except to France, whose interests he constantly upheld. But it would be too much to expect from statesmen the virtues that we honor in private life; and the "last of the Machiavellis" of Europe cannot be denied his part in the salvaging of the France of 1815. Nevertheless, not even a Talleyrand could have done anything for Germany in 1919, for the popular diplomats would not listen to any German spokesman, refusing to meet representatives of the "enemy" until they had settled the terms of their *Diktat*, and in 1945 they promptly put the competent German diplomats in prison.

We are now in a position to judge the Conference of Versailles (so called, although it was held in Paris) against a background of diplomatic history, and to see how the new diplomacy fell far short of the old diplomacy, which we have been taught to scoff at as both antiquated and wicked. The old diplomacy was antiquated in the sense that each age has its own problems, and that it would have been folly to have applied the solutions of 1815 to the problems of 1919. It was only wicked in the sense that no diplomatic solutions of international problems can be perfect; they are conditioned by the sort of danger which seems greatest, the sort of "ideology" that is prevalent in ruling circles, the physical as well as the moral possibilities. But the new diplomacy of 1919 was still more antiquated, in that it was a throwback to barbarism —the *vae victis* of the Gallic chief who took Rome in 390 B.C.—and it was incomparably more wicked in that it was, under the mask of "popular" opinion, vengeful and blind to the future coëxistence of victors and vanquished in a world where their peaceful coöperation was needed.

Much has been written about the Versailles Conference, which I followed from beginning to end from a post of vantage; but we can now see it in better perspective. We have seen the poisonous fruits it produced—the second World War, with a third World War in sight. Moreover, although so much has been written, certain vital comments have never been made—or if they have been made (some of them by me), they have attracted too little attention and have not been appreciated at their right value as guides to diplomatic conduct.

By far the most important comment is this: that, for the first time in history, the peoples (I mean the peoples on the winning side) flooded into the Council Chamber at Versailles. It was not Wilson alone who invited them; all the would-be statesmen called the peoples to their aid, and openly played their game in accordance with what they believed (they were not always right) to be the best electoral card.

Hitherto, able diplomats had sat behind closed doors. Now, the doors were flung wide open. Hitherto, careful cogitation had been undisturbed by the shouts of an excited populace. Now, the delegates were the willing victims of the most voluble advisers. Hitherto, peacemakers had thought in terms of peace. Now, they thought in terms of war. Hitherto, they had taken long views. Now, they were only responsive to immediate acclamation.

It is a truism that peace cannot be concluded in an atmosphere of war. Diplomats ought to be able to escape from the atmosphere of war sooner than the masses. Peace cannot be concluded unless all parties, victors and vanquished, are in substantial accord on what is practicable. But the men of Versailles, oblivious of everything but their excited publics, continued the war on another terrain. They had no wish to close a chapter of misery and suffering. Catherine de' Medici once said: "Very good, my son; we have cut the cloth, now we must sew it." She knew, with that wisdom she had inherited from her Italian family that, after destruction must come reconstruction, and that a final agreement by both sides to a dispute, however bloody, is of the highest necessity. How can the fighting men fresh from their trenches, how can the public, bitterly resentful with good cause, forget in a moment its animosities, unsay all it has said and been taught to say? For that matter, how can politicians, clever though they may be in turning partisan and ideological somersaults, suddenly change their tune? They have been cheered for the most irresponsible statements designed to stir up anger; the incense of the people's praise has delighted their nostrils; and on the renewal of the applause hangs their chance of securing a new mandate.

Surely, I need not insist, though apparently the lesson has not been learned, that leaders in war cannot be leaders in peace. Their own lethal imagination has been kindled; in firing the crowd they have taken fire themselves. They are quite unfit to make a settlement that will promote reconciliation. They will be bent on revenge or, if perchance they can rid themselves of such inappropriate feelings, they must still reckon with the untrained and untamed impulses of the herd they have excited.

Wilson, who came with high-sounding words and admirable intentions, was an astute politician, though he made an egregious mistake in coming to the Conference and in putting forward propositions that aroused antagonism in Europe and hostility in America. He had no experience in diplomacy, he had little knowledge of the countries for which he proposed to legislate. Clemenceau was an old parliamentarian whose career had been checkered, but he had won the esteem of the French people by his undying hatred of Germany and his wartime efforts. Lloyd George was flushed with his success at the polls where he had obtained votes by the most unstatesmanlike utterances—promises of the execution of the Kaiser who had fled to Holland, and the bleeding white of the German people. Orlando was, likewise, a seasoned parliamentarian who dared not go home without the spoils which had been assigned to Italy in the Secret Treaties and the Italian people logically expected.

How could they think seriously? How could they disentangle the skein of tangled problems of which they were as uninformed as the mob which shouted counsels to them? That mob was indubitably represented in the Conference. It was, perhaps, the only genuine party in the deliberations. That is why I affirm, as one who followed the discussions from beginning to end, that the Versailles Conference was a veritable revolution in international relations and procedure. It changed overnight the whole conception of diplomacy, and the revolution still continues with ever more dire results. How can the mob be excluded from international conferences again?

It may, of course, be supposed that the Big Four (for in spite of professed concern for the "good little nations" there were only four powers admitted to the making of real decisions) realizing their lack of knowledge, would have turned to their advisers at the Quai d'Orsay, at the British Foreign Office, at the American State Department. Certainly, they were briefed, but they took little notice of their briefing. The consultations were of the most superficial character, merely on points of fact; and the conclusions drawn were the work of the principal delegates. Much more important than the diplomatic advisers were the deputies in the Chamber, the Senators, the members of the House of Commons and

Congress and, behind them the weight of public opinion, that is to say of public anger.

Besides, it seemed to me that the advisers were generally men of restricted vision. They might prepare an able summary of the case for this or that, in accordance with the preconceived views of their masters, or their own personal biases, but they were careful, for the most part, not to commit themselves to views that were contrary to those already held. They emitted no warnings. That was not their job. They were functionaries, each serving the policy of their chiefs, and those chiefs were often at logger-heads. Their facts and figures did not conform to those of other delegations.

Even with such facts and figures to help them, the Big Four displayed their ignorance on many occasions. Thus Lloyd George naïvely asked: "Where is Teschen?" though the district of Teschen was the main stumbling-block in any agreement between the new Poland and the new state of Czechoslovakia. He confused Silesia, in Germany, with Cilicia in Asia Minor. Wilson never understood why the Italians, after warmly welcoming him as the savior and friend of their country, turned and rent him when he refused to ratify the pledges of France and England in respect of Fiume, Dalmatia and Smyrna. Nor could the opponents of Italian ambition understand why, after taking a stand which nearly wrecked the Conference, he finally agreed, contrary to his principle of "self-determination," to place the Brenner frontier and Southern Tyrol under Italian control. It was an American professor, Robert H. Lord of Harvard University, who drew up the preposterous plan for a Polish corridor dividing Germany, and the equivocal status of Danzig, which was recognized by all sane observers from 1919 onwards to be the potential cause of a new war.

Always looking over their shoulders to see how the deputies, M.P.'s and senators were taking it, always listening for

the echoes of the mob, the Big Four consented to the imposi-
tion of "reparations" on a ruined country ten times greater
than the debt to the United States that England was unable to
repay. On the folly of this measure, which meant the bankruptcy of Germany without helping either France or England, a few British economists, notably John Maynard
Keynes, who at any rate were used to counting, warned the
statesmen, but to no avail. To make Germany pay was the
simple demand of the public unversed in high finance, and it
was useless to protest that there were only three main methods of payment—in goods, which nobody wanted, since a
flood of importations would upset national economy; in services, which would, by instituting a system of foreign slave
labor, create unemployment, notably in France; or in gold,
which did not exist in any proportion to the amount required. "You cannot cut beefsteaks off a cow and expect to
milk it" was one familiar way of expressing the reality of
"reparations"; but nevertheless, in obedience to popular diplomacy, Germany was saddled with impossible debts, and
the life of Europe was thus bedevilled for many years.

I must here briefly refer to a story I have already told in
my book, *In My Time*, since it illustrates the attitude of the
public and the parliamentarians. The public was, of course,
physically present at Versailles in the shape of newspaper
men. Now I am not reflecting on the ability of a profession
which I followed myself for several decades when I suggest
that the swarm of "special correspondents" in Paris were just
as uninformed as the readers of their journals. How could
they have had any experience with economic and diplomatic
matters? How could they think differently from the mass of
their readers? They made no pretense to knowledge; they
were content to take their "directives," if not their instructions, from the press agents which each delegation enrolled
as liaison officers between the statesmen and the newspaper
men. They were (as the phrase went) spoon-fed. Personally,

I decided from the beginning to stay away from the "press conferences" which merely wasted the time of those who wished to follow the proceedings intelligently, and to rely on a few independent sources of information and my own interpretation of matters which I had studied.

The question of reparations did open the eyes of Lloyd George to realities. One day he met the newspaper men and talked to them over the tea cups. He had just circulated a letter to his colleagues pointing out the importance of making a treaty that Germany could observe: "No *Germania Irredenta* which would provoke a fresh war in a few years, no reparations which would shatter European economy." He tried to convey to the newspaper men that we must forget the wartime propaganda, the rash and inconsiderate election promises, and get down to "brass tacks." Every time he began to speak of a just peace, a durable peace, a possible peace, there were snickers. This new kind of talk sounded like a joke. Now Lloyd George, the old politician, had his "antennae" well developed, and he soon saw that he was mistaken in thinking that he could unsay all he had said. He was faced with a wall of incomprehension, and he decided to talk of other things.

As my own mind had moved in the direction which Lloyd George was now taking, rather belatedly, I at once discerned that something had happened of the greatest interest, and I remained behind after the others had left. "You tried to say something that you eventually decided would not go over," I said. "Perhaps you will tell me." And, then and there, the British Prime Minister poured out his soul to me. My interview, which was described as being with a "High Authority," made an enormous sensation. Yet it did no good. On the contrary, a great majority of the newly elected House of Commons called on Lloyd George to repudiate the sentiments and reasoning of my article. What could he do but bow to the storm? He boldly asserted that he had never said the things attributed to him and it was not until three years later that the publication of his circular, in the very terms I had employed, proved the accuracy of my recording.

Surely no better demonstration of the evils of popular diplomacy could be desired. A public crying in its ignorance for what would be revengeful and dangerous; politicians, equally ignorant, pandering to the public prejudices, their very existence linked with the public prejudices; parliamentarians preventing the conversion of their ministers to reason; and a press accustomed to receive the "hand-outs" of the governments as gospel truth: that sums up the imbecility of Versailles, in particular, and of popular diplomacy, in general.

As for the territorial changes, they were deplorable. Some of them did not threaten later war, but there were others, which chiefly concerned the Polish Corridor and the break-up of Austria, which were bound to bring disaster on Europe. Groups of voluble agitators, in the name of nationalities long ago defunct, made claims which reduced Eastern Europe to a mosaic of rival states without force. Certainly, the Austro-Hungarian Empire was tottering, but precisely when it was most necessary for Europe to form larger unities, it was thought fit to encourage the sentimental cry for "small nations." Reforms were badly needed in the Austro-Hungarian Empire; they could have been imposed. This hodge-podge of races, Germanic and Slav, was falling to pieces; that was the best of all reasons for consolidating it by removing all disabilities on the subject peoples.

It is axiomatic that you cannot leave a great gap in Central and Eastern Europe without some great nation, whether it be Germany or Russia, moving in to take control. It is axiomatic that, if you try to fill it up by a number of feeble countries, these countries will offer a standing temptation to their more powerful neighbors. The opportunity of creating a happy confederation, which would be at once a bulwark against a future Germany and a safeguard against a future Russia (for Russia too, though, at that moment down and out, might be expected to recover) was unique. It might never occur again. The whole trend of the nineteenth century was towards unification, against divisions, against frontiers, against barriers of any kind. America had, indeed, fought the bloodiest of civil wars to oppose the splitting up of the Republic. Germany had finally been constructed, Italy had been unified.

But now, popular diplomacy was fascinated by the multitudinous demands for "freedom"—freedom to separate, to contract out, to form little communities jealous of their neighbors and oppressive, in their turn, of the minorities which must necessarily be placed within their borders if they were to be framed at all. Thus Czechoslovakia, carved out of the Austrian Empire, was principally composed of populations that by no stretch of imagination could be described as Czechs. There were Slovaks who asked why they, too, should not be "free." There were Germans, numbering several millions who had been there long before the Czechs. In the old Serbia, now called Yugoslavia, there were Croats who demanded their "freedom." Austria proper was reduced to a tiny state that could not live on its own resources; in form it was like a tadpole with a huge head and no body to speak of, a great capital, Vienna, without a country. It was plain enough that she would, sooner or later, ask to be brought into the German fold. Hungary was cut to the bare bones. Rumania, which happened to be on the Allied side, was given areas of land that were Russian. It would not have been easy, and it would have required wise diplomacy, to aim at the federation of the Balkans. Instead of this, popular diplomacy prevailed, with dire results that were readily foreseeable. In the end, it was Pan-Slavism, which was anathema to the old diplomacy, that was the gainer, and the whole of the Balkans were eventually Russianized. But this took place only after a calamitous war which stopped them from being Germanized.

"Open decisions openly arrived at . . ." proclaimed President Wilson in his revolt against so-called secret diplomacy, which really meant discreet, prudent, farsighted, dispassionate, expert diplomacy. That there was much to criticize in the diplomacy he denounced, I should be the last to deny; but, whatever its faults, was it sensible to rush to the opposite extreme and try to make peace in accordance with unproven theories, by men who had not served their apprenticeship in the art of international relations, who were improvised dabblers in geography, history, economics, and the psychology of any people other than their own? Was it sensible to work in a hubbub of noisy and vain newspaper comment, in a confusion of conflicting claims, against a background of popular applause or hissing? Surely the answer is plain.

Remark also that not only were the decisions manifestly erroneous, the source of future wars, but they were also, from the viewpoint of the promises made in the famous Fourteen Points and other pronouncements that had induced the Germans to surrender, eminently mendacious. If it is argued that the Germans would have had to surrender, with or without these promises, the truth or falsity of the argument cannot release us from our pledges. Virtually all the Fourteen Points were broken.

It is not my purpose to enumerate the foolish and baneful articles of the Treaty; but I must lay stress on one, the most vicious article of all, which embodies in itself the whole spirit of Versailles, the vicious article that is the perfect poison-fruit of popular diplomacy, the vicious article that is, if not the cause, at the very root of all our woes—the article which attributed the sole guilt for the onset of the first World War to the German people.

To protest against it in 1919, to suggest that perhaps it was superfluous and therefore mischievous, was to draw on one's devoted head the hideous charge of pro-Germanism. A pro-German was then the worst kind of traitor. That is why, perhaps, even those who ventured to criticize the Treaty in detail, were strangely silent about its most outrageous clause. I hope it is not necessary, now that everybody can see where that monstrous clause has led us—to Hitlerism, to the Second World War, and a third world war looming ahead—to state that, for my part, I have never been pro-German. My culture, my affinities, my birth, my upbringing, my spiritual sympathies, have been quite un-German. But neither have I been anti-German, for that is not a sensible historical or philosophical position. One should today, as in 1914, in 1919, at all times, think not in terms of what will profit England or France or Russia or America or any other section of the human family, but in terms of what will benefit the whole of humanity. And from this standpoint I affirm that it is anti-human to brand any nation as possessed of an exceptional dose of original sin. We can discuss the facts of history, we can show where this or that country went wrong, but we cannot, without damage to the human race, pretend that this or that country is fundamentally wicked. Yet, that is precisely what the peacemakers at Versailles did. Without awaiting the verdict of an impartial jury of historians, they put in the forefront of their Treaty a sentence that condemned the German people, without trial, without evidence, without admitting any defense, as outlaws from humanity.

It was natural that the victorious peoples, after a long and cruel war, should regard their defeated adversaries as criminal. But it was the business of statesmen to refrain from any endorsement of the moblike view of the masses. They should have deliberated in a calmer atmosphere, free from the dust and turmoil of the battle-field. They should have risen above the turbulence and excitement of the arena. They were there to make a practical settlement, not to pronounce moral judgments.

To inject moral judgments into diplomatic arrangements is one of the most pernicious practices of our age. It is, unfortunately, an integral item of popular diplomacy; it is the mainspring of mass emotion. Let it not be supposed that I think that morality has no place in international relations. On the contrary, there cannot be international relations without some morality. But our conceptions of morality are affected by our interests, our susceptibilities, our sufferings, our hatreds, and our affections; and, by the well-known psychological process of projection, we are inclined to blame others to cover up our own guilt.

So it was in 1919. Without entering into any discussion of the causes of the war, which are multiple, without attempting to attribute its due part to Germany, or Russia, or France, or any other country, it was certainly ill-advised, and indeed immoral, to cast all the blame for its outbreak on the Germans as a people. Even if we allege that morality demanded a search for the culprits, the search should have been seriously undertaken by impartial judges. But the men of Versailles did not hesitate. The first thing to be done was to justify any iniquitous conditions that might be laid down in the Treaty by arraigning Germany before the bar of public opinion.

Arraigning? Public opinion? Neither expression is appropriate. The public opinion was that of the victors. It took no heed of the long train of circumstances. It did not call in the archivists, the historians, the few neutrals. It gave no place to the public opinion of the beaten countries which presumably was altogether different. It based itself on a moment of time in certain countries, without asking whether at a later moment of time, in different conditions, public opinion was susceptible of change. It worked in the immediate present, in a state of emotion which might be fanatical and ephemeral, and it solemnly set down forever, in the indelible ink of a signed and sealed Treaty, a curse which purported to be the curse of mankind. Germany was henceforward to be the Cain among the nations, with the frightful mark of God set on her forehead.

Arraigned? No, all justice calls for a hearing of the accused. But, in Paris, no German was asked to explain his conduct, or to exculpate his country were it possible. It was taken for granted that Germany was a criminal, and nothing remained except to pass sentence on her without a hearing. When German representatives begged to be allowed to state their case, they were indignantly repelled. Popular diplomacy had spoken, and there was no more to be said.

It is amazing, in looking back to these early days of popular diplomacy, to reflect that whatever bitter wrangles there might be among the statesmen at the Conference on the measures to be taken against Germany, no voice was raised against the blanket condemnation of Germany. Nobody seemed to realize that we would have to live with Germany again, that she could not be suppressed, put beyond the pale of human relations. Nobody paused to consider that we must again work with Germany, trade with Germany, march forward together with her to our human destiny. It will hereafter appear incredible, if it does not already so appear, that men of presumed intelligence could gather to make peace without imagining for a second that there are at least two partners to a peace, and that to endeavor to erect it solely on the foundations of a condemnation, just or unjust, is to build it on shifting sand.

Even worse: that the Allies should unilaterally condemn Germany without restriction, without extenuating circumstances, was bad enough; but that she should be denied even the opportunity of protesting her innocence, her relative innocence in any case, an opportunity not denied to the convicted murderer, is something which belongs to the realm of phantasmagoria. Nay more: it was decided (as in the mock trials in the countries behind the Iron Curtain today) that justice would not be satisfied unless Germany signed a confession, full and unreserved, of her criminal nature.

The choice was given: either to take the Treaty as it stood without debate, or to submit to the continuation of the state of war with all that it implied after the surrender. Even the unconditional surrender of 1945 did not go as far as this: Germany in 1945 was not called upon to append her signature to a document attesting her incurable blood-guiltiness, her incorrigible turpitude. The men of Versailles were in a position in which they could command. Their *Diktat*, backed by the might of popular diplomacy, had to be swallowed willy-nilly, and there had to be found two unfortunate Germans who would put their names to the avowal that Germany was the eternal felon of nations. One of them spoke to me sadly as he left the Palace of Versailles. "It will seem so different twenty years from now," he commented. Twenty years! Whether by extraordinary prescience or by mere guesswork, he had estimated correctly the number of years that would elapse before the world would be plunged into a still more dreadful conflict.

A great deal happened in those twenty years, and it might have been possible, had we been wiser, to undo much of the physcal harm that was done by popular diplomacy in 1919. But I do not see how we could undo the moral damage that was caused by the clause that was designed to make of Germany the pariah of nations. Material wrongs can be righted; many of them were. Time might efface the traces of injuries deserved or undeserved. Germany might grow strong again—as indeed she did—and enforce the rectification of boundaries and the removal of disabilities. But nothing could obliterate the memory of the proscription unanimously laid on Germany, not only their rulers, and form of government, but on the whole German people everywhere. On this text Hitler could well base his most extravagant diatribes. In this uniqueness and solidarity in ostracism he could well stimulate the German people to rebel against the very essence of the Treaty. Every other nation was bidden to regard the Germans as accursed; in Germany a deep sense of inferiority was stirred.

How could peace be made and preserved by such a refusal to coöperate with Germany as a country which enjoyed the same rights, which might have the same aspirations, which possessed the same human qualities as the rest of us? Many times, when I have heard eloquent pleas for equality, for a united Europe, for one world, I have smiled bitterly, and asked myself how it was possible to join hands with an un-repentant wrongdoer, a self-confessed worker of iniquity. It could only be brought about by inviting Germany to for-get that she had been damned as the world's malefactor. We spoke often, without accomplishing much, of a revision of the Treaty, but the first act of revision, which conditioned everything else, was the annulment of the War-Guilt Clause. Had we done that, history might have taken a vastly different course. Mankind might have entered on the road to freedom, prosperity, and happiness. While the Guilt Clause stood, hopes for the future were utterly vain.

The disgust with which one of the old diplomats regarded the theory of unique German war guilt and the War-Guilt Clause of the Treaty of Versailles is well brought out by Harold Nicolson in his *Portrait of a Diplomatist* where he is discussing the attitude of his father, Sir Arthur Nicolson, British Ambassador to St. Petersburg and one of the last of the outstanding old diplomats. As early as 1917:

> He was incensed by the theory, which was even then being propagated, that Germany had provoked the war. He set himself to write an article . . . in which he put

the German case more fairly. He concluded this article with a note of warning.

All are anxious for a durable peace, but there will be little hope of durability if it were thought to impose on great communities terms which would be regarded as intolerable or humiliating and which would sow the seeds of revengeful animosity. . . .

He was appalled by the Treaty of Versailles. Particularly did he resent the paragraph which obliged Germany by force to admit that she was solely responsible for the war. He considered that paragraph both undignified and meaningless. "I cannot understand it," he would say, "you cannot impose a moral judgment on a whole people. I feel sure that we old diplomatists would not have done such a thing."

It is strange that, in the name of morality, we should have destroyed our prospects of a better world. In condemning Germany, we condemned ourselves to misery. One may argue as one pleases as to the causes of the First World War, but there can be no argument as to the causes of the Second World War. The culprits were the men of Versailles, who brought to ripeness the poisonous fruits of popular diplomacy. The others, the Hitlers, are only secondary causes, or rather consequences, of the original cause, which I have named, correctly I believe, popular diplomacy.

Incidentally, it is interesting to note that the Versailles Conference not only produced a revolution in diplomatic methods but also launched the epoch of bad manners in international intercourse which continued until, as one talented observer remarked, the representatives of states spoke to each other in peacetime in terms which, a few decades earlier, would not have been used in the midst of a war. Such were the bitter remarks made by Goebbels against the Russians, which were returned in kind, Churchill's denunciations of Russia before 1941 and of Hitler before 1939, Roosevelt's use of such term as "rattlesnakes" to describe the Nazis with whom the United States was still at peace, and Truman's reception of foreign diplomats by denouncing their system of government and political chiefs before they had laid down their hats and gloves.

The representatives of the Big Four, spurred on by the clamor of their publics for revenge or spoils, had many heated exchanges. Perhaps the most dramatic was the occasion on which it is said that Clemenceau attacked Wilson and tried to choke him.

The Travels of Mr. Dulles—In 15 Months, 4 Times the Distance Around the World

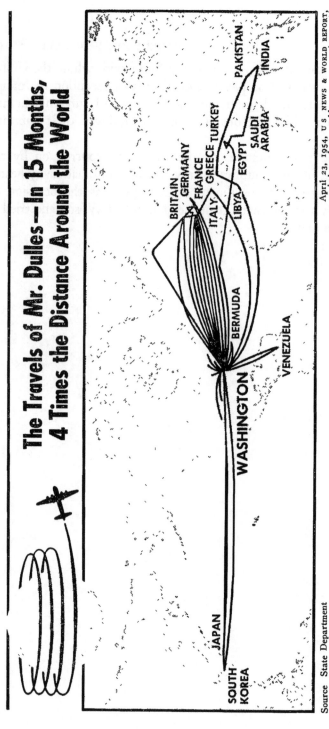

Source State Department
© 1954, By U.S. News Pub Corp

April 23, 1954, U S NEWS & WORLD REPORT, an independent weekly news magazine, published at Washington

6

TROUSERS AND TRAVEL
PERIPATETIC POPULAR DIPLOMACY

A̲ll̲ t̲his̲ is very well, a reader may protest, but you are merely criticizing high political decisions. They are of vital importance, it is true, but are such as must be taken only on exceptional occasions. It may be that wrong decisions are made under the stress of public emotions which influence statesmen, and that statesmen themselves, being human, are swayed by such emotions. It is possible that in a great crisis they may fail. Without minimizing the gravity of their failure, is not the normal work of diplomacy efficiently carried on day by day by a highly trained and competent body of diplomatic agents and officers?

Such, in theory, is the case but, in reality, the new diplomacy has taken the direction of affairs out of the hands of able and trained public servants, has stripped them of real initiative and power, has converted them into mere cogs in a complicated machine which turns in the void and grinds out noisy verbiage. Without an efficient head, without a definite policy, without clear aims, without continuity, without fixed purpose, without responsibility, without an absolute assurance of ministerial backing, the best and most elaborate diplomatic corps can function only in a futile and vacillating manner.

Now the new system of perpetual conferences, frequent meetings of ministers, public discussions, parliamentary questioning, press propaganda, and unceasing agitation, has made of foreign offices and state departments little more than publicity bureaus without any inspiring and guiding principle. They have no sound mind or sincere soul. They are subjected to political—that is, popular—interference at all times. The temporary parliamentary chief may utterly ignore their recommendations, since he takes his instructions or at least his cues from what is loosely called public opinion. Never have there been such huge organizations as the diplomatic and consular services of today, but never has their trained weight been less felt in public life and world affairs. There is an old story of the out-of-work actor and the bedraggled lady of the streets sitting on a park bench bewailing the ruin of two of the oldest professions in the world—by amateurs!

The business of the diplomatic corps is to gather information in every capital. From the embassies and legations a steady stream of naval, military, commercial, as well as political reports, comments, interpretations, perhaps recommendations, flows to the home office. The representatives of each nation keep in close personal contact with the significant personalities in the countries to which they are accredited. They are usually of good social standing and sometimes of more than average intelligence. It is not on the ground of insufficient machinery that the diplomatic service of today is to be criticized; but it goes without saying that, however able and extensive the personnel may be—though it is not always such—it can not by itself produce permanent results of any kind, bad or good. Everything depends on how it is operated. If the final control of international affairs is assigned to a steady and competent chief all may be well. If, however, it is handed over to a nominal chief who, whether with the advice or against the advice of the experts, obeys only the will, or the whim, of the public, all may be ill—and usually is.

In my own day I have discerned a definite deterioration in the quality of diplomatic officers. This I attribute to their awareness of their ultimate futility and impotence under our system of popular diplomacy. If the man in the street is to decide, the work of the man in the bureau becomes little more than superficial. Or, if ministers come on the scene, routine agents must retire into the wings. Of what avail is finesse, if the provocative and noisy debates of the forum are to shape policy? So, while the diplomatic services have become more extensive, they have become less important and effective.

Nor can I overlook a growing and rather silly preoccupation with social conventions. They have their place, no doubt, but they are all too likely to play too large a rôle. I remember that, when I took charge of the foreign bureau of a newspaper, I found the following ludicrous correspondence: "May I advise you, as your duties are chiefly diplomatic," wrote the editor to my predecessor, "to model yourself sartorially on the Embassy." To which my predecessor, being a man of humor, replied: . . . "touching the matter of trousers, would you advise me to take for model the Ambassador, who usually wears checks, or the First Secretary, who prefers stripes."

I myself shocked one attaché by wearing brown tweeds at lunch. How often we are told that Mr. X . . . is the best dressed man in the foreign office or that Mr. Y . . . of the state department changes his tie every day. The Homburg hat, since the passing of the silk topper, is the badge of the tribe, and the black coat is *de rigueur*. And, touching the matter of ties, it is considered desirable in England that the candidate for a diplomatic post should be able to sport an "Old School" tie, a splash of neckgear color which marks him out as a product of Eton or Harrow, or one of the other leading "public schools" to which rich or noble parents send their children.

In short, the English diplomatic service is pretty much closed to men of ability who do not come from the "upper classes." There are, of course, exceptions, but those who adopt diplomacy as a career must at least appear to be "gentlemen," in the English acceptation of the term. It is, as a rule, so in France; and even the more vigorous type of American diplomat cultivates, as an essential virtue, a manner which reveals his profession to the most casual eye. The training and manner are much the same in other countries, with the exception of Russia, where rudeness rather than courtesy would seem to distinguish a Communist emissary, at least since 1945. I well remember the astonishment with which George Tchicherin, one of the earlier representatives of Bolshevism, was greeted because he was "well bred." Most of the Russians sent abroad to negotiate since V-J Day have made up for his lapses into good manners, and are the more appreciated at home the more they provoke "slanging matches."

This education in suavity, even in banality, which the candidate for career diplomatic offices receives, has its excellent side, but it has also its lamentable defects. By dint of inculcating the habit of understatement, all color and all meaning tend to be washed out of the perfect product of the art. I could mention many egregious blunders that were made in our dealings with men like Mussolini through our capacity for toning down our complaints or our warnings. The method leads to a lazy placidity in face of peril. Many diplomats of the new dispensation positively think it creditable not to look far ahead. "Sufficient for the day is the evil thereof." This is a singularly poor motto to follow in international affairs.

Lord Salisbury, one of the great of modern English diplomats who headed the Foreign Office for fifteen years, protested against this policy of "floating downstream, occasionally putting out a diplomatic boat hook to avoid collision." In France, the blunter André Tardieu, referring to Briand, characterized him as "a dead dog floating with the current." Dead dog or lazy punt, it is obvious that in these strenuous times the system of evasive passivity on the part of professional diplomats is no more defensible than the blatant and noisy publicity seeking of the "clamor boys." Mr. Herbert

Morrison, for once, hit the nail on the head in telling England that we are not living in the nineteenth century when it sufficed to send to the scene of our blunders a menacing gunboat. Gunboats, in this sense, are out of date in this age. It would appear that the American equivalent of the gunboat —namely, a loan or a gift in dollars—will soon also be out of date.

Once, when what I considered to be a particularly dangerous policy was being pursued, I spoke to a very high representative of the English Foreign Office. "Do you not see that you are pushing Italy into the arms of Germany?" I asked. "Will that not increase the chances of war?" To my observation, which the sequel has shown to be only too well founded, the very high representative languidly replied: "When we come to that bridge we will consider how it can be crossed." There was nothing more to be said. Against such a passive and evasive mentality expostulation and argument would be useless.

A chess player who refused to take into account the next move of his opponent would have no chance of becoming a champion. The whole business of diplomacy, as of chess playing, is to think out several moves ahead, and certainly not to push a piece complacently into difficulties. I had then, and have had since, many reasons to believe that the spirit in which many diplomats—as well as the politician-diplomat who confines himself to the present—play the game on which depends the future of the world is that of my above-mentioned interlocutor in the Foreign Office. There are circumstances in which, limited as is our foresight, cramped as are our means of action, it may be well to reassure ourselves by saying: "Don't worry—it may never happen." But to adopt as a basic rule such a mentally passive attitude in public life and diplomatic policy, with the responsibility for the welfare of millions resting on our shoulders, is a folly beyond my comprehension.

I have personally known many ambassadors and a number of high officials in the British Foreign Office, the Quai d'Orsay and the American State Department. With the exception of three or four, they have all been short-sighted, indifferent to consequences, provided the immediate advice, decision, or evasion, saved trouble for the moment.

The professional diplomats are usually—if not invariably —men who enjoy at least some small income of their own. For the higher posts they are often taken from outside the service, for they must spend more than their allowance warrants on entertainment. Both in the United States and in England these appointments are usually made as a reward for political services, and not necessarily for merit or fitness. Nevertheless, such is the contagion of the system that they generally soon take on the tone of the professional diplomatic *milieu*. Rarely do they display any real initiative. They are not expected to do so and, if they did, probably the result would be unpleasant. They must keep to their dual rôle of glorified messenger boys in diplomatic uniform and of distinguished social lions.

I do not know how it could be otherwise for, amateur or professional, they are usually quite devoid of any real knowledge of the country to which they are accredited. They have no genuine contacts with the life of the people. By their functions, by their standard of behavior, they are debarred from moving in all classes of society, even if they had any desire to acquaint themselves with the views and feelings of common folk. It is superfluous, as is now the case in Russia, officially to restrict their movements, to mark out the bounds beyond which they must not go. Those bounds are invisibly set in all countries. The farthest and most daring expedition permitted is to visit a fashionable night club which, like the political, social and official circles, is entirely unrepresentative of the true life of a nation. A French writer once drew a sharp distinction between the "legal France" and the "real

John Foster Dulles

France," and it is a valid distinction which applies to England, the United States, Germany, Italy, as well as to France. The position and status of diplomats, from the ambassador to the third secretary and the attaché, isolate them. They must, normally, be the least informed of all foreign residents. Even when the diplomats do inform themselves carefully and fully about the country to which they are accredited, ignorant cabinet officials may arrogantly disregard their information and advice. This was well illustrated by the excellent and informed advice on Japan sent to Washington by Ambassador Joseph C. Grew and Counsellor Eugene Dooman, most of which was contemptuously disregarded by such uninformed men as Secretaries Hull and Morgenthau. The result was Pearl Harbor and all the subsequent disasters to mankind.

So much is this general diplomatic ignorance the case that at one period, an ambassador—wild horses would not induce me to say whether he was American or English—used to ring me up every morning to ask me what information I could offer him. It was plentiful, and he tried to repay me by telling me whatever he had heard. There was, at that time, little that I did not already know, but it pleased him to imagine that he was being helpful. I did not disillusion him, since the relation was useful in other ways. Yet, morning after morning, he ended his conversation with the words (it was his ritual): "I need hardly remind you that whatever has been said has been said in confidence—it is off the record and must not be repeated." And, morning after morning, I replied (it was *my* ritual): "Of course I cannot accept that. You know who I am. It is my business and my duty to gather news and to report it. Besides, I may learn everything you have told me elsewhere. No, I do not bind myself to respect confidence." He grunted, and the next morning we exchanged exactly the same set of words and remained quite friendly.

Apart from the official news which came to diplomats from government quarters, and the unconfirmed rumors they might have heard, there were the newspapers of the country. They had some importance and reliability, but only on condition that one knew enough to read between the lines and be able to guess the reasons which prompted the editorial writer to take this or that view. The background, the party and personal affiliations, the financial interests of each newspaper, must be known before one can attach the right value to its opinions, even to its news or rather, its selection and presentation of the news. The capacity to know and critically evaluate newspaper opinion and policies cannot be learned in a few months, perhaps not even in a few years. I have even been acquainted with embassies where nobody was formally assigned to read the press of the country and, therefore, in the end, had to call in outside help to obtain a digest and appraisal of the newspaper views expressed. I have no doubt that these digests were scrupulously forwarded to the head office and were scanned by somebody.

Now, in my experience, it has become evident that the most important news in any country is not some spectacular occurrence or pronouncement which happens on a given day. It is a trend of thought, difficult to discern at first, but steadily mounting. I am sure this kind of news is seldom recognized in most embassies, and that they are surprised when it suddenly reveals itself in action.

It may fairly be deduced that, although I regard most of the professional diplomats as estimable and companionable fellows, able to plunge into small-talk with their neighbors at the dinner table, correctly dressed in their striped trousers and black coat, I have serious doubts about their ability and usefulness in informing and guiding their home governments relative to the country to which they are accredited.

A recent French novelist has written a cruel caricature of the ministers, of whom he was one, in a certain country. I withhold the name of the author and the title of the book for several reasons. I do not know his motives, I do not know whether his facts are, even in transposed form, reliable. There are references to persons which may be libelous. But distorted though his account certainly is, in some respects, it cannot be altogether brushed aside as fiction. There are, in every embassy, petty jealousies, ridiculous questions of precedence and procedure, rivalries of influence between the various members of the diplomatic corps, trivial personal pursuits, absurd tasks of receiving visitors, of attending ceremonies, and, in spite of the cautiousness which becomes second nature, the possibility of falling into the most serious errors in the transmission of information.

In former days, an ambassador had a highly responsible duty. But, today, the existence of the telephone, the telegraph, the airplane, is reducing his function to that of a forwarding agency and a dignified delegate of his country on official occasions. He appears to be an anachronism in an age in which heads of state can speak instantly and personally by wire or wireless with other heads of state, and in which ministers can fly in an hour, or in a day, from their capital to another capital. He has come to be looked upon as a survival, an antiquarian reminder of the picturesque customs of other days, in his cocked hat and gold braid, like the Lord Mayor's Show in London.

This, I believe is a great mistake. I think the traditional training, quality, and functions of ambassadors should be reviewed in the light of the needs and realities of the twentieth century. The ambassadorial institution is admirable, but it is out of date in its present form. The ambassador should have greater powers and, subject to the approval of the foreign minister, should be empowered to negotiate without the deafening publicity accompanying all international arrangements since 1919 on matters that concern the welfare of the nations. The public demands immediate results; it cannot understand delay, time for reflection, patience to allow the ripening of problems. When the "stars" of diplomacy come on the scene, it is expected that they will quickly return home in triumph. The public imagines that its view or interest must prevail quickly and spectacularly whenever its champion descends into the limelit arena.

There was, indeed, after the Versailles Conference, a temporary attempt to restore to the diplomatic corps something of its prestige, something of the competence which had marked it in earlier peaceful years. A Conference of Ambassadors was established which was to work on the loose ends left by the prime ministers and presidents, after the ill-fated meeting. But it would require an effort of memory of which I am incapable to recall anything important that it accomplished. The prime ministers and presidents had reveled in the publicity; it was not likely that they would now forego the pleasures of popular acclaim; and they quickly resumed their peregrinations in Europe and in America.

And not only did prime ministers and presidents begin to treat ambassadors as negligible quantities, or as hotel-keepers who should put them up for the night: senators, parliamentarians of all categories, took a hand in diplomacy. Embassies were for them a sort of Cook's Tourist Agency. They had, perhaps, heard the French proverb: "*Les voyages forment la jeunesse.*" Why should not travel "form" their mature years as well? Yet, they were not really to be "formed" by travel. They knew about everything in advance, and they made the "grand tour" not to learn, but to teach. I well remember—the name is of no importance—a visitor who was afterwards a candidate for the Presidency of the United States. We met at the dinner-table of an ambassador and he at once began to tell me of his inquiries into the state of Europe. "I have particularly gone into the question of the Ruhr," he told me. "In the Ruhr a plebiscite is to be held to determine whether it should be French or German."

"Excuse me, Governor," I interrupted, "you mean the Saar."

"I mean the Ruhr," he testily replied. "I know what I am talking about. Well, as I was saying, it is certain that the inhabitants of the Ruhr will vote an overwhelming majority for French nationality. . . ."

I tried again. "Impossible, Governor; the Ruhr is purely German. So indeed is the Saar, but there may be some doubt about the sentiments of the people there. You have confounded Ruhr and Saar."

"Do you suppose that I have been wasting my time since I have been over here? I tell you it is the Ruhr. . . ."

"Have it your own way, Governor," was all I could say; but I was saddened by the realization that it was thus, and that by such persons European problems were now to be settled.

I regarded then, as I regard now, the Versailles Conference as a disastrous example of popular diplomacy. Its failure, in my eyes, was unquestionable, but I could not fail to recognize that, for most of my contemporaries, it was deemed to be in the right line of diplomatic progress. However much they were disappointed by the results achieved, they believed that, on the whole, it had upheld democratic principles of justice. It had "made the world safe for democracy"—although the Russian Revolution had brought Communism to a great nation, later to menace the globe, and the products of Versailles were later still to bring Fascism to Italy and Nazism to Germany, and another World War, with still another in its train.

Versailles was to vindicate the rights of peoples to "self-determination," to assure to smaller nations their liberty. Somehow, the world persuaded itself that these ends had been achieved, though it was obvious that populations had been "bartered like chattels," more people had been placed under subjection, and more causes of strife had been created than ever before existed. It had been a "war to end war," although it opened up a vista of endless wars. Versailles had completely missed its objectives.

Yet, at first, few saw the truth. When I analyzed the promises and the performances, I discovered that virtually none of the promises and expectations had been fulfilled. It was then, and not years afterwards, that I came to the conclusion that the failure was not due solely to untoward circumstances, which might (especially after the propaganda of the war) have ruined the high hopes that we had entertained, but should be attributed chiefly to the methods employed—namely to the system of the new diplomacy of the market-place, the discussion of foreign policy from the house-tops.

It was not to be expected that the right explanation would be given by those who were conscious of the collapse. We had entered on a slippery path which we would continue to take for many years. The paroxysms of popular diplomacy would grow more and more violent. Yet, I am convinced that these convulsions, however prolonged, are the convulsions of a dying monster which should never have been born. As we shall see, matters were to get far worse; they do not yet appear to be getting better, and it may be they will never get better before they lead to the ultimate catastrophe of a third World War. Nevertheless, I believe that the decline and eventual fall of popular diplomacy may be (though hidden from many observers) dated from the day when the Versailles Treaty was signed.

The sequel to Versailles was a series of conferences in all the spas and casinos of Europe, and the United States was included in the itinerary of the travelling statesmen.

The proof that no good results could be obtained from this kind of wandering diplomacy should have been sufficient to discourage the official tourists. Pascal has written that most of the mishaps of men arise because they leave their homes. The statement is far too sweeping; on the contrary, it is often by seeking adventure abroad that one finds wisdom and happiness. But, for the politician-diplomats, the axiom is not without point.

Wilson, because he was not content to stay at Washington, to remain in his distant rôle of arbiter, was disowned by the Senate, and died amid the wreckage of his ideals. The lesson ought to have served his successors. Alas, men do not learn from the experience of others, and the nomadic impulses of a later President landed him in terrible blunders that have wrecked more than his ideals—have perhaps shattered our Western civilization.

Orlando was forced out of parliamentary life by the advent of Mussolini. Clemenceau, who was indeed on his home ground, was under continuous pressure not only by the visiting teams, but by the two stalwarts on his own side, Poincaré and Foch, and was promptly kicked out of office and denied the presidency which he coveted. As for Lloyd George, his gypsying was fatal to him and to his party, the great Liberal Party, which had contributed to the prosperity of Britain, now shattered into fragments, its power and traditions both lost. Even from the short-sighted political viewpoint, popular diplomacy does not pay. It cannot avert the consequences of its errors and, sooner rather than later, they come home to roost.

As my own work compelled mè to follow the roving diplomats in their pilgrimages, I can testify that it made no difference whether they met in Spa, in San Remo, in Locarno, in Venice, in Cannes, or even in Washington; the problems somehow refused to change whether they were considered in Genoa, London, or Paris. The implicit confession of these excursions was that Versailles had solved nothing, and neither did the diplomatic joy-rides that filled the post-war years.

This is not a history, and I will not count the one-day or one-week stands that we made in the quest for an elusive agreement that would undo the work of Versailles. At the time, I considered them utterly useless. The procedure was always the same.

The trains started with flag-waving, photographing, optimistic declarations. But no sooner were we comfortably ensconced in our luxurious hotels than there were notes of disillusionment. A crisis was announced. The cables were overcharged with our pessimistic reports which were, I presume, eagerly read by an anxious world. Editorials were written informing the statesmen what was expected of them and they were forbidden to yield an inch under pain of being repudiated by their parliaments. On the third, or maybe the fourth day, it was intimated that an accord was possible. Finally, a *communiqué* was issued affirming that all was for the best in the best of possible worlds, that although no definite decisions were reached the atmosphere had been excellent.

In a word, everybody had tired of the charms of (for example) Stresa, and had agreed to disagree. No genuine progress had been made, no genuine progress could be made between two trains. Yet, satisfaction was expressed as the red carpets were laid down and the band struck up at the departure in the railroad station; and we waited for the next conference of the diplomatic nomads.

Such was the routine, until at last even the public became tired of the same comedy played on different stages. The actors were replaced from time to time, but the piece was dreadfully monotonous and boring. The newspapers, not too quick to discern the increasing apathy of the public, continued to send their "special correspondents," who managed to have an exciting time, and many columns about the abortive proceedings, together with descriptions of the delegates, of the scenery, of the dishes served, of the dresses worn, were printed. I think that what broke down the seriousness and determination of many editors was a front-page story in a respectable English newspaper, written on a note of virtuous indignation, of a luxurious lupanar hastily decorated and furnished with girls of all the nations—a feminine

League of Nations—for the accommodation of delegates from many countries in a Calvinistic city. The description, in which the writer gloated over the spicy details in mock horror, was followed by the announcement: "Other Conference News will be found on Page Ten." Thereafter, it was felt that, perhaps, public interest was flagging in the diplomatic doings of the peacemakers.

The Treaty of Versailles had called for impossible reparations, in obedience to the wishes of the masses, and now Germany was bankrupt, and American money was being poured into the German industries. Austria and Hungary could not continue to exist without aid, especially after the first Bolshevik incursion into Hungary. International loans were called for. Poincaré would not budge; reparations had been awarded and must be paid. Commissions sat in Paris, the Ruhr was occupied, and Dawes and Young were sent to ascertain the real resources of the recalcitrant country. The economic dislocation of the world was felt on Wall Street, and the crash of 1929–1930, which sent shares to rock bottom and closed numerous banks, had to come before the experts finally imposed their views on the politicians and virtually wiped off both the war debts and reparations. Surely, this financial disaster—which was the starting-point of still graver disasters—could have been avoided if, instead of allowing diplomacy to be dictated by the people, or by politicians who were intent on giving the public the illusory verbal satisfactions it wanted, the question had been left, without haste or publicity, without any attempt to make political capital out of it, to sane economists.

The same follies were to be repeated about disarmament. To please the public, Germany was disarmed. There was much to be said in favor of disarmament; the difficulty was that it is impossible to disarm only a single great nation for long; and Germany was soon manufacturing heavy arms in Russia. But there was not only intense anger against Germany, and a call for her disarmament; there was, also a demand from the war-weary and the pacifically-minded for the disarmament of the Allied Nations. Both these decisions were put into the Treaty. When it came to carrying them out, it was found that clandestine arming by Germany could not be stopped, and any real disarming by the Allies was deemed suicidal.

Probably the wisest course would have been to effect a compromise with Germany. But that would have offended two sections of the public—the furiously anti-German section and the pacifist section. Votes would be lost whatever was done. So, the subject was evaded for years, and then disarmament conferences, with the customary tam-tam, were convened, to waste more years in sterile discussion, while the two sections of the public shouted critical counsels at the top of their voices. Nothing was ever sillier than these conferences. The petitions for disarmament were stacked up; they were delivered in huge crates from the four quarters of the globe. On the other hand, there were just as many protests from men and women, who had suffered from the war and had reason to fear a German attack in the future, against the stupidity of weakening our defenses.

Why, if there was no prospect of adjustment and pacific arrangements, bring together delegates from the ends of the earth to make speeches which could have no practical conclusion? Again, why not entrust the task to a small body of experts, if the matter had to be discussed at all, so as to arrive quietly at a give-and-take accord? The new diplomacy, parading on platforms, was opposed to sensible silence; the new diplomacy, also creating divisions of opinion on technical matters, prevented the slightest progress.

A main trouble is that conferences, although they are brief and abortive, as they are usually meant to be, nevertheless produce incalculable mischief since they stir up unnecessary heat and dissension in every nation and thus engender animosity and exasperation between nations.

I wonder whether we could not, after all, make better use of a diplomatic corps? It would have to be very different from the diplomatic corps of today, and would have to attach less importance to trousers and travel. Probably, the human material is there if it were trained to the specific task of reaching reasonable agreements, without publicity, and were given full responsibility and adequate authority, divorced from politics.

7

THE LEAGUE WITHIN THE LEAGUE
A DYNAMIC COMMUNIST FRONT

In 1949, there appeared a book by the English publicist and novelist, George Orwell, entitled *Nineteen Eighty-four*. It purported to describe the world that had taken shape by 1984, though Orwell recognized that the trend and pattern had already become well established by 1948, and he originally intended to give his book the title of *Nineteen Forty-Eight*. His publishers persuaded him that his startling statements would meet less public resistance if they were put in the form of predictions of things to come rather than as a description of what is now taking place.

Orwell's main thesis is that the social and economic system is maintained by perpetual phony war and that this is made possible by a régime of "doublethink," in which public policies are presented in a light precisely the opposite of the reality. Thus, the leading public slogan is that "War is Peace," and the War Ministry is called the Ministry of Peace.

Events since the publication of the Orwell masterpiece have amply borne out his analysis and description. Although the whole world is now on a war footing, although expenditures for armament for the imminent next World War are astronomical and exceed the wildest dreams of the "merchants of death" of a generation back, and although a bitter war was waged in Korea—which has already been called by responsible political leaders the prelude to the third World War—the myth was officially maintained that all this was being done in the interest of peace. Both the American bloc of nations and Russia and its satellites maintained this fiction with a straight face.

Yet, long before Orwell's book was brought out, this system of doublethink and the creation of a war psychology and war system behind the false front of an alleged world organization for peace had come into existence at Geneva. This is the most essential and yet the most ignored fact about the realities in the history of the rise and fall of the League of Nations.

Nearly everything of historical or "ideological" interest has been written about the League of Nations except the most essential and ominous fact. This essential fact, from which we have averted our shocked eyes, is that the existence and operation of the League were a direct and leading cause of the Second World War.

That is a harsh charge and I hasten to add that there were many other causes, earlier and later—most of all, of course, the War-Guilt Clause of the Treaty of Versailles. But I repeat, with due emphasis, for an understanding of this central thesis is vital if we would repair our errors, that the League became the principal war-making machine, and that on its platforms and in its lobbies were forged the mentality and policies that produced the clash of arms in 1939.

In an effort to placate those readers who think I exaggerate, who resist the thought that, out of so many peace protestations, out of an assemblage of men and women many of whom were sincerely desirous of better international relations, there could have evolved a fanatical determination to smash, by every possible means, those forces which they held in horror or disdain, I will go so far as to admit that the most baneful influences of the League were to be found in the lobbies rather than on the rostrum. Yet, I do not absolve the platform—on the contrary the platform provided the necessary publicity to support and publicize the operations of the secret conclaves of conspirators.

By what singular and evil perversion, it will be asked, could an association founded in good faith for the establishment of peace hurry us into war? The experience with the League from 1921 to 1939 is not the first nor the last time that paradoxes of such a character have been observed by those who endeavor to penetrate below the surface of things, who examine actual results rather than empty words. In our time, as George Orwell has explained, slogans which have been invented may mean exactly the opposite of what they purport to mean. There is nothing so dangerous as a crusade. In the name of good, men are prepared to commit any evil, evil that could not be committed in the name of evil. Our age is an age of masks. Many of the wearers of the masks first don them in all innocence.

At first sight, it is indeed curious to observe how ignorant every epoch is of itself. I am certain that most of the cruelties of history have been perpetrated by men who imagined themselves appointed by God to fulfill a noble mission. The witch-hunters of Trier, Würzburg and Salem, the heretic-burners of the Inquisition, the soldiers of Mahomet, to take only a few examples, did not regard themselves as evil men. Nor were they bad; they were so filled by the sense of their duty to an ideal that they were blind. In the two decades that I spent, on and off, in the former seat of the ruthless Calvin (another virulent reformer!), I was greatly impressed by the admirable intentions of the bulk of the League supporters; but I was also painfully aware of the perils of the path on which they had entered.

It would appear that the more earnestly one strives for peace, the more likely one is to provoke war. The greater one's love for the community of minds that think and feel like oneself, the greater the detestation of those who think and feel differently. "Be my brother," cried the French Revolutionaries, "or die!" As the inevitable upheavals, consequent on the Versailles Treaty and the Russian Revolution, came to Europe, there was a crystallization of sentiment in Geneva against the heretical wrongdoers that threatened peace.

I watched the process with dismay. I am not being wise after the event; as early as 1921, I wrote an article in the *Atlantic Monthly* pointing out the danger. It is true that I did not then foresee the positive conspiracy of the Communists and the crypto-Communists, ranged against the "Fascists," a term of opprobrium applied to everybody who did not accept the Russian viewpoint, irrespective of whether the person so designated had any sympathy with "Fascism" or not. I did not foresee, as I was later to witness, the sharp division of the League into two clans, according to the conflicting "ideology" of its members. The Russian followers adopted the motto: "He who is not for us is against us"; and eventually they won the greater number of adherents in political circles, all the way from the delegations to the secretariat, from the camp-followers to the accredited correspondents. Now the main purpose of the founders of the League was ostensibly to prevent such cleavage. The whole purpose of the League should have been to minimize differences of political thought and to reconcile men and women in a united effort towards agreement.

I did not foresee this development, which manifested itself clearly only in the latter part of the second decade of the League. The first half of the existence of the League was relatively harmless. Its record was chiefly negative. It was content to move around in circles. Even its most ardent advocates were able to laugh, rather wryly, at the jibe: "It touches nothing that it does not adjourn." There was a period of euphoria, in which it was veritably believed that a new era had opened for mankind and that there would be no more quarrels among the nations. The Wilsonian conception of international agreement through public debate, which was not without nobility as an abstraction, had not yet convincingly revealed itself as impracticable. When lack of progress was charged against the League, it was replied (for there are always appropriate *clichés*) that Rome was not built in a day. Here, however, was a case when Rome should have been built in a day—or never; for the League had postulated a change of heart, a complete conversion, of all its members.

As another excuse, the apologists pointed out that the United States had refused to join the League proposed by their President: that was a formidable handicap. I could not see why it should be a serious handicap if the assumptions which went into its making were correct. If all the other nations were ready to forego a portion of their national sovereignty and obey the universal conscience of mankind, how could it matter that there were here and there defections? The fact is, of course, that no nation, big or little, really meant to abdicate its sovereign rights or to act except in its own interests. Not by merely bringing together forty or fifty nations could they be welded into one, with a single standard of political morality, with single eye to the welfare of the world. They still remained at Geneva forty or fifty nations, in unselfish accord on nothing that seriously interested them.

The truth is that the League was, at the best, a League of Foreign Offices, and it is the business of a foreign office to pursue its national purpose. The League offered a convenient maneuvering ground in which the foreign offices could wheel and intrigue, form coalitions against other groups, and promote their particularist policies by making use of the international platform obligingly provided. Since each nation employed the League to justify its selfish policies, there was necessarily a deadlock on whatever truly concerned a group of nations. The League, which was meant to promote peace and impose principles, shelved the pleas of minorities against its members. It was silent in face of the defiance of Italy in

Corfu. It allowed Poland to seize Vilna. Sanctions were not invoked against Japan for her action in Manchuria. Although the earlier system of "alliances" was supposed to be ruled out, not only were the member-nations busy constructing networks of alliances, but the League kindly consented to register them. Live and let live, was the *leitmotif* of the League; but, since the peoples back home expected something more, there were countless hypocritical speeches containing the proper vacuous catch-phrases.

Another and more valid defense of the League was found in the excellent work done by some of its departments. On non-controversial subjects the League was indeed exceedingly useful. It coördinated international activities, it collected information, it adopted irreproachable measures. Yet, all this contributed little or nothing to the fundamental purpose of promoting world peace. It was not for the sake of this kind of organization and activities, however admirable, that the League was founded: it was founded to deal in a new and more peaceful way with serious international differences, flagrant international injustices, and ominous international tensions. It was precisely these things that it dared not touch if one, two, or more powerful nations chose to use their veto. On any question except those of procedure, unanimity was the rule.

It followed that the revision of the unfortunate treaties, notably that of Versailles, which had been promised in the Covenant, could not be frankly broached. Whatever was bad, whatever might be a cause for war, had to remain as though the League did not exist. There would always be some nation, in default (if such default can be imagined) of France, which would prevent any reconciliation with Germany—or block any alleviation of the Austrian or Hungarian situation. Therefore, it rapidly appeared that the League was merely (in this respect) a new and gigantic Holy Alliance whose object was to maintain a *status quo* rightly judged by enlightened observers to be both unjust and perilous.

It is hardly necessary to point out that the "mandates" system, by which England and France and other nations were to govern, subject to League control, various territories, including former German overseas territories—an alleged improvement over the old colonial method—presented no features that could command our respect. The "control" was no more than perfunctory. How could it be real and effective? Japan, perhaps only more outspoken than other nations, boldly threatened to leave the League if there was any interference with her mandates, and there was no interference.

Nor is it necessary to recall at length the fate of the Disarmament Commission when the matter was referred to the League. The long-drawn-out debate was nugatory. Each nation did exactly what it pleased.

There is one subject much discussed in the early years on which I must linger, since it has received its more complete illustration in the later United Nations Organization—the U.N. of today. From the beginning, the French were particularly insistent on the need of a League Army. It was called "putting teeth into the Covenant." Obviously, the French were thinking of the possibility of a German recovery. Would it not be an advantage to create on the French side an international military force to resist "aggression" and, incidentally, to keep Germany in subjection? But surely that would be making of the League an instrument of war, when its whole purpose was to be an instrument of peace?

The confusion of thought here which I noted then prevails today, as we have seen in the Korean War. There were then many objections. In the first place, there were those nations (not many) which did not intend to repress Germany forever. How could we know in advance what changes on the international checkerboard might be made? In the second place, who would supply the men, and who would command them? Was it likely that any nation would go light-heartedly into war unless its immediate interests were at stake? Again, if the question ever arose, would not some countries prefer to remain neutral, and others vote against the use of troops? It was wrong to assume that the membership of the League implied a single opinion, solidarity of interests, readiness to make sacrifices. On whom would the ultimate burden fall, assuming that there was unanimity on the launching of hostilities? Would an international army be efficient?

These and other doubts arose, but the most conclusive argument came—curiously enough—from a Frenchman, Jacques Bainville. "And what if the League army should be beaten?" What indeed? That simple question gave the exponents of a militarized League pause. The event was not improbable. The quality of a heterogeneous army, supposing it was in being and that it had been directed to take the field, was doubtful. Had such an army rushed against Germany in 1939, one may ask, would it not almost certainly have been defeated? In Korea, in 1950, the American army came within an ace of being driven into the sea, and it was, however much we may admire the small contingents from other nations, an American army with all the mighty resources of the United States behind it. Even so, the experiment, after much bloody fighting, seems to have resulted in a stalemate.

The idea of an international army did not include the idea of a bloody war or of a stalemate; it signified a sort of police force that would impose the decisions of the League without much trouble. The idea of starting another World War was, it must be charitably supposed, foreign to the advocates of an armed League. Irony or doublethink can hardly be pushed farther than the conception of a League, the League to keep peace in our time—and in all future times—by its fiat initiating a conflict in which all the nations of the earth should automatically join. Persistently there rang in my ears the questions: And what if there should, at the show-down, be two Leagues, perhaps three Leagues, dissidents who would choose to stay out of the fighting, dissidents who would range themselves against the "good League" and prefer to enroll themselves in support of the "hosts of evil"? And what if the "good League" should be beaten?

Of course, no one fully visualized such a grim picture. We were idealists, we were illusionists, we believed only what we wanted to believe, and saw ourselves as good-natured policemen telling bellicose or disorderly persons to "move on, please." In any case, we were all agreed on one point: if ever there were fighting it would be clean fighting, confined to well-conducted soldiers. No more indiscriminate bombing, for example, no employment of weapons that might hurt civilians. Women and children and property would be respected. We tried to draw up lists of prohibited weapons—prohibited to the prospective enemy, of course, for our own weapons, directed in the right sense, were peace weapons. We made, at least in our minds, rules for war. Under our guidance, war would—if it came, which was almost unthinkable—be a gentlemanly sport under strict Queensberry rules.

Well, we have seen to our dismay and shame what became of such delusions. The story is best told in the book written by an able English lawyer and publicist, Mr. F. J. P. Veale, entitled *Advance to Barbarism*. It was first published in England in 1948, when the author wisely decided that it was most discreet to use the *nom de plume* of "A Jurist." A greatly enlarged American edition was brought out in 1953, and so general has become the recognition of the truths stated in the book that no less a personage than Dean Inge consented to write a laudatory foreword for the American edition.

Now, the mischievousness of the League can be classified

under many heads. First, there was the propagation of those dangerous myths which turned us from the grim realities. Second, there was, under the velvet glove, an iron fist, a definite diplomatic menace to those who did not accept the doctrines of the League. I soon learned to shudder when I heard the word peace, because it clearly meant war. Third, the soft speeches persuaded men that there was no need to tackle urgent problems—a phrase was actually coined according to which frontiers had no importance, and, by a slight extension, wrongs were rights since we were now all one big family. What was lost to Germany, for example, was gained for, let us say, Czechoslovakia—which was nearly the same thing. If everything was going to be arranged in this friendly fashion, why worry about a few apparent immediate injustices? Fourth, we were so convinced of our own morality that anyone who disagreed with us was regarded as an unredeemed sinner who merited condign punishment.

There are other evils that could be itemized but these will suffice: the point is that, in the first period of the League's existence, immobility was assured. In a changing world, the League stood still. I have no doubt whatever that, without the League, without the sounding-board of an international hall where everyone preached for himself under the cover of generous generalities, a few real statesmen—diplomats of the type of Bismarck, Disraeli or Salisbury—could have quietly got together to make the necessary readjustments. In the poisonous atmosphere of pompous publicity at Geneva, nothing could be done. The utterances of Geneva were not the words of statesmen, but the vacuous rhetoric of vulgar tub-thumpers. The Leaguers had to take, at once and without due deliberation, a public stand, from which they could not afterwards retreat. The proposal of a militaristic League was, in fact, abandoned, for the keynote of the League was facility, complacence, inactivity, lack of dynamism. Do noth-

ing—but talk—was its *raison d'être*. The pouring out of plat-
itudes, pleasing to the masses, was its occupation. And it
must be confessed that there was much enthusiasm for such
a League. When once it was seen that the League would alter
nothing, the governments favoring the *status quo* played up
to its devotees.

Yet there did linger in the minds of the foreign offices the
possibility of converting the League into a definitely coercive
organization that might save them much trouble. France, for
instance, felt that, without undue effort on her part, she
might, through the agency of the League, keep Germany in
order. England, in the end—and it was the end of the League
—instead of dealing directly with Italy who offended her
in Africa (and it would not have been difficult to reach a
direct agreement) called upon the League to coerce Italy,
a task for which the League proved its incapacity; its failure,
by demonstrable stages, brought us to the Second World
War.

I am anticipating: for the first half of its existence, while
Europe was relatively quiet, before the struggle of the
"Haves" and the "Have-Nots" began, the greatest defect
of the League, inherent in its constitution, was that it
"clamped the lid" on the world, refusing to recognize that
the balance of forces was changing. In spite of its fine
speeches, it was essentially conservative, a stumbling-block,
an insuperable obstacle to treaty revision in the silence of
the cabinets. All this made negotiations between two or
three powers virtually impossible, since forty or fifty opinions had to be publicly reconciled. It helped the statesmen
to justify their selfish or obstructive attitudes by resounding,
if misleading, proclamations from a world platform, thus
bringing the most delicate foreign affairs into the domain
of mass emotions.

But there was to come a period, in the 1930's, when the
decline and eventual fall of the system of popular diplomacy

could not be concealed. Europe was stirring again. Neither Germany nor Russia could be excluded from the League any longer. The closed corporation of the 1920's was ripped asunder. At once it became evident, for those who had eyes to see (alas, they were a minority) that, while League methods might succeed when Europe was quiescent, the moment there was strong and determined opposition the League would fly to pieces. The League was a screen to hide these disconcerting facts. It was to be roughly knocked down when Hitler, whose advent to power was entirely due to the refusal of the Allies to deal honestly with the "democratic" governments of Germany, obtained ascendancy in the Reich, and when Mussolini began to clamor for the fulfillment of the promises made to Italy. It was the blindness of the League, which conditioned the blindness of the powers, that made a clash imminent. "The League is only what the powers make it—the League is not to blame," was a favorite argument. But how could one separate the League from its members? And was not the existence of the League a convenient excuse for the powers to procrastinate, lolling back lazily on the deceptive comfort of the League cushions? The League could not logically be regarded as both an autonomous entity and merely a meeting-place for the powers, each with its separate and selfish policy.

The League, in its earlier years, was, whatever the theory might be, an instrument of the *status quo*, and was, therefore, automatically opposed to Germany and Russia which were outside. Now it was thought wise to remember that it should be universal—or at any rate as universal as possible—and, one after the other, Germany and Russia were admitted to membership. As if such admittance could alter the fundamental antagonism of the German and Russian conceptions, on one side, and the conceptions hitherto maintained by the League! Germany, then more brutal in diplomacy than Russia, followed the lead of Japan, who had tiptoed out of the League in quiet protest against League rebukes, but Germany's exit was noisier. Germany slammed the door, and began to act for herself without asking the permission of the League. She began the long series of violations of the Versailles Treaty, against which the League was powerless and against which the Allies, after their protracted reliance on "collective" methods, were afraid to move.

The peoples had been taught that the League was there to do their work without any effort on their part, and it was impossible to tell them now that their security lay, as always, in their own hands, and not in the hands of forty or fifty nations. In my view, they should have shown far more of the spirit of conciliation while Germany was at their mercy, and far more of the spirit of determination to resist when Germany began to take unilateral action. Whatever concessions—no, that is the wrong word—whatever arbitrary reversals of Allied decisions were imposed by the will of the Germans on the Allies, Germany owed the Allies no thanks. Earlier, the voluntary surrender of positions that could not in justice be defended would have led to European peace. Now, the enforced evacuation of these same positions led only to war in the end.

For the older enlightened diplomacy of the council chamber, there had been substituted popular diplomacy with its illusions, its snares, and its perils; and the League was doomed.

Russia was wiser than Germany—unless indeed Germany was certain of securing everything she wanted without war, or of winning a new war. It should be remembered that Fascism and Nazism, detestable as they are, in that they imply a totalitarianism destructive of human personality, the complete submergence of the individual in the mass, came after Communism, which was equally totalitarian. Dictatorship, whether attained by the ballot or the bullet, shocks our sense of freedom. My libertarian personal political philosophy is in complete opposition to Communism as practiced in

Russia, Nazism as practiced in Germany, and Fascism as practiced in Italy. Nevertheless, it should not be forgotten —as it too often is—that Fascism and Nazism came as a *reaction* to Communism, and were largely the product of the instinct of self-defense of European peoples against Bolshevism.

Whether in Germany, Italy, or Spain, where a terrible civil war was fought, ranging the adversaries of Bolshevism on the side of Franco, or in other European countries, where Communism was making headway, the national forces were mobilized against the Russian menace. Fascism, said Mussolini, is not an article of exportation. Communism certainly was, and is, and its main tactics were to establish a Fifth Column, a Trojan Horse, in all the countries that might oppose it. More: Lenin had never disguised his intention of spreading Communism to the ends of the earth. It was a universal creed. Clemenceau had tried, by the *cordon sanitaire*, the first Iron Curtain, erected not by the Russians but by the Allies, to "contain" Communism. I thought the scheme bad and ineffective. Yet, it was generally recognized in Europe that the greatest danger lay in Russia. Russia was, therefore, surrounded by a chain of states, from Bulgaria to Poland, which were for a time militarily strong enough to hold Russia within her borders. Communism had indeed infiltrated, yet in spite of weaknesses here and there, Russia was, before the 1939 War, "contained."

Now, I have always regarded Maxim Litvinov as the most astute of the Russian diplomats. Whether he was the inventor of the Russian strategy I do not know, but he certainly came to Geneva prepared to execute it, and execute it he did, brilliantly. He could not openly and directly "sell" Communism to the League, and thus to the European countries, but he could and did "sell" anti-Fascism. Distracting attention from Communism, he denounced, both publicly and privately, in Genevan circles, the danger of Fascism. There rallied to him some of the *élite* of the League. It was not long before I was conscious of the existence of a League within the League— a League of anti-Fascists. In this League were the representatives of various countries, mostly those of Central Europe, but also members of the delegations of France and, I suspect, of England. There were friendly journalists, including Americans. There were, naturally, exiles from Germany and Italy. Anti-Fascism is not Communism, but it inevitably became associated with Communism, and in the late 1930's it was almost inseparable from Communism.

The enemy was "Fascism" in all its forms, in France, in Germany, in Italy, in Spain, and against this enemy there must be unity of action: "Let us forget whether we are Communists or not; let us make a Common Front against Fascism. If Russia is not exactly a democracy, as we define democracy, if there is little liberty in Russia, if there have been mass atrocities and brutal imprisonments, let us conveniently put aside these unhappy facts and memories; let us consider only that we are faced with the most hideous monster of all time—namely Fascism." On this ground, under this banner, we were invited to join hands.

Communism was thus gradually transformed into the chief opponent of Fascism; Communism, the ally of all anti-Fascists, little by little was accepted as a friend by the democratic countries. As between Communism and Fascism, the intelligentsia of Geneva, and eventually the Socialist and Labor movements, seemed determined to choose Communism. If they did not become Communists, at least they were co-workers with Communism, "fellow-travellers," in the fight against Fascism. Finally, whoever was not Communist, or at least a sympathizer with Communism, was dubbed a Fascist, and a Fascist was whoever was opposed to Communism. *Fronts Populaires*, which brought into association radicals and moderates, were formed, and thus

Communism, whose militants were a minority, obtained control of the sentiments of the masses—and often even of the "classes."

Here lies the cleverest political and diplomatic operation of my time and it was the work of Litvinov. Whoever does not grasp its implications and its consequences cannot hope even to begin to understand the age in which he now lives. Nor was Litvinov, or his directors from the Kremlin, content with this cunning maneuver. He identified Russia with peace.

All the pacifists of the League were bound to applaud when Litvinov called for "collective security," which meant that all countries (with a mental restriction in favor of Russia) should jump with both feet into any local war and destroy each other. He coined another clever and seductive phrase, "indivisible peace," which signified much the same thing. For my part, I held that "collective security" was really "collective suicide," and that "indivisible peace" amounted to "indivisible war"—war on a bigger and bigger scale, world war whenever two or more tiny states started a dogfight. But the most responsible ministers from the Great Powers piously repeated the words after Litvinov, and the most earnest peace-workers in Geneva thrilled at the prospect of an all-nations war.

"Russian Communism emerged from the First World War; World Communism will emerge from a Second World War," said a cynical Russian observer. The unexpressed condition was that Russia should keep out of the Second World War after having provoked it. The subsequent lamentable history of the League should be read in the light of what I have written. This proper and vital interpretation of the League's historic evolution has been ignored. Litvinov became, in its later stages, virtually the League. And, though he is now dead, he still influences most of our political thinking on world affairs. We continue to inquire first of all of any country whether it is anti-Fascist or pro-Fascist, whether it is anti-Communist or pro-Communist is of secondary importance.

We shall deal later on with the United Nations Organization. But even here we will do well to point out that most of the evils of the League of Nations persist in this international organization which grew out of the Second World War—in some respects they have even been aggravated.

We have seen that political and diplomatic lethargy, and the resulting impotence, were the main traits of the League in the 1920's. That the United Nations would be impotent was assured from the beginning by permitting any Great Power to veto positive action in restraining an aggressor. Soviet Russia has been accused of having foisted the veto trick on the U.N. in San Francisco, but actually at the time the United States was also favorable to the idea. Only the unexplained absence of the Russian delegate from the Security Council in June, 1950, made possible the U.N. intervention in the Korean War. Probably the absence was due to the shrewd perception that such action would greatly drain and weaken the United States, would train the new Chinese military machine, and would solidify Chinese public opinion behind the Communist régime, while imposing no serious burdens on Soviet Russia.

The "league within league" nature of the League of Nations has been intensified in the U.N. In the 1920's, with Germany and Russia still out of the League, there was some pretense of unity at Geneva. The U.N. has been split into two bitterly antagonistic groups from the start. War talk and charges of mutual aggression have been hurled back and forth from the outset. All major meetings have mainly provided a forum for the fomenting of a war psychology. There has, probably, been less hypocrisy than at Geneva. Though the U.N. was established to preserve peace, it was soon admitted by both sides that peace was most likely to be maintained by wars against aggressors and by gigantic military preparations. The Orwellian slogan that "War is Peace" was, consciously or unconsciously, from the beginning adopted by both conflicting groups within the U.N.

Due to the growing hostility of the United States and its satellites in the U.N. to Soviet Russia, and the resulting Cold War, the U.N. is not the relatively united pro-Communist front that the League became in the late 1930's. But, even so, the hatred of the anti-Communist contingent in the U.N. is greater against even the memory of Nazi Germany and Fascist Italy than it is against the existing reality of Communist threats today. Russia and its satellites are members of the U.N. in full standing; Franco Spain, the last of the main Fascist nations, is still excluded. And a veto by Russia and its satellites can prevent the admission of new members to the U.N. if they are deemed unsatisfactory in their attitude toward Communism.

8

CROWD PSYCHOLOGY
THE KEY TO POPULAR DIPLOMACY

I$_F$ WE WISH to comprehend fully what has happened in the first half of the twentieth century, we could hardly do better than consider the following syllogism: (a) all crowds are irrational; (b) this is the age of crowds; (c) therefore, our era is irrational.

This may appear to be a bold saying, for it has become sheer blasphemy to criticize the working of democracy. Yet Lincoln, one of the ablest champions of democracy, wisely pointed out that democracy implies an electorate which is moral, intelligent, and rationally patriotic. In England, one of the most illustrious pioneers of democracy adjured the working classes to make a wise and unselfish use of the political power they were winning.

Can we honestly affirm that democracy has grown up? Can we suppose that the masses are capable of comprehending and solving without bias all the difficult and complicated questions that present themselves in our modern world? Since we are agreed that any people has the right to live its own life and should not be forced to live in slavery under any master, however far-seeing and well-intentioned he may be, we should, after the free presentation of the various arguments for or against any reform, permit the people to decide its own mode of existence. Its domestic affairs are its own concern, just as the private affairs of every man are his own concern—with, however, the important proviso, laid down by John Stuart Mill in his famous essay on *Liberty*, that he should do no wrong to others. I agree that this definition is extremely vague, for nearly all of our acts, if not most of our thoughts, may touch in some way the existence of our fellows.

There is, I remember, a story by the German author, Arthur Schnitzler, which relates how a youth was warned by an invisible mentor not to go into a wood, on pain of bringing the kingdom to destruction. Laughingly he disobeyed. What relation could his walk in the wood have with the fate of his native land? It turned out that his presence frightened a butterfly, which flew into a garden, and there laid her eggs. Some time afterwards, the king's wife came to the garden to await the birth of her child. The larva of this particular butterfly crawled over her in her sleep; she awoke in alarm, and premature pangs killed her and the unborn child. The kingdom passed into the hands of a tyrant, who, by his folly, ruined the kingdom.

This is far-fetched fantasy, of course, but it does illustrate the strange and unforeseeable sequence of events that may spring from our most innocent actions. No one is isolated; we are all links in a chain; and we cannot tell the ultimate result of our lightest word or deed. Nor can we be expected to peer precisely into the seeds of time. I merely wish to suggest that even a country's domestic affairs, and our own private affairs, cannot be regarded as without consequence to others. That is why I have never envied the politicians who, usually without special competence, pretend to direct the destinies of nations.

In foreign affairs it is clear that we and our rulers may easily take a course that will bring catastrophe upon the world in general as well as upon us. I have often, from my own knowledge of contemporary history, allowed myself to speculate on the trivial circumstances that have determined mighty upheavals; kidney stones or an ill-timed indigestion— I have specific cases in mind—have been responsible for irrevocable and disastrous decisions. Certainly, we cannot change these laws of nature; but I do suggest that our international relations should not be made to depend on the whims of an uninstructed public opinion. At the best, the ablest minds are hesitant and uncertain. It was my privilege to be acquainted with one of England's foremost statesmen, a man who possessed an exceptional brain. He once told me that, when he was puzzled in some matter of high policy, he threw a coin into the air and acted accordingly. "There is often just as much reason," he said, "for taking the right turning as for taking the left." He was an incorrigible skeptic, and was speaking half in jest.

Does it, then, matter overmuch that the public, which cannot possibly weigh with knowledge and wisdom the arguments for and against, which is the victim of its own impulses, presses its untutored views on the statesmen? Surely, for practical purposes, it does matter. It is true that the wisest men may many times be wrong, but it is highly probable that the masses, swayed entirely by unreason, by emotion, will usually be wrong. Coleridge wrote: "The multitude are always under the domination of some one feeling or view; whereas truth, and above all practical wisdom, must be the result of a wide comprehension of the more or less, the balance and the counterbalance." Or, as Renan put it: "Truth and wisdom lie in nuances." For the public there is only black and white. For the statesman who is not governed by the sentiments of the public there are an infinity of shades. Alas, such statesmen are rare! It is easier to "follow in front"—if the expression be allowed—in the direction of the crowd, than to strike off at a different angle and find oneself left alone.

In describing the twentieth century as "the era of the crowd" I pretend to no originality. As early as the last decade of the past century, a remarkable French philosopher and social psychologist, Gustave Le Bon, already discerned the beginning of a tendency which has never ceased to accelerate its speed. His book on *The Psychology of Crowds* (1895) remains, in my opinion, in spite of many later studies of the same character, the classic treatment of the mental traits of crowds. Yet Le Bon's writings on the crowd are seldom mentioned today when most of his alarming prophecies have come true and most of his ominous observations have been confirmed.

It is very important to note that Le Bon's famous analysis of crowd behavior, with its high suggestibility, its irrationality, its impulsiveness, and its capacity for remarkable feats of public heroism or iniquity, was written when modern journalism, with its world-wide coverage, sensationalism, and mass-circulation was just coming into being. While the telegraph was widely used, wireless was unknown, and telephones were a rare luxury. Moving pictures, the radio and television were completely unknown. All these new media of communication have since served to facilitate and intensify crowd-mindedness and mob-psychology and give greater weight to Le Bon's assertions.

Moreover, they have produced crowds and mobs of vastly greater extent than were ever known in the previous history of mankind. The mobs that killed the brothers Gracchi in ancient Rome, the fanatical religious mobs that wiped out the Albigensians in the thirteenth century, the mob that sacked Magdeburg in the Thirty Years' War, the mob that carried out the massacre of St. Bartholomew's Day, and the mobs of the Reign of Terror during the French Revolution were small and petty bands, however horrible their acts, compared with the crowds and mobs of today. By the use of contemporary media of communication whole nations are now reduced to a great crowd in normal times and may be goaded into becoming a vast national mob by sufficiently dramatic and unscrupulous leaders. Now that television is becoming universal, there seems little doubt that the national mind will become and remain truly and permanently a crowd mind, always in danger of being inflamed into mob-mindedness.

The great French contemporary of Le Bon, Gabriel Tarde, wrote a book on *Opinion and the Crowd* (1901) in which he distinguished between the crowd and the public. He held that a crowd is a definite physical assemblage of persons gathered together in a given place at a given time. The public is made up of citizens who are dispersed in space, even though they read the same news and interpretations thereof and thus arrive at some unity of belief and potential action. Since members of the public are to a certain extent isolated when they form their opinion, they have greater opportunity for deliberation than crowds operating under the influence of physical contiguity, psychic contagion and the personal suggestion of leaders.

This was probably a valid differentiation when Tarde wrote his book over fifty years ago, and his contention was shared by the famed Italian student of crowd psychology, Scipio Sighele, in his books *The Criminal Crowd* (1891) and *The Intelligence of the Crowd* (1903). But, with the arrival of the sensational mass-journalism, the movies, the radio and, above all, television, any such thing as a rational and deliberative public is fading out, or has disappeared altogether, and nations have become crowds in both policy and behavior. In other words, while we still continue to talk about *public* opinion, and university text-book writers produce learned tomes describing its origins and operations, there is in reality, today, little save *crowd* and mob opinion. And what still remains of *public* opinion is rapidly being snuffed out by the growing impact and influence of television.

Because something important has been said before we should not refrain from saying it again, saying it until it sinks into the consciousness of men. There can be no doubt whatever, that, for better or worse, our own epoch is distinguished from preceding epochs by the overwhelming influence of the masses on our communal life. Until the last fifty years or so, the majority was content to entrust its fate to the hands of those in whom it recognized superior talents in the art of government. Now, although it has leaders, its leaders are those who do its bidding, whether that bidding is openly and vociferously expressed or, still hidden in the subconsciousness of the crowd, is "divined" by the leaders. There is a correspondence of thought and feeling between crowds and leaders, without which the leader would be rejected.

Perhaps all great leaders of men have possessed the ability to "divine" the wishes of the people, but they have not hitherto been obliged to rush into follies against which their better judgment protested. They could afford to ignore the crowd when the crowd was palpably wrong. Today, no politician who values his post can risk unpopularity. Willy-nilly, he must "follow in front" or be dismissed from office. Usually, he seeks to inflame the sentiments of the mob, and is counted the more successful the more he strikes the note which pleases the crowd. To please the crowd, it need hardly be remarked, is no guarantee that either he or the crowd are right. On the contrary, there is a serious presumption that they are both all too frequently wrong.

Before any science of psychology as applied to crowds had appeared there were leaders who instinctively realized the nature of the crowd. That is why (to confine ourselves to modern history) Napoleon, by his flamboyant utterances, captured the imagination of the masses and led them to face danger and death. Nevertheless, national ways of thinking and feeling are far more accessible to gifted leaders than the ways of thinking and feeling of foreign nations. Napoleon, to keep our example, understood the French: he completely misunderstood the English, the Spaniards, the Russians, as did Hitler in our own day, and as, perhaps, the Americans now misunderstand the sentiments and temperament of the nations on the Continent of Europe.

Le Bon shrewdly points out that great changes, the downfall of empires, the collapse of civilizations, do not come from foreign invasions, from the overthrow of dynasties, the military defeat of nations, the sweeping away of régimes (i.e., Communism, Nazism, Fascism, etc.)—spectacular events that may figure prominently in the manuals of history. The real transformations are the result of a gradual modification of ideas. Christianity, to take an instance, did not spread and triumph in the Western world by the sword. It was no sudden blinding revelation that displaced the mighty Roman Empire and its pagan gods. There was a slow gnawing away of ancient beliefs, ancient ideals, ancient virtues. As I see it, it matters little today whether Communism, Nazism, Fascism or any other 'ism, including our own, is demolished in its material form by tanks and bombs; whatever most appeals to the emotions of the crowd will eventually win.

Even the most obtuse observer must now be aware that the old nineteenth-century world, with its stable institutions, its revered laws, its moral discipline, its relative political apathy of the masses, is dead. The old Liberalism, the old *laisser-faire*, has gone, never to return within any predictable time. Something new is stirring. Mankind is on the march again. It would be absurd to predict its destination. I confess, however, that repulsive to me as are the doctrines of Communism, Nazism, and Fascism, and detestable as has been the conduct of the countries which have adopted totalitarian methods, it is childish to have instituted anti-Nazi courts, as we are today setting up anti-Communist courts, to condemn the adherents of these doctrines, and to "de-Nazify" or "de-Communize" them. A more fatuous fight against ideas was never invented and, as the records of mankind amply show, the making of martyrs never converted anyone to the contrary doctrine.

How the world will be shaped tomorrow is a theme for the Jules Vernes, the H. G. Wellses, and the Aldous Huxleys. We do not know today. But we do know, for the fermentation is already visible, that it will not be shaped as we believed in our youth, when we thought it had already been shaped to endure forever.

For bad or for good, our former social order is in a state of liquidation, and I am tempted to affirm that our twentieth-century wars are not the main cause of the liquidation—they are only outward symptoms of the fundamental inward changes in society. The salient factor in the unseen revolution, a revolution whose consequences are incalculable, is the breakdown of restraints on the functional character of the crowd. The crowd has come into its own, its voice has become louder and louder, its action is felt stronger and stronger. The collective mind is our new ruler. Nothing is left of the intellectual aristocracy of the nineteenth century; nothing remains either of the monarchs by divine right or their agents who shared, in the eyes of the crowd, something of that divine right. Today, the people—that is to say the crowd—is the natural heir of that divine right, and woe betide those who set themselves up in opposition to the masses!

At present, the manifestations of the crowd are contradictory, confused, apparently meaningless. In European countries with which I am particularly acquainted, they have resembled the antics of Bedlam. Everything which we held sacred has been called into question. After the *débâcle* of 1940, men who remained to face the German invaders in France were dubbed traitors; men who fled abroad to live safely, if not in pampered luxury, were hailed as heroes. The French Communists, of course, boasted loudly of their patriotism, seeming to forget that they had just collaborated with the German allies of Russia and now collaborated with Russia, the enemy of Germany after June, 1941. After 1944, obedience to authority between 1940 and 1944 was punished as a crime. Dissidence was glorified. Lawlessness and disobedience were proclaimed as virtues. France, for the first time since Joan of Arc, is today unable to raise and support an adequate army. While I hope for a return to sounder principles of society, after a temporary lapse, it is plain that, throughout Europe, the destructive termites which attack the foundations of civilization have been at work. Nobody except those who are blind to the recent ravages in Europe will be surprised at the final upshot of a revolution whose signs are written in letters of blood and fire on the European sky.

It should be emphasized that, although the crowd is composed of individuals, the individual is not, as such, a mathematical portion of the crowd. The individual may be—must be—quite different in quality from the multitude, and the multitude is not the individual multiplied by a hundred, a thousand or a hundred thousand. The crowd is another creature, a psychic monster which is more easily excited, performing good or bad deeds that the individual would normally shun. It may, as the eminent Italian social psychologist, Scipio Sighele, emphasized, be heroic on occasion or it may be criminal. It is capable of violence from which most of its members, taken separately, would shrink, often in horror. So great is the power of psychic contagion in crowds that the most eminent, the most placid, the wisest of its component parts, are swept on to deeds, sometimes sublimely courageous, sometimes incredibly atrocious, that they would never have dreamed of performing in their calmer moments in solitude. The mere existence of numbers metamorphoses men. They come under the spell of mass hypnotism.

Doubtless a mysterious atavism operates here. Deep down

in us all there is an ancestral urge, primitive and savage. It is buried under layers of civilization, concealed and controlled by centuries of education and culture. Yet there, among the tangled roots of tradition, lurks in the shadows the instinct of the herd, so well described by Dr. Wilfred Trotter, and a word, an image, will awaken it and bring it to the surface.

When this happens, in exceptional moments of keen suggestibility, we revert, in a crowd of our fellows, to our barbarian emotional heritage. I have been in several countries, in the exercise of my journalistic duties, during periods of revolution, and again in the troubled atmosphere of war, and I have watched with amazement the behavior of ordinary citizens. It hardly seemed possible that these frenzied, pitiless creatures were the same kind compassionate men and women I had known in normal communal life. There came to my mind the wildest pictures of the French Revolution when men became worse than beasts, pictures which had once perplexed me. Now I understood; I realized that no extraordinary manifestation of bravery—and, likewise, no extraordinary manifestation of ferocity—are impossible when the crowd is inspired by a collective purpose, whether good or evil. On the good side we may put—as does the historian G. M. Trevelyan—those "two million peasants, scarcely emerging from serfdom, together with a few score thousand Huguenot refugees, inhabiting certain sandy regions of North Germany," who defied for seven years the onslaught of Austria, Russia, and France. It may well seem a miracle, but it is a miracle that has often been repeated from the days of Thermopylae, where Leonidas, with his 300 Spartans and Thespians, faced the host of Persian invaders.

The same irresistible and irrational qualities, subdued to the color of more peaceful times, are to be found in the crowd which forms what we call the electorate today. Now and again they break forth spontaneously, violently, and the business of the statesman is to direct their impetus and actions into channels where they can do least harm.

An excellent example, on a small scale, was furnished me in Spain. A friend of mine, an American antiquarian who had long lived in the country, was happily present when a revolutionary mob set fire to a convent in which were stored priceless treasures. Everything would have been destroyed, had he not taken the lead and given the words of command. "Make a bonfire of whatever I tell you," he cried, "but not of what belongs to the nation." And he indicated the poor beds, the miserable or indifferent furniture of the convent, and willing hands threw them from the windows, while the jubilant throngs danced around the flames. In the meantime, he was busily salvaging the pictures and other works of art. Everybody was content—the mob which had wreaked its symbolic vengeance, my friend who had preserved the best of the treasures, and the nuns who had saved the most valuable objects of their convent.

In the course of a long reportorial career, I have seen popular anger flashed on nearly every country in turn. It must not be supposed that because we are friends today we shall be friends tomorrow. It must not be assumed that because we are foes today we shall be foes forever. We properly try to forget the past differences, but I have seen in my lifetime international animosities directed against almost every country, including England and America, which, had the conditions been propitious, might easily have resulted in war. Popular sentiment, at any rate, would not have been hostile to any strong measure, had such action been possible. It is better not to enumerate these disputes; the list would show that war between any nations, is not, as we like to declare, "unthinkable"—except on purely material grounds. Passions are quickly inflamed; the crowd is impulsive, irritable, touched in its *amour-propre* by an alleged affront, far more quarrelsome than are private persons.

It is not sound national interests with which the crowds are most concerned—although national interests do play their rôle in its anger; sometimes it is ready to act against its national interests. There is, in the hours of mass wrath, no premeditation; there is no cold calculated policy; and, indeed, generally, when nations go to war, the lack of preparation is woefully apparent.

Happily, such outbursts of temper are usually short-lived, for another characteristic of the crowd is its fickleness, instability and volatility, its capacity to forget injuries. Even after the bloodiest of wars, in which the most frightful cruelties have been perpetrated, after which it would seem, if peoples were rational, there could be no forgiveness and a rankling acrimony would continue for generations, an attempt to effect a rapprochement may often be soon observed. There are notable exceptions; between the French and the Germans a lasting resentment would appear to have arisen; but both English and Americans have, after two wars with Germany, in which bitterness was pushed to the point of folly, extended a helping hand to the defeated adversary. The crowd is fickle in its hatreds as in its loves. That is why no statesman with a sense of history should ever, in the heat of the battle, pronounce absolute dicta, terms or conditions which he may soon be compelled to revoke, or seek in the moment of victory to impose unbearable servitudes on the "enemy."

"Enemy" or not, nations have to live in the same world together, and they will have need of each other. The degeneration of our civilization is plain to all who think, when we compare the wars of today with those of yesteryear. Then, the old diplomacy discounted popular indignation or made a careful and judicious use of it. Now, popular diplomacy obliterates any notion of prudence in the minds of the rulers, who do not hesitate to pander to popular indignation, to fan it into uncontrollable flame, and to demand the unconditional surrender of the foe and the complete destruction of his armaments and industry. Then, a few years later, we are obliged to rebuild the armaments and the industry and to beg the help of the vanquished foe.

The most conspicuous example of such folly is to be seen in the change of emotions and policies toward Germany since 1941. At Casablanca, in January, 1943, "unconditional surrender" was demanded of the Germans. This prolonged the war for some two years and led to vast destruction of life and property in Germany. The Stalin-White-Morgenthau Plan, adopted at Quebec in September, 1944, called for the total destruction of German industry and mining and the reversion of Germany to a pastoral and agricultural nation—something which would have involved the starvation of tens of millions of Germans. German industrial plants were wantonly dismantled, some of them even being moved into Soviet Russia. It was loudly announced that Germany would be disarmed forever. Then came the rising Russophobia and the Cold War. It was seen that only a rearmed Germany could be effective in holding back the tide of a Soviet invasion of Western Europe. Whereupon, the Western Allies, but mainly the United States, began to spend billions to help rebuild the destroyed and dismantled plants, and Western Germany was virtually begged to rearm.

The crowd flies to extremes; it has few doubts or hesitations; it is exaggerated in its judgments, now too unfavorable, then too favorable. Its absence of critical discernment, of logical thinking, is reflected in the men whom it places —or who find themselves placed by accident—at its head. The crowd can pass from fear to hatred, from hatred to compassion, from compassion to respect, from respect to admiration, from admiration to love, without much delay. The intermediate stages are usually brief. The transitions are swift. The pendulum does not stop. Yet how many difficulties has popular diplomacy made for itself as a result of the foolish and heedless fluctuations of its likes and dislikes!

Certainly, it is impossible to ignore the crowd, with its irrational impulses. It demands that its thoughts and feelings should be taken into account. There is no returning to the centuries when the masses could be disregarded and public policy pursued in this sense or in that without much thought about the people who were there to supply the cannon-fodder. The crowd must be listened to, it must be consulted. Nevertheless, it should now be apparent to anyone who is fit to aspire to leadership in a nation that it may be fatal to succumb to the caprices of the crowd. Whoever, for the sake of some temporary acclaim, is weak enough to stimulate its most reprehensible ardors is a malefactor and may contribute to the ruin of his own nation as well as to the ruin of the rest of the world. There was never a period of history when such great skill in the management of public affairs was called for as in our time. A terrible responsibility lies not only on presidents and prime ministers but also on ordinary senators and members of parliament, on politicians of all ranks, on trade unionists, writers, priests and pastors —whoever has the slightest influence on the molding of "public" opinion.

It is no longer necessary to deliberately incite the crowd to war, as may once have been deemed necessary when grave issues of national prestige and profit were at stake; it is now more necessary to apply the brakes, to restrain the bellicose instincts of the crowd.

One of the beliefs most strongly held at Geneva, was that the masses are spontaneously opposed to war. Women in particular, were held to be peace-loving and it was asserted their vote would render war impossible. Today, we still hear of "peace-loving nations." These assumptions are quite untrue. There are, naturally, periods of war-weariness, when peoples who have suffered in spite of their victory just as much as those who have suffered from defeat, lick their wounds and temporarily permit nations which are in a more enviable position to insult them, to defy them, and to rob them.

Except for such breathing-spaces, contrary to all our professions, the crowd is essentially belligerent. The lessons of history and particularly of recent history, leave it unmoved. If it has to submit to hardships, if it is on the edge of bankruptcy, if it loses its liberties one after the other, it never stops to ask itself whether it is in some degree to blame. It does not stop to ask whether its chiefs who, after all, have embodied its profoundest sentiments, have misled it. I am not inquiring here whether and why and how we went wrong —if we did go wrong; I simply remark that neither in Germany nor in France nor in England nor in America, are there any serious regrets for entering the late war—though there may be sadness and pehaps bewilderment in the contemplation of its disastrous consequences.

The dangerous deception in regard to the alleged peace-loving character of the crowd is at the root of most of our misunderstanding of our age. If it is accepted, it implies that the crowd, in every nation, has been innocently taken into war by unscrupulous governments willing to sacrifice a reluctant people to their foolish ambitions. That is not the judgment of the crowd; nor is it mine. On the contrary, less than fifteen years ago, Chamberlain in England and Daladier in France were execrated in many quarters as "appeasers" because they had averted war at Munich; and, even today, the term *Munichois* is one of obloquy. It is true that, with the fickleness which marks the crowd, there was a sigh of relief when, in September, 1938, we were on the very brink of war and then suddenly learned that the catastrophe had been postponed; but within a month or two the men who had temporarily warded off the peril were regarded as betrayers of the public conscience. Nothing seemed more odious to the crowd than "appeasement," nothing more contemptible than to shrink back from war.

In America, as I write, there is, I will not say a conscious war party, for that would be an exaggeration, but there is at least a growing conviction, which does not arise from propaganda alone, that there must be no weakness in dealing with potential adversaries, and that nothing must be done to give the impression that we are not prepared to carry out N.A.T.O. and E.D.C. policies with a high hand (which means the dropping of a few atom-bombs), whatever the outcome. In Europe, the crowd is as yet divided; still, in many quarters the tendency even here is toward the forcing of a "showdown." The memory of the last war is too vivid in Europe, the ruins are too conspicuous, not to awaken doubts, not to arouse a spirit of hesitation. Besides, the prospect of another early defeat, with the ultimate American liberation taking place in lands which will have become little more than cemeteries, gives continental Europeans pause. The material means for another war are obviously insufficient. These considerations, however, do not stifle the fundamental fact that, already, the European crowd is summoning up its courage to face another war.

My contention is that, in the new era of the crowd, the principal duty of a statesman, who must weigh the consequences of his utterances and acts, is no longer to push the people into a trial of arms, but to restrain bellicosity and to guide the people with a tight rein along a road strewn with danger.

Monarchs, before the feelings of the crowd were a decisive factor in public policy, could use the crowd, could drive it as they thought best, well knowing that they could pull it up when and where they pleased. Statesmen worthy of the name today must realize that the crowd is all too likely to take the bit in its teeth, and plunge us all into the deepest ditch. They must recognize that the crowd is unruly, is not quiet in harness, and does not require the whip and wild shouts to hasten its pace. The doctrine that the crowd is "peace-loving" is, then, one of the most mischievous ever invented. An expert and comprehensive knowledge of the psychology of the crowd in this era of mass domination should be required of any aspirant to statesmanship.

It is equally fallacious to hold that women are more peace-loving than males. The First World War came during the very period when women were getting the right to vote. In most civilized countries they had obtained this right by the early 1920's. But this did not prevent the preparations for, and onset of, the much more bloody and destructive Second World War. Women are, if anything, more subject to the bellicosity of crowd stimulation and more sadistic than males. Philip Wylie, in the chapter on "The Moms," in his *A Generation of Vipers*, deals with this matter in very realistic, if somewhat caustic, fashion.

It is easy enough to manipulate the crowd, and to find some temporary profit in such manipulation, in the sense of yielding to popular diplomacy; but to manipulate it in the sense of the general welfare is an exceedingly difficult art. When we consider the state of the world—Europe and Asia in particular—much of it behind an "Iron Curtain," most of it improverished, once proud empires pitifully diminished in extent, power and wealth, morality at a lower ebb than it has been since the Dark Ages, our conceptions of civilization menaced if not shattered, we must deplore the work of a half-century of popular diplomacy. There has been a new invasion of the barbarians, but the barbarians have not invaded us from the exterior—they have surged from the interior.

Vox populi, vox Dei. Was ever a greater or more dangerous falsehood ever uttered?

Any discussion of crowds and their relation to contemporary government and popular diplomacy would be quite incomplete and inadequate without consideration of the leadership of crowds. By themselves alone, crowds, whatever their potential irrationality and explosive impulsiveness, are an inert mass. They emerge into vigorous action, for good or evil, only under the stimulation and incitement of leaders. But, in this era of crowds and mobs, the latter inevitably beget a type of leader suited to the age. If he were not attuned to crowd psychology, he could neither become a leader or long maintain his rôle as such.

Though there have been spellbinders from the days of Demosthenes, the great rhetoricians of antiquity appealed chiefly to the literate minority. Prior to the emergence of nose-counting democracy, leadership was based in large part upon superior wisdom, sagacity and shrewdness, as applied among relative equals. Rationality and factual relevance played a significant rôle in establishing and maintaining leadership. Today, all this has passed away and the successful leader is the one who can best exploit the suggestibility, impulsiveness, irrationality and sadism of the crowd.

Le Bon gave this subject his attention. He held that the leaders of crowds are almost invariably rhetoricians or agitators obsessed by passion rather than well-informed persons, careful thinkers, or public-spirited citizens. They may gain the attention of crowds and the consequent ability to manipulate them by superficial types of prestige and sensationalism, such as military prowess and other achievements which have little bearing upon ability or preparation in the realm of statecraft or diplomacy. The most successful leader of a crowd, as Hitler well demonstrated, gets the latter to accept his leadership and program by constant and repeated affirmation of his convictions and dogmas rather than by any reliance upon reasoned analysis. Once an idea is accepted by a crowd, it spreads with great rapidity as a result of the psychic contagion which is characteristic of crowd psychology.

Le Bon leaves us with the pessimistic contention that the

present era of crowds may deprive us of any informed, rational or intelligent leadership in the future. According to the laws of the psychology of crowds, the individuals assembled in a crowd are governed by their emotions rather than by their intellectual faculties, and the emotional traits of the most erudite do not differ materially from those of the average individual. As Le Bon puts it: "In a crowd, men always tend to the same level and, on general questions, a vote recorded by forty academicians is no better than that of forty water-carriers."

The improvements in the means of communication since Le Bon's time have increased the power of the manipulators of the masses in playing upon the irrationality and suggestibility of crowds, whether local or national. Hitler, perhaps the most powerful and sinister manipulator of crowd psychology who has ever lived, relied especially on the loudspeaker and the radio, a matter touched upon in another chapter. Joseph Goebbels, another most ruthless and successful manipulator of crowd psychology, relied on all means of communication save for television, which came too late for his malevolent exploitation. Franklin D. Roosevelt and Winston Churchill, the other two outstanding manipulators of national crowds and mobs, owed much of their political power and international renown to their clever use of radio. Television is already increasing the power of leaders to sway crowds and is making a crowd out of nations.

All trends and examples in recent years have amply proved that he who seeks success as a political leader must work upon the emotional suggestibility of crowds rather than appeal to facts or reason. Therefore, when, in the remainder of this book, we speak of crowds and the impact of crowds on diplomacy, we have in mind not only the masses themselves but the leaders the crowd era has brought forth and who conform in their behavior to the requirements of successful demagoguery in our era. In our usage here, then, the crowd is an inseparable couplet composed of the masses and their manipulators, the traits of the former begetting the tricks and techniques of the latter. The combination has all but ruined scientific statecraft, rational diplomacy, and the prospect of world peace.

The techniques employed by the leaders of crowds, which also means nations today, can all be summed up under the head of propaganda or, as Aldous Huxley designated it, "emotional engineering." Propaganda goes back to the earliest Oriental days. Hebrew prophets and Mesopotamian war lords were able and ardent propagandists. More talented were orators like Demosthenes and Cicero, and more violent were the champions of the Catholics and Protestants after 1500.

But propaganda in international relations first began in a serious and extended form in connection with the wars of the French Revolution and the Napoleonic periods. These ended the era of small, paid, professional armies and introduced the era of mass, conscript armies. In order to make the latter fight effectively, they had to be misinformed, deceived, or both, in regard to the purposes of the wars and thereby made to hate their enemies. But, due to the paucity of long and bloody wars between 1814 and 1914, propaganda in world affairs tended to simmer down until the rise of sensational or "yellow" mass journalism in the 1880's and 1890's. The powers of the sensational press in propaganda for hate and war were first demonstrated on a large and impressive scale when Hearst and Pulitzer played the leading rôle in putting the United States into the Spanish-American War in 1898.

But international propaganda only came into full bloom with the First World War. Here the Allies vastly surpassed the Central Powers who proved notably scanty and stupid in their propaganda efforts. Britain played up effectively the invasion of Belgium and Chancellor Bethmann-Hollweg's ill-considered remark about warring for "a scrap of paper," although we now know from John Morley and John Burns that the British decision to enter the war was made without any discussion whatever of a possible impending invasion of Belgium by Germany. Moreover, Germany had proposed to respect Belgian neutrality in return for British neutrality. Then came the notorious myth of German "atrocities" in Belgium and elsewhere, the validity of which was attested by no less an authority than the respected Lord Bryce. The falsity of such charges was later fully revealed by another Englishman of as high character and more discernment, Sir Arthur Ponsonby, in his *Falsehood in Wartime.*

The press in Britain and the United States wallowed in the opportunity for sensationalism provided by all this, and the newspapers were guided by Lord Northcliffe, George Creel, and others. "Top-level" leaders also took a powerful hand in the proceedings, notably President Wilson and Sir Edward Grey. They developed the famous, but deceptive, "war aims" of the Allies: "to make the world safe for democracy," "a war to end war," and the like, culminating in Mr. Wilson's Fourteen Points which were conveniently forgotten after the Germans had accepted the Armistice which was based on them. The propaganda of Lloyd George's "hang the Kaiser" Khaki election proved stronger than the noble war aims. The story of propaganda in the First World War has been told in such books as Sidney Rogerson's *Propaganda in the Next War;* Mock and Larson's *Words that Won the War;* and H. C. Peterson's *Propaganda for War.*

Even professional historians were enlisted in unabashed propaganda, the most systematic program being that of the National Board for Historical Service, organized in the United States by James Thomson Shotwell and others. This emotional orgy of the historians has best been described by Dr. Harry Elmer Barnes and C. Hartley Grattan. What happened at the "top-level" peace conference held in Paris on the heels of this propaganda has been described in a previous chapter. It led to the Second World War and all the ills that accompanied and followed it.

Indeed, the most conspicuous examples of propaganda between the two World Wars grew directly out of the mistakes of the Versailles Treaty. Italy, disgruntled and disorganized by the failure to get what was promised her under the Secret Treaties, fell under the sway of Mussolini, with his talents for rhetorical bombast and showmanship. But, as a propagandist, he was far outshone by Hitler and his Nazi entourage. Hitler made great use of rhetorical denunciations and affirmations, symbolism, and the limitless resources of the press and radio, a matter we shall discuss later on. Joseph Goebbels, Hitler's Propaganda Minister, was the most successful and ruthless of all mass-propagandists. He not only made use of the laws of crowd psychology but frankly exploited the baser simian traits of mankind. Nazi propaganda was directed mainly against Soviet Russia and the Jews, and was returned in kind.

When the Second World War broke out in 1939, the resources and mechanisms of propaganda were utilized on a scale without precedent in history. The media of communication used in propaganda had enormously expanded between 1919 and 1939, social psychologists and advertisers had reduced propaganda to something of a science, and veritable manuals of propaganda had been prepared. National and international organizations for propaganda, euphemistically called "War Information" bureaus and the like, were established by the warring governments. The material for propaganda was more voluminous and sensational. The actual atrocities of the Second World War were far more numerous and horrible than the imaginary and fake atrocities of the First War.

The propaganda ferocity was so great during the Second World War that it made impossible any general peace conference afterwards or even a bad peace treaty. It made feasible the fatal Stalin-White-Morgenthau Plan for Germany, and the notorious war-crimes trials which are an enduring menace to the peace and safety of mankind. Wartime emotions have not yet subsided enough to permit the preparation and publication of a comprehensive account of the propaganda during the Second World War, but a preliminary survey was presented in Harold Lavine's and James Wechsler's *War Propaganda and the United States* and Walter Johnson's *The Battle Against Isolation.*

After the War came the cold war, which involved the exchange of bitter propaganda charges between the American and the Soviet blocs of nations. The United Nations provided a forum and platform for hurling the invectives of propaganda. Next, the Korean War continued and intensified the propaganda of the cold war, and Communist China replaced Japan as the most hated of the Asiatic nations.

Crowd psychology and international propaganda took complete control of popular diplomacy. The old diplomacy, based on concessions and adjustments, was absolutely ruled out as unworthy, if not criminal, "appeasement." The world was well on the way into the régime pictured by George Orwell in which it is openly proclaimed that "War is Peace," the waging of war is entrusted to the Ministry of Peace, and the whole political system, domestic and foreign, is controlled by ruthless propaganda, intimidation, and torture. As Le Bon was the prophet of popular government and diplomacy in the first half of the twentieth century, it may turn out that Orwell best predicted the trends in the second half.

9

REJECTION OF DIPLOMATIC READJUSTMENT
OR PREVENTIVE WAR BRINGS WORLD CHAOS

It is no purpose of mine to discuss in this place the mistakes made by this or that country, or to attach special blame to persons in regard to the events that brought us into the Second World War—a war that Mr. Churchill later described as unwanted and unnecessary; but certain general observations can best be illustrated by reference to the incidents that are familiar to every literate person of our generation.

I affirmed in my last chapter that the public needs no encouragement towards bellicosity and that it will readily enter a war without first asking what means it has of pursuing the war to a satisfactory conclusion, or, especially, inquiring as to what sort of conclusion will be satisfactory. But I refrained from any insistence on the opposite trait and tendency of popular diplomacy, namely, its reluctance to show a bold front when such a display would, perhaps, avert war, or at least make victory certain without paying an excessive price.

I deliberately set aside the extreme pacific viewpoint, not necessarily because I condemn it, but because I do not think it is a viewpoint taken, save in the interval between wars, by the vast majority. It does not, for better or for worse, conform to our human nature and the present political situation in the world. In any realistic approach to our problems, we must take the world as it is, and not create an imaginary ideal world.

Now, in the actual world, antagonisms exist between nations that may inevitably, sooner or later, result in a trial of

163

strength. To assume the contrary is to close one's eyes to implacable facts. My indictment of the diplomacy of the crowd, as I have defined it, is not only that it makes war when it would have been wiser to strive for reasonable adjustments and continues that war until all rational arrangements become impossible; it is also that it refuses to bestir itself in time to stop a war while it has the power to do so, or to choose a moment for making war when it could win without a great expenditure of men or money.

The crowd may be lazy, indifferent, without foresight, and its alternations of apathy and belligerence are frequently badly timed. It may be lackadaisical when it should be alert, it may be bellicose when it should be cautious. It is all too likely to make the wrong war at the wrong time and in the wrong place.

When Germany was feeble, after the First World War, it would have been, not magnanimous, but simply sensible, to revise the terms of the Treaty of Versailles which were clearly unjust. When Hitler succeeded in restoring strength to Germany, it would still have been possible to convoke a conference resolved to remove once and for all the legitimate grievances on the distinct understanding that any subsequent breach of the agreement voluntarily reached would be resisted by an immediate armed intervention. But, during all those years, popular diplomacy did nothing, it was not antagonistic or, on the whole unsympathetic to Germany; it was merely in one of its periods of mental indolence. The crowd was slothful, letting events overtake it while it slumbered. When, at last, it was aroused from its comatose condition it struck out furiously and found itself involved in a needless conflict which ended like a Shakespearean tragedy, the stage littered with corpses.

It is now over twenty years since I wrote a little book entitled *War Unless*, in which I advocated an immediate settlement of post-war disputes or—though I hoped that the alternative would be rejected—immediate war. Preventive war? The suggestion was received by most with horrified silence. Doubtless, it is a dreadful thing to make war deliberately; but it is no less dreadful to stagger inertly along the road to war and then to be rushed headlong into a flurry of frantic, indiscriminate and fruitless slaughter.

Let me affirm that I am not an advocate of preventive warfare. I am not an advocate of warfare at all—certainly much less an advocate of warfare than the majority of "peace-professors" who, after a great deal of "high-faluting" peace talk, finish up by plunging neck and crop into supporting the most unintelligent kind of warfare. But this being said, I confess that I do not share the verbal indignation that is usually aroused by the very mention of the possibility of preventive warfare. Warfare, if admitted as a public reality, and it is of course admitted by nearly everybody, may be of two kinds: (1) calculated and directed towards a purpose, or (2) senseless and without any logical goal.

I am constantly and sadly reminded of the stupid discussions at Geneva, in which men and women, otherwise presumably reasonable beings, tried to establish humane rules for warfare, as though it were a sort of international boxing-match. This weapon was fair, that weapon was inhuman. It was assumed that it makes a great difference to a combatant whether he is killed by a bayonet or a bomb! That civilians should be spared as far as possible, in harmony with what was long the European code of civilized warfare, may be granted. In any case, whatever rules we lay down will infallibly be broken—by both sides—if war actually comes. The strange mixture of bloodthirstiness and humanitarianism that inspires such debates as those at Geneva is no more than nauseating humbug. If you accept war, you must exclude sentimentalism, you must accept it as a life-and-death struggle without endeavoring to extenuate its brutalities.

So with preventive war. You can take your choice between

peace and war. You can, moreover, choose between one kind of war and another. For my part, my plea has always been for peace; but for those who prefer war, it is only logical to make war when the "enemy" is least prepared to resist. It is quite idiotic to wait until his strength has developed to the full —even help him to develop it—and then attack. That is precisely what France and England—i.e., the crowd—did in the six years that preceded their declaration of war on Germany in September, 1939.

When Hitler decided to re-arm, the only sane choice was between an offer of a final adjustment of past injustices with Germany and an ultimatum. When, in violation of the Versailles Treaty, he marched his troops into Rhineland, the clear choice was between a sweeping revision of the Treaty and a military expedition to force him out of Rhineland. Had the French moved at that moment, the Germans would have retreated—they had definite orders to withdraw should they meet opposition. A preventive war would then have been bloodless. When Hitler, emboldened by unopposed success, imposed the *Anschluss* on Austria, we could have called a conference to re-shape central Europe, once and for all, or we could have intervened with Anglo-French armies. We—the crowd—unable to look ahead, and enjoying our fatal inertia, did neither. When, justly or unjustly, Hitler lopped off a huge slice of Czechoslovakia, we could still not make up our minds whether to stand firm in resistance or to embody the unilateral Munich decision in a general European re-settlement. So Hitler went on from conquest to conquest, and we looked on listlessly, for such was then the mood of the crowd. When he annexed the whole of Czechoslovakia we still remained inert. Who shall acquit us of acquiescence, and therefore of complicity, in a series of operations that were bound to end disastrously? After calmly tolerating and acquiescing in all this, Britain and France made war on Hitler for demanding the return of Danzig and a motor road through the Polish

Corridor—certainly the most reasonable of all Hitler's demands from 1933 to 1939.

Preventive war? Surely not if there is a workable alternative; but, if there is no alternative, or if we cannot resolve to take the alternative, then preventive war is the only sensible course. I have already said that popular diplomacy rarely takes the sensible course. It is slow to understand. It is torpid. It continues to live in a fool's paradise until it suddenly awakens from its dream and wildly runs amuck. In this case, the crowd allowed Germany to become once more a mighty military nation. Then, ill-equipped, defective in morale, in danger of reverses in the early years, and threatened with ultimate defeat, it rushed into battle to save Danzig from becoming a German city, which it was and had been for centuries. That is how the mind of the crowd can work. It can act most rashly and precipitately after remaining inactive and heedless. It oscillates between supineness and fury. When it eventually goes crazy, when it "sees red," as the saying is, it throws reason to the winds, and accepts any odds against victory. The result of starting hostilities in 1939 is that, after all the expense, mortality, and devastation of the most pitiless and destructive war of all time, Danzig has been lost, after all, Poland is lost, the Baltic States are lost, the Balkan countries are lost. If England and France are said to have nominally won the war, they are both actually in the most perilous condition they have ever known and are threatened with a far more cunning and formidable foe than Hitler ever was or could have become.

Preventive war? Certainly a preventive war—if it prevents a war a hundred times more costly. Or, as the alternative, for there was, and probably always is, an alternative, a genuine attempt to reach an acceptable settlement by mutual and fair adjustments. I am unable to understand, therefore, the outcry of popular diplomacy against a preventive war which may save us from a war of extermination. But, of course, in order to strike at the right moment, the crowd would have to possess intelligent foresight, keep a cool head, and know exactly what it wants and how it can get it. But these are the very qualities that the crowd apparently can never possess, or at least very rarely indeed.

That is why popular diplomacy, obedient to the instincts of the crowd, must necessarily, through a brutal and stupid peace, lose every war in which it engages. Whatever we may think of war as a means of settling quarrels—and I personally do not think much of it—we should clearly understand that war—especially after victory—calls for the greatest intelligence. It is the science of obtaining by force precisely what is desirable and of never going beyond this objective; of timing one's stroke, of limiting the consequences, of vacillating as little as possible, and of concluding a stable and just peace at the earliest opportunity.

Say these things to a nation at war, however, and you will certainly be arrested, and possibly executed, as a traitor to the country. Clemenceau all but hung the ex-Premier of France, Joseph Caillaux, for alleged treasonable relations with the enemy which were, in reality, a statesmanlike effort to achieve a negotiated peace before both France and Germany were ruined. When Lord Lansdowne proposed peace negotiations in November, 1917, a move which would have averted the vicious Treaty of Versailles and in all probability have prevented the rise of Hitler and the Second World War, he became overnight the most unpopular and hated man in England—for having made the most statesmanlike suggestion set forth in England from 1914 to 1952. Likewise, no statement of Woodrow Wilson brought him more bitter criticism than his wise declaration that the only just and permanent peace that could grow out of the First World War was a "peace without victory." War should be the art of attaining possibilities, but the crowd caught up in war rashly demands impossibilities and is carried on to its ultimate ruin by its hatreds and fantasies. Instead of following Lansdowne and Wilson in their moderation, the crowd backed up Lloyd George in his insane demand for a "knock-out victory," which knocked out Germany, but with results which nearly knocked out the world in 1939–1945, and may still complete the job. It followed with equal fatality the demand of Roosevelt and Churchill, the Casablanca demand for the "unconditional surrender" of Germany, Italy and Japan.

Today, a similar situation—or rather an infinitely worse situation—presents itself, and the mind of the crowd is confused and troubled. It has discovered that the last war ended badly, but it seems to have no idea why it ended badly. It attributes the disappointment of its hopes—if it had any clear hopes—to fatality, the perverseness of events. It has no appreciation of the law of cause and effect. It cannot analyze its own mistakes—or the mistakes of those who purported to guide it. There is, amazingly, no general reaction against the rulers who helped it to go astray.

In this absence of reaction against guilty rulers, the crowd at times, is, broadly, if unwittingly, right; for the rulers of Britain and France in 1939 were only the mouthpieces and instruments of the crowd. In condemning its rulers, it would actually be condemning itself, and that the crowd never does. In France, after the collapse of 1940, Marshal Pétain pronounced a *mea culpa* on behalf of the French people—and he died in prison. No people will search its conscience to find where and why it has gone wrong; and anyone who ventures to show its errors and who preaches penitence will, after the first hour of anguish has passed, be repudiated. There is here an object-lesson for politicians who would succeed for the moment; never confess that the fault lies in us! It lies in the treachery of the "enemy," in traitors in our midst, in some arbitrary behavior of fate; not in us.

But we cannot completely excuse *all* leaders from personal responsibility in entering the Second World War. The crowd in the United States remained overwhelmingly against entering the conflict until Pearl Harbor. The pressure for intervention was headed up by President Roosevelt and his intimate entourage of Harry Hopkins and others. It was motivated by a desire to preserve the tenure of the Democratic Party after the New Deal was rebuffed in 1937 and 1938, by the Anglophilism of Eastern seaboard financial and political leaders, and by the anger of certain ethnic groups over Hitler's treatment of radicals and minorities. But, once the welcome attack on Pearl Harbor took place, the American crowd entered the hostilities with great zest and emotion, from which it has not even yet sufficiently recovered to be able seriously to consider the responsibility for policies and actions which cost the United States many lives, vast natural resources, and hundreds of billions of dollars to do battle and to repair the damage done to the Old World through unwise policies in both war and peace.

Although it could be demonstrated in some convincing detail how and why "we got like that," it would be both thankless and useless to undertake the task, except as a historian dealing with far-off days. American historians have shown more alertness than Europeans here. In such books as Doctor Beard's *President Roosevelt and the Coming of the War, 1941*; Professor Tansill's *Back Door to War*; George Morgenstern's *Pearl Harbor*; Doctor Sanborn's *Design for War*, and W. H. Chamberlin's *America's Second Crusade*, the facts about the causes of the Second World War are set forth in what must remain substantially the final verdict of history. We can do little more than point to the basic essentials of the post-war problem as it now faces us, and to suggest remedies which will probably be ignored.

From the breakdown of government in Russia, the Russia of the Czars and the moujiks, the Russia without a middle class, to the war that broke out in Korea in 1950, is a far cry. But we might trace every link in the chain: (1) the Bolshevik Revolution; (2) the ill-conceived attempt in 1918–1919 to isolate or destroy the Communist State, with the result that Communist-Nationalism was born and flourished; (3) the bad peace of 1919 which enfeebled Germany which might have been a bulwark against the spread of Communism; (4) the rise of Fascism in Italy and of National-Socialism in Germany as a counterblast to Communism; (5) the desperate struggle in Spain against secularism, radicalism and Communism; (6) the ambitions of Italy in Abyssinia and the resulting "sanctions" which failed in their purpose but ranged Italy with Germany and thus removed the barrier to the *Anschluss* of Germany and Austria; (7) the refusal to listen to the pleas of "democratic" statesmen in Germany, and the consequent rise of Hitler; (8) the opportunity offered Japan to expand by the inability of the Western world to put its house in order; (9) the increasing hostility towards Japan in the United States and the American support of the corrupt régime of Chiang Kai-shek in China; and, finally (10) the coöperation of anti-Bolshevik countries following June, 1941, with Russia, thereafter extolled for several years as the most progressive of nations and the champion of "Democracy" against "Fasnazism."

At every stage of this confusion of tongues and reversal of rôles it would be easy to show the blunders of popular diplomacy. We should not fasten on the "leaders" of the past thirty or forty years the exclusive blame for blunders which belong in large part to the easily excited and inconsistent feelings of the masses who have been the veritable rulers since the turn of the century.

In my youth there were fiery campaigns against Czardom, the grand dukes, and the great landlords of Russia who governed their serfs by a plentiful use of the knout. Then, in the First World War, there was nothing but praise for the mighty nation that was our ally; nothing had changed in Russia, but we had changed. Later, when Russia made a separate peace with Germany at Brest-Litovsk, we had no words too harsh for Russia, now fallen by sheer Czarist incompetence into the hands of the Communists. Afterwards, for a long period, the chief peril to Europe was considered to be Bolshevism. Nevertheless, in France and in Italy, the doctrines of Communism won millions of sympathizers. In Germany, too, Communism implanted itself.

When Mussolini and Hitler arose to stem the rising tide of Communism, they were abused by the Communist sympathizers—rightly abused for their violence—but they were commended by many of those who feared lest the masses should adhere to Communism. I could cite many passages from speeches and writings of men who later on ranged themselves temporarily with the Communists, full of unmitigated condemnation of the Moscow régime. They were thankful that at least Japan in the Pacific, Italy in the Mediterranean, and Germany on the North Sea presented ramparts against the Communist menace. Especially notable among those who bitterly condemned Soviet Russia and rejoiced in the rise of Fascism and Nazism as a bulwark against Communism was Winston Churchill.

And, then, the tide turned again; strangely enough, it turned when the Russian Communists, after the dethronement of the King, went to the assistance of the radical "Loyalists" in Spain, who were also assisted, in different degrees, by France and England, while Germany and Italy went to the aid of General Franco. It is true that nominal "neutrality" was proclaimed, but it is equally true that, from then on, popular opinion took sides; and the two "crowds" ranged themselves in fighting mood in Europe—Italy, Germany, and Franquist Spain, opposed to England, France, Russia, and the so-called Spanish Loyalists.

This line-up was incredibly unreasonable; it could not have been the work of skilled diplomats; it was a spontaneous manifestation of popular diplomacy which was not appalled by, but rather rejoiced in, the creation of a small-scale battle-field in Spain, the model for the future vast battlefield of Europe and Asia. All judicious observers grieved at the spectacle, but there is no remedy against the suicidal senti-ments of the masses. It is odd that, although years have gone by, the field has changed, and Franquist Spain is an essential factor in the strategy of the third World War which many people foresee, the old resentment against Franco persists. It is the more curious in that while Italy and Germany, who fought against us, are now received back into the fold, Spain, which remained aloof from the European strife and greatly aided the Allied cause, is still the object of our enmity.

Naturally, the common sympathies of France, England, and Russia in the Spanish Civil War, gave a remarkable im-petus to Communism. Communism then became a respect-able creed in Europe, and "Fasnazism" was irrevocably our enemy. Although European countries, unlike America, were rather indifferent to the operations of Japan in Manchuria and China, the smearing of Japan as a militaristic and authoritarian country, as distinct from China, also governed by war-lords but sufficiently in confusion to be considered "democratic," brought grist to the Bolshevik mill. For my part, I regretted that Japan, once the "trusted ally" of Eng-land, who also stood for order, the only stable element in the Far East, should have fallen under the displeasure of the United States—or at least of President Roosevelt and Secre-taries Hull, Ickes and Morgenthau. Although public senti-ment on the European Continent was not particularly strong against Japan, that country was, nevertheless, ranged by popular diplomacy as among the "enemies" to be overthrown at the first opportunity.

The French, when they wish to survey the world with detachment, imagine themselves looking down from the celestial heights of Sirius—the dog-star. I, too, like to sit in a corner of the heavens and watch the strange doings of men.

Everything seems so different when seen from that coign of vantage.

The observer on the dog-star first saw Russia—that is to say Communism—of which everybody was afraid, fenced in by Turkey, jealous guardian of the Straits, Greece, Bulgaria, Rumania, Yugoslavia, Czechoslovakia, Poland, France, Italy—though there were advance-guards of Communism in some of these countries—Lithuania, Latvia, Esthonia, the Northern nations such as Finland, Sweden, Norway, Denmark, Holland, Belgium, and, above all, Germany. Germany was the solid barrier. Germany alone seemed able to prevent Communism from breaking through. The same observer, glancing eastwards, saw China in chaos, but still non-Communist; Indo-China, Malaya, and India, still under the British crown; and, above all, Japan, the solid barrier to Bolshevik encroachments in that half of the world.

Looking again, a few years later, the observer on Sirius saw that the might of Japan had been broken, partly by the dropping of atom-bombs by America, long the arch-enemy of Communism. He also saw that Germany was a sheer wreck shattered by obliteration bombing, while the cordon of states which were to protect Europe from Bolshevism— the Baltic States and the Balkan States—were now virtually part of a great sprawling Russian Empire, now much the strongest power in the Old World.

The old anti-Communist Europe had shrunk to the smallest proportions, and was living on American charity. Even England was compelled to take subsidies from America to keep alive. In short, Europe, as he had known it, would have disappeared entirely, swallowed up in the Communist maw, had not America, chiefly for American rather than European reasons, decided to save what could yet be saved. America was the benevolent Providence for Europe. And, when the observer on Sirius inquired how this change had been brought about, he was informed that America and England, not content with shattering anti-Communist Germany, the barrier to Bolshevism, had made a present to Russia of nearly two-thirds of Europe, that America and England had vied with each other in loud praises of Russia, and that the erstwhile Communist tiger was regarded after June, 1941, as a soft-furred, purring pussy-cat, finally domesticated and perfectly harmless.

Gazing eastwards again and a little later, he saw that China had been conquered by the Communists, that Malaya was the prey of terrorists, that Indo-China was the theater of bitter fighting, that India was no longer British and was not altogether outside the sphere of Communist designs; that, in fact, the whole Far East was seething in revolt. Nor was this all: the Arab countries, in the Near East and in Africa, countries which had hitherto been fairly quiet, guided to-wards their independence by the Western nations, were rising up against their rulers and might well be amenable to Communist agitation.

The ferment of Moscow was felt all over the globe. Misery was a breeding-ground for Bolshevism, and misery was more widespread and more intense than ever before in human experience. The restraints of religion, of morality, had been loosened in most lands.

And again, when the observer on Sirius asked how this transformation had been effected, he was told that such had been the will of Western civilization, which had suddenly conceived an extraordinary affection for Communism, and implicitly and blindly trusted in the good faith of Bolshevik Russia.

But, as the observer continued to regard the world scene, he observed a curious commotion. The confidence in Russia had gone, there was now fear. Emissaries hurried to and fro, seeking to reconstruct the factories demolished in Germany, begging Germany, their defeated and disarmed enemy, to re-arm in haste, trying to build up another Japanese army to help them in their belated resistance to Communism. After doing everything in their power to suppress and destroy the anti-Communist countries, they now belatedly besought them to play their part in the protection of the world.

"What fools these mortals be!" exclaimed the onlooker, perched aloft on the dog-star.

The oddest of all was the attitude of the Western countries towards their citizens who had once believed that Communist Russia was their friend. These unfortunate, slow-minded persons, formerly seeing that it was good form to be Communist, or sympathizers with Communism, as their leaders had taught them to be, did not change in time. When they did change, they found they could be punished retroactively for their former opinions which had been patterned on the opinions of their chiefs. They were liable to imprisonment or at least to ejection from their jobs. "When Father says turn, we all turn," was the motto under an election poster in my youth which depicted a swarm of children in the same bed. Those who do not turn today, at the word of command, are ruthlessly thrown out of bed.

Confucius once remarked dolefully that it is hard to strive with all one's heart for the wrong results. Obviously, even the crowd did not fight valiantly over nearly six long years deliberately to bring about the fatal international results which we have briefly catalogued above. Yet, it is not by mere accident that we have tied ourselves up in knots that perhaps we cannot untie. I submit that any cool-headed philosopher-statesman could have foreseen in 1939 or 1945 precisely what would happen. Indeed, it was impossible not to foresee it if one were guided by reason. The explanation is, of course, that the flux and reflux of popular sentiment are responsible for the disaster, and that no prominent philosopher-statesman has dared to oppose himself to the current of popular sentiment. Had there been a guiding hand—or rather had it been possible for any hand to be strong enough to direct the masses—we would have been steered to some clear goal. Not fate, but popular diplomacy, has brought us to this unhappy pass at the mid-century.

"We have killed the wrong pig," is the sad confession attributed to one of the Allied leaders in the Second World War; it is probably apocryphal, nor does it much matter whether it was ever made; our politicians are not even now willing to make such avowals. Nor should it be taken as embodying the whole truth. There were forces in the world which had to be crushed, if we could crush them; but it was not necessary to destroy whole nations, to break down all barriers, to raise up another potential enemy more formidable than the first. There was no need, in the words of the French apologue of Gribouille, to plunge into the lake to escape from the rain. There was no need to conduct one war in such manner as to render another and more horrible war almost inevitable.

Nevertheless, I maintain that the onus of the defeat we found in victory cannot be fixed squarely and solely on the shoulders of one or two or three persons. The onus also lies on us all, that is to say on the crowd whose irrationality is amply proved by the terrible tragedy of errors that leaves us floundering in an unprecedented international tangle. We have marched on, by many devious routes, into a quagmire, and how we shall now extricate ourselves no man can predict. Of one thing we are sure, that even when we emerge from the morass, we shall still be in piteous plight.

That brings me back to the subject of preventive war against Russia today. Many people see it as the only solution. Timely opposition to Hitler, either by a just settlement or by the earlier acceptance of the risk of war, was undoubtedly called for in the 1930's. But, with the lesson of the last war now before us, who will dare to affirm that another war would not be equally ill-conducted, and that our last state might not be worse than the first?

We could easily have stopped Russian expansion in 1944 and 1945. There ought never to have been any dangerous Russian expansion or a Russian menace. Now it is too late to recover lost ground by preventive war. We have dealt out the cards. We needlessly gave Russia the aces; so we cannot complain because she played them to her advantage. It is one of the supreme follies of the post-war popular diplomacy and crowd psychology to blame Russian Communism for the inevitable results of the colossal mistakes of Roosevelt and Churchill, predominantly those of Roosevelt, at Casablanca, Cairo, Teheran, Quebec and Yalta (and the affirmation and perpetuation of these at Potsdam by Churchill, Attlee and Truman). We cannot just kick over the card table and start a fight. We must put up with our losses, and they are grievous, since we chose to enter the game under conditions of our own making; but we can play the cards that remain in our hand with greater skill—if we are capable of greater skill.

We should insist, however, that the crowd at the elbows of the players must remain silent, for it is the excitability of the crowd, its cries and counsels, that have jeopardized the game. The kibitzers (the crowd) at the diplomatic game under popular diplomacy may be even more dangerous than the reckless gamblers themselves who are dealing the cards and playing the hands. This was notably true at the time of the "Peace Ballot" during the diplomatic crisis over Ethiopia, and when the British and French radicals and warmongering conservatives denounced the peaceful policies of Chamberlain and Daladier at Munich in 1938. Popular diplomacy, the most pernicious of public evils, must be repudiated and abandoned, and the conduct of the game left to the experts.

POSTSCRIPT

It is no part of my purpose to comment in detail on current policies, but I must make an exception to call attention to certain misconceptions in the United States about the strength of Europe's defenses.

Even Great Britain is far behind on her program of rearmament, while there is in the country a large group led by Mr. Bevan which believes that any rearmament that impoverishes the nation will be worse than useless. Moreover, so long as there are millions of Communists in France, firmly resolved not to fight Russia, but prepared to sabotage French defenses, it is unlikely that Great Britain will risk her twenty to twenty-five divisions on the Continent, where they would be at the mercy of a "Fifth Column" on their flanks and in the rear.

Two years of sterile discussion about the size of the French army have been wasted; promises, poor as they were, have not been fulfilled; and it is doubtful whether ten French divisions, properly equipped, are at present available. There were one hundred well-equipped French divisions ready to defend France in 1939.

The Germans, still suffering from the ruthless destruction of the war, are, whatever political accords for their conscription are reached, reluctant at present to be rearmed and so place their country in the forefront of an attack by the mighty land forces of Soviet Russia.

Assuming that the extraordinary reversal of the policy of the Allies to keep Germany disarmed forever is put into execution, in spite of the opposition of the French who place every obstacle in the way, how can it be supposed that Germany will be an obedient collaborator with the Western Allies? The key to national unity, for Germany, lies in the hands of the Russians—not in our hands; and the realistic course for Germany to pursue may well be to seek an agreement with the Kremlin by which her unity would be restored in return for her benevolent neutrality in the event of war between East and West.

Real-politik would recognize these facts, but again we indulge in sentiment, and imagine that Germany will be so grateful to us for past damage and injustices that she will plunge into civil war (for there are, thanks to our diplomacy, two sorts of Germans, Eastern and Western, as in Korea there are North and South Koreans) and once more offer her country as a battlefield to those who shattered it to pieces only a few years ago.

What other forces count in Western Europe? Certainly not Turkey and Greece, whose rôle would be purely local. Spain? But Spain is still ostracized by England and France for reasons that are quite senseless.

Thus, we loudly advertise plans that are, to say the least, ill-conceived and probably entirely inoperative. It would be humorous were it not tragic on a world scale.

10

DICTATORS AND DEMOCRACY

At this point it is incumbent on me to discuss dictatorship and to clear away some misconceptions that hamper our view of the world as it is. I deprecate dictatorships, not only because they are un-democratic, but also because they are the ultimate flower and fruit of democracy and crowd rule. In other words, the dictator is the most complete incarnation of the spirit of the crowd.

It is possible to imagine a dictator imposing himself on a nation by deception, by conspiracy, or by the organization of forces which are interested in his maintenance. But such a tyrant, whom we suppose to stand in total opposition to the thoughts and wishes of the people, could not last for long. You cannot, as the Holy Scripture has it, kick against the pricks. In modern social conditions there are many ways of dethroning a despot, but I need only mention the method of a general strike. "You can do many things with bayonets," said Bismarck, "but you cannot sit on them." The would-be dictator must place himself on a more comfortable throne. It must be the throne of the people's will if it is to endure.

Democracy may be of many kinds; the democracy of America, where the president, elected by nation-wide suffrage, is the supreme figure, to whom secretaries of state are responsible. He can veto if he chooses the laws passed by Congress, and is a much more powerful personage than, for example, the president of the French Republic. The latter is elected by the two chambers, has no control over the prime minister or the members of the cabinet, normally overthrown every few months by the shifting combinations of a dozen groups. He is mainly a decorative figurehead, though a strong personality with powerful political connections and affiliations, like Raymond Poincaré, may exercise great influence on affairs of state. Nor does the democracy of England, for England is veritably a democratic country in spite, or perhaps because, of her king, strongly resemble that of any continental nation: the king fulfills traditional rites and sentimental functions binding together the peoples of the Commonwealth on a plane above politics, but the prime minister, the head of the party which can command a majority in the House of Commons, is the real ruler.

There are a variety of ways of voting, direct voting for particular candidates, proportional distribution of seats over wide areas according to lists drawn up by caucuses, or voting by the second or third or fourth degree. Some of the methods are fair, others strike one as unfair; but, whether the elected person has obtained an absolute majority of votes, or merely a relative majority when there are three or more candidates, or even a minority of votes, as in some countries in Europe where the elections are deliberately rigged against the strongest groups, it is rarely that the successful party represents much more than fifty per cent of the electorate.

An American president winning with 60 per cent of even the vote cast, for example, would be regarded as exceptionally favored, and only in mere formality can he ever be regarded as acting with the consent of the whole national community. After the last English election I read statistics purporting to show that the triumphant party had received fewer votes than the defeated, and the argument based on them may be taken to be substantially correct. In France, especially since the last war, the government may represent only a small fraction of the people. In round figures, a third of the electorate may be so disaffected that it does not vote. A quarter of the electorate may vote Communist, without

receiving any place in the government at all. A similar per-
centage may vote Right or Gaullist without having any
effective voice in the conduct of affairs. The Center parties
may be at variance with each other on almost every subject,
yet agree to work together. A former Prime Minister,
André Tardieu, wrote a book to prove that usually not
more than 10 per cent of the population is represented in any
French Government.

Now these facts—and they are facts—have no real consequence in ordinary times, for the governments are not
concerned with a section of the population: once elected
they are bound to obey—on pain of being rejected on the
first occasion—what they feel to be the general will. They
may, and do, often go wrong, misinterpret the general will,
sometimes ignore it for sectarian purposes, and, if they are
foolish, struggle against the general will; yet the golden rule
of popular government remains true—it must be the general
will that prevails in the long run.

In times of exceptional stress, notably during a war, two
or more parties may unite in a common purpose. These
coalition governments, or biparty agreements, surely resemble dictatorships in actual operation. It was thus that Mr.
Churchill was the unquestioned chief in Great Britain from
1940 to 1945. It was thus that Mr. Roosevelt was the virtual
dictator in the United States from December, 1941, until his
death in April, 1945. It had to be so. Everybody knew that
if there was to be unanimity of will it had to be expressed
through one person.

I do not see how this situation differs fundamentally from
the fact of dictatorship—except that it is more temporary.
Mr. Churchill, after the war, could be dismissed by the electorate. But so, with or without elections, would any dictator be dismissed if he did not truly continue to embody the
overwhelming aspirations of the crowd. Witness what happened so suddenly to Mussolini in July, 1943. If, then, democ-

racy is to be taken seriously, it is obvious that it may well be carried to a higher pitch in dictatorial countries, where the popular will is concentrated on a few simple objectives, focussed in one man who has most keenly sensed and expressed them, than in other countries where the popular will is less sharply defined, or emerges precisely only in special circumstances.

I am not arguing in behalf of dictatorships; they bring abuses and inconveniences and a persecution of minorities that shock all lovers of individual liberty. But so also, to some degree, do democracies in the accepted sense; it was a democrat who cried: "Minorities are born to suffer." The individual of independent mind and character is everywhere faced with the brutal intolerance of the crowd. I am only pointing out that the difference between democracy and dictatorship is one of degree and that, if democracy expresses the inexorable will of the common people, it is much more likely to be displayed in conditions of peril or conditions that call for united resolve than in the workaday world of give-and-take. A dictatorship may, then, only be democracy pushed to an extreme. Our democracies may be only pale shadows of the dictatorial ideal. Happily for us, it is seldom that circumstances require the full application of the principles of democracy, and there is usually left some small margin of freedom for the non-conformist—the man who does not think and feel with the crowd.

These are not merely pleasant paradoxes; they are the realities which are essential to an understanding of our time. It was because we considered Hitler and Mussolini to be eccentricities, passing phenomena, political mutations, that we managed to deceive ourselves, hoping that they would quickly be discarded. They were not discarded or disowned by the people, except during the agony of the defeat of their cause, that is—the cause of the people they represented. The notion that they were usurpers of authority could arise only from the loosest kind of thinking and lack of knowledge of the facts. The memory of Hitler and Mussolini, for aught I know or anyone else knows, may ultimately be execrated or revered; it may pass or it may linger. Yet, veritably, these men were, in certain circumstances, a moment of history. You cannot separate Germany from Hitler—that is to say the Germany of his day: he was, while he lasted, Germany, and Germany was for the moment summed up in Hitler.

Yet we should beware of falling into the opposite fallacy. If, on the one hand, there was not simply a handful of bad men who contrived to seize power or, on the other hand, a multitude of good men, who were oppressed by the Hitler "gang," neither does the Germany of the Hitlerian epoch correctly reflect the "eternal" Germany. There are many phases in the life of a nation, and it is superficial to judge a country by a single brief period. In the history of every nation there are many "ages," and, just as it would be absurd to seek for the "true" America solely in the Pioneer Age, the Colonial Age, the Age of Expansion, the modern Industrial Age, or to look for the "true" England only in the Elizabethan, the Cromwellian, or the Hanoverian Ages, or in the Churchill episode, so it is absurd to think of Germany exclusively in terms of one of its historical epochs. As well judge France by the abominable inhumanity of the Revolution of 1789 or of the Liberation of 1944. The disabilities under which Germany was placed by the Versailles Treaty, the prolonged suffering, the sense of humiliation, were bound to produce an emotional complex which came to a head in Hitler.

To put it in the language of our thesis, as a result of defeat, disgrace, betrayal and depression, the Germanic crowd, with a single purpose towards whose fulfillment it strained every effort, could not fail to recognize as its leader the man who was visibly animated in the fiercest and most concentrated form by the same purpose. The statesmen who did not realize by the late 1920's that the advent of a Hitler—in whatever shape he appeared, whatever name he bore—was as inevitable as the rising of the sun, were singularly ignorant of the psychology of the crowd. A science which they should never cease to study was practically unknown to them. About Germany they still labor under the most stupid delusions.

It is our business, as students of the crowd mind, neither to approve or disapprove the existence of Hitler or Mussolini, or Stalin, but rather to try to understand and explain them. From the beginning, it was plain to me, as a reflecting observer, that, in Germany, Hitler (perhaps in another body, with another name) could not fail to focus in his person the converging sentiments of the crowd. He did not assume power by a *coup d'état,* but by the most orthodox parliamentary methods. His party—or rather his person—gathered to it the cumulative forces of revolt against the Versailles *Diktat* latent in the crowd. Those politicians in Europe who attached much importance to little setbacks here and there, insignificant political incidents, were befuddled by their own petty parliamentary preoccupations. Here was something on a totally different plane, although for the moment it seemed to be following conventional lines. When, at last, Hitler attained power, the majority of even the most reluctant Germans ultimately rallied to him. They could not do otherwise. The crowd willed it.

I was astonished that European politicians, whose primary job was to watch events, should express skepticism at the size of the vote for Hitler whenever he chose to test public opinion by a plebiscite. I am far from thinking that the plebiscite is normally the fairest system of voting; it is, however, a sure guide to the feelings of the crowd in particular circumstances. When Hitler polled from 90 to 99 per cent of the vote, there were loud cries of incredulity from the amazed politicians whose utmost ambition was to receive from 51 to 60 per cent—when they were not content with 15 to 25 per cent—of the votes. There must be cheating, there must be undue pressure, they protested. I was myself in the Saar, then under French and League control, when the plebiscite was taken there, and I can testify that without vigorous German pressure, practically without systematic propaganda, the result was the same vast majority. Surely, the eyes of the most obstinate should have been opened by the Saar plebiscite. Surely, it should have been seen that the crowd, as distinct from political parties, was taking a hand in the game. Alas, the wilfully blind cannot be made to see.

What! cried the blind; we would admit 51 to 60 per cent —that would be democratic; but 90 to 99 per cent is quite undemocratic. It is "phony," it is fake. No politician ever received so many votes . . . That is how they now talk about the 99 per cent Russian approval of Communism in the Soviet plebiscite.

Yet, an elementary knowledge of the psychology of the crowd would have taught politicians that unanimity is natural whenever great issues are at stake—and sometimes even when only trivial issues, which happen to move the crowd, are involved. I read in the English press the story of a foolish young fellow who put himself in opposition to the sentiments of the crowd on the occasion of the royal funeral, that of George VI in 1952. The crowd had decided that silence and immobility for two minutes would be a fitting mark of respect for the late King. This was a perfectly proper gesture, against which I do not demur. But our foolish young fellow, quite logically and quite legally, argued that it was not for the crowd to dictate how he should express his personal feelings, that he was a free citizen, that he was not bound by some anonymous and spontaneous decree of the crowd. He, therefore, continued, without provocativeness, to walk on his way. Thereupon, the crowd, made up of presumably peaceable citizens, turned on him and rent him. They, illogically and illegally, forgot their own vow of silence and immobility, and spent the two minutes in trying to lynch him. One can suppose that in this crowd there were lawyers, clergymen, sweet young women and amiable housewives; but they were part of the crowd, and their feelings were outraged.

Here is an excellent illustration, though on a relatively small matter, of the contagious character of any popular movement. I should add that, when the foolish young man was rescued, he was taken into custody and fined for "insulting behavior," though in the law there is no obligation to observe a two minutes' silence and immobility, and in strict logic one might hold that he was the insulted party. What we must bear in mind is that, far more important than law and logic, is general sentiment. It is dangerous to take up a non-conformist attitude in the face of crowd emotions—and the inclination to do so is always rare in any country.

In Germany there were unquestionably many professional men, many industrialists, many pastors and priests, many intellectuals, many trade unionists, Socialists, Communists, who at first resisted the Nazi current; but, as it grew in volume, as it became really national, they joined it not because of coercion but out of emotional conviction. It is gratuitous to imagine that they were insincere, or frightened, playing for safety; once the crowd was formed, they could only think and feel with the crowd, however independent their nature, however distinguished their position, however high their intelligence. Their education, their affinities, their philosophy, counted for little or nothing once the crowd surged around them.

We must not interpret Germany, or Italy, or Russia, as exceptional. We must regard the countries which have gone behind the Iron Curtain as composed of ordinary men and women. There will always be a few "foolish young men," whether in England or America, who will, in times of national crisis, try to stand outside the current, refuse to share sentiments that they hold to be unwarranted, set up their independent judgment against what they deem to be mass hysteria. But they will succumb quickly to the general feeling, will prudently keep their opinions to themselves, or will be excluded from the community. Given the proper moment of history, given the appropriate conditions, there is nothing mysterious or inexplicable, there is nothing surprising, about a 99 per cent vote of approval. I am persuaded that Churchill would have obtained such a vote at certain hours of British peril from 1940 to 1945. Probably, in America, although the danger was not so real or immediate, Roosevelt would have come fairly close to obtaining a 99 per cent approval. Rational politics, after all, are for periods of calm, not for periods of tempest. Nor are they for periods of great national exaltation, such as may follow periods of abasement.

Were I permitted to change a word in Burke's dictum, I would say that you can, indeed, indict the crowd. You cannot indict a nation because a nation is not something fixed in time; it has a past and a future, it goes through many experiences, it has many moods, it is composed of many elements. But the crowd is a definite point in time, it is one and indivisible. It can, therefore, be indicted. When a people is passing through great emotional stress, it is, as Scipio Sighele contends, only the crowd that can properly be indicted. Its individual members should be immune. They are not responsible as individuals; they are responsible only as members of the crowd—that is to say, they are not responsible as private persons.

The French, after the Liberation of 1944, introduced into their jurisprudence the principle of "collective responsibility." They were right. But they were assuredly wrong when they proceeded to accuse of "war crimes" individual members of certain organizations that had doubtless been guilty of "war crimes." The organizations were guilty; the individuals—no. The French courts even went so far as to hold guilty members of such organizations who could prove that they were not present at the moment of the crime and had in no way participated in it. "No matter," argued the prosecuting attorneys; "you were a member of a guilty association." Now, I think this doctrine of "collective responsibility" both right and wrong; right, in so far as it puts the blame on the collectivity, wrong, in so far as it puts the blame on the individual. And I would go so far as to declare that the individual who has, in fact, committed crime, or participated in a criminal act as a member of the organization, is not actually guilty. He is not acting in his own person; he is acting as an irresponsible member of the crowd. His thoughts and feeling are not his own; they are those of the crowd. He is an automaton, a blind instrument of the communal will.

But, someone will object, you cannot punish the crowd; you must therefore punish the members of the crowd. I will admit that you cannot punish the crowd—not even a more or less organized crowd such as a regiment or a nation; but that does not seem a good reason for punishing an irresponsible member of the crowd. Although I will not be drawn into a discussion of the Nuremberg trials, I think they open up the gravest perspectives for the future, not only because the judges were parties to the case, as prosecutors, but because they condemned generals who obeyed the instructions of their superiors, and their superiors who obeyed the will of the crowd. The precedent will surely have the most serious consequences as Mr. Veale has revealed in detail.

Plutarch wrote parallel lives of Greeks and Romans, showing how two men whose careers were not dissimilar resembled and differed from each other. Were it relevant to my theme, I, too, would write the parallel lives of Hitler and Mussolini. Although outwardly they seemed to resemble each other at many points, they were opposite in character, and I have never understood why popular opinion should have chosen to employ as the generic term of abuse, the word Fascism, rather than the word Nazism. For Mussolini was, as compared with Hitler, an ordinary political adventurer, and Fascism was, as compared with Nazism, an ordinary political party. Neither Mussolini nor Fascism was inspired by one unchanging purpose; whereas Hitler and Nazism were.

In my travels in Italy, in my encounters with the Duce, I never felt that the movement transcended the rational. I never felt—except at one moment during the war with Ethiopia, when the hostility of England and the abortive "sanctions" did unify the nation around Mussolini in a mystical manner—that Mussolini and his followers were anything more than very skillful political opportunists who had managed to seize power and to use it efficiently. That is, of course, much: it differentiates them from the rest of the inefficient politicians and political parties.

But Mussolini was an exceptionally gifted administrator, with a remarkable sense of showmanship, and a wonderful talent for maneuvering among the shoals and shallows of national and international affairs, rather than the mystical embodiment of the nation. He was a twentieth century *condottiere*, of splendid intelligence, usually knowing just how much he could do, getting it done, and striking impressive dramatic postures. His intelligence broke down in the end, but although one must deprecate some of his methods, and regret that he led his people into a calamitous *cul-de-sac*, in 1940, it is impossible for the impartial historian not to admire his personal qualities when they were displayed at their best.

These qualities were in sharp contrast with those of Hitler, who was not so much intelligent as intuitive. He was a political "medium" in the spiritualistic sense. I realized the difference when I saw them meet at Venice. Hitler was modest in his demeanor, not choosing to put on airs, whereas Mussolini was the man of the theater, posturing, superb, or, as the schoolboy would put it, consciously "showing-off." One almost felt sorry for Hitler, shabbily dressed, shrinking, one might have supposed shy, beside his proud-strutting compeer. Mussolini cast himself deliberately in the role of Superman. Hitler was content to be the demi-God, revealing himself only when in action on the platform.

Yet of the two, one felt that the dramatic gestures and resounding phrases of Mussolini made a far less profound effect on his audience than the deep note of inward passion and whole-hearted sincerity of Hitler. I am not judging the ends to which their capacities were directed, I am not estimating the good or harm that these two men wrought. I am merely suggesting that Mussolini loved power for the sake of power and did not feel himself inspired by a great purpose; whereas Hitler was the madman with a mission, heedless of everything except what he conceived to be his mission. One had an unconquerable belief in himself; the other trusted implicitly in his Daemon.

Mussolini, though he ultimately failed tragically, would never, I think, have fallen into the inhuman excesses of Hitler. He was overmastered by circumstances, he miscalculated badly and was driven on to ultimate folly; but, though his intelligence did not save him, it might well, had fate not been against him, have extricated him from his difficulties. He was sacrificed by the King and the treacherous Fascist Council when things went wrong; had he not been, it is probable that his Machiavellian intelligence would have found a way out of the imbroglio. Not so Hitler: had he been a Mussolini he would again have driven a bargain with Stalin, in 1944, which was indeed a possibility even in the last extremity: but when his Daemon deserted him, Hitler preferred to perish, like a Wagnerian hero, in the flames and havoc of a ruined world.

Two men, two manners: yet they both knew that the

masses have need of gods and heroes. If Hitler cut deeper furrows in the consciousness of Germany than Mussolini cut in the consciousness of Italy, it was because Hitler was, in reality, the incarnation of the Germanic mind at a given moment of history. Mussolini, like all men who unscrupulously grasp power, can be reproached with a few crimes that shock the conscience of mankind; he, like Napoleon, had his Duc d'Enghien. Yet he did not commit or countenance wholesale atrocities as did Hitler; his crimes, so to speak, were the inevitable incidents of his career.

Hitler's career was not a personal career; it was the fulfillment of a "mission," and horrors piled on horrors' head could not deter him. He regarded the Jews as an obstacle to the fulfillment of his "mission;" therefore, the Jews must be repressed. He regarded the Poles as the "enemy" of Germany; therefore, the Poles must be destroyed by fire and sword. Though he was induced to make a short-lived bargain with Russia (as Germany had done first at Brest-Litovsk, then at Rapallo, and now at Moscow), he was determined (to his undoing) to seize at no matter what cost the best lands of Russia in order to allow Germany to expand eastwards. How far he ordered, and how far he ignored as of no consequence, the ignominy of the concentration camps, often camps of torture or extermination, I do not know. It does not much matter whether they were the work of over-zealous and criminally-minded lieutenants, or whether they were part of his design; we may be sure, given his "mission," that he cared nothing for atrocities. That millions should perish, whether they were Germans in the snows of the Russian steppes, or "enemies" in a gigantic holocaust, could not give him pause—the glory and the grandeur of Germania (or if you prefer, the ignominy and the dishonor of Germania—it was all one to him) demanded the action no matter what price.

It must be admitted that, however great our detestation

of many of the practices of Fascism, they remained far more closely within the bounds of conventional reason than the insanity of Hitlerism pushed to the limits of human fanaticism; and the opprobrious term of "Fascism" instead of "Hitlerism" is wrongly used by the adversaries of dictatorship.

We come back to our original question: how far were the followers of Hitler, which means 99 per cent of the German people, responsible for his misdeeds? Now it will appear to the impartial observer that Hitler, unlike Mussolini, was neither his own good executive officer nor a shrewd critic of the men about him. All he asked was that they should agree with his ideas and carry them out to the fullest possible extent.

Among the Nazi leaders were many of the worst kind of go-getters, sadists, and some unspeakable criminals over whose activities no moderating hand was placed. The result was that a coterie of quasi-gangsters, often unchecked by the most elementary notions of decency, was allowed undisputed sway at times, and that Hitlerism was doomed to disaster from the beginning. For these conscious criminals there can be no excuse. But for the crowd, anonymous, confiding, we can make some excuse, at least to the extent of seeking to understand its behavior. The crowd, after a period of oppression and misery, hailed, as all crowds must do, its Great Man who promised a larger and fuller life, who was apparently equipped to lead the German people out of the slough of despond. I do not think we can be too harsh towards individuals who could not discern the dangers of the course on which they embarked with Hitler at the helm. They were not aware of the worst features of the régime—in fact, the shocking revelations of the later years of the war and the post-war period were barely suspected before 1940, even by the hostile Allied nations.

We can, assuredly, indict the Germanic crowd during the Nazi régime, for it permitted when it did not commit many atrocious acts. It is fairly certain that the mass of Germans had no knowledge of the more brutal atrocities when they were committed, but it is probable that they would have condoned them had they known, since the crowd is capable in any country of enacting or approving the most hideous deeds. The Germanic crowd was certainly aware of the persecution of Jews, ardent democrats and liberals, and radicals by Hitler and his government. But, of course, more guilty than even Hitler or the German people, were the Allied statesmen who made the Versailles Treaty and prevented its amelioration between 1919 and 1933, thus making it possible for a man like Hitler to attain power in Germany and develop a Germanic crowd of hysterical unity and ferocity. The indictment of the Germanic crowd under Hitler cannot logically, if my assumptions are right, be extended to individual Germans who were caught up in the crowd psychology of the time. This may not exculpate Nazi leaders, but it does expose the folly and injustice of trying and convicting thousands of petty Nazis who, as individuals, would have recoiled in horror from the atrocities ordered or permitted by Himmler and his like.

To refuse some degree of confidence to a misguided people is to refuse to believe in humanity, for humanity seeks gods, and if it has abandoned its faith in religion ("the opium of the people," said Karl Marx), it will find other and false gods. In the whole world of today there is this despairing search for idols. In the absence of God from the universe, the crowd makes gods in its own image—that is to say, gods devoid of the principles of morality and of reason that have guided us, for better or for worse, along the perilous path of human destiny. It was Thoreau who declared that God has no sympathy for popular movements, and popular movements have no sympathy for God. The development of science, the inventions and the discoveries of our age, the transformation of life by the multiplication of machines and amusements, have given to many of our contemporaries a purely materialistic conception of the world. The airplane, the cinema, the automobile, the radio, television, which might have enriched our existence, have impoverished it, since, instead of taking them as accessories, we have accepted them as substitutes for the spiritual.

We have—in all countries—worshipped fetishes, whether in the form of men like ourselves or in the shape of empty words, but these false gods cannot satisfy our soul, more naked and solitary than ever in a Nature which, after all, remains inscrutable and perhaps hostile. All that excites our passions, hatreds, brutality, cruelty, an economy which is often inhuman, the collapse of former values, the mockery of ancient virtues, the augmentation of symbols of wealth without corresponding augmentation of real wealth, have hastened the downfall of our civilization. A society that is not built on the solid rock of honesty, of the ancient values and virtues, and of sound public morality, must break down. That is what we are witnessing in many lands where the old landmarks have been removed. It is thus that, for countless millions of peoples inside and outside Russia, Stalin, who preached the gospel of materialism, became the new god. The masses must have a "mystique," and when the "mystique" is not that of supernatural religion, it is that of some secular program and its hero-leader is a Mussolini, a Hitler, or a Stalin. As Harold Laski has pointed out, Communism takes, for many people, the place of Christianity, or some other sincerely held religion: Communism has actually become a religion. It is a religion built on the tenets of materialism, and it may fall and bury us all under its ruins. To this impending new Fall of Man has the uncontrolled exercise of popular thinking and feeling brought us, and it could bring us nowhere else.

11

USES AND ABUSES
OF PROPAGANDA

W HEN, IN 1865, Clerk Maxwell was studying the phenomena of electro-magnetic waves, he never dreamed that he was thus revolutionizing the relations of the governed and the governing. Two years later we find Heinrich Hertz, equally unconscious of the perturbations his discoveries would bring in the field of public affairs, both domestic and foreign, engaged in the same fascinating study of physics. The practical consequences of their researches were not unfolded for many years; indeed, within the past twenty years the president of an American university, who had been a professor of physics, was chiefly concerned with the pedagogic confusion into which he had fallen by reason of the changes in scientific thought.

"I had to modify my teaching several times," he confessed to me when I was dining with him in New York. "The very foundations of our knowledge have been shattered, and I am now too old to begin to learn again. Science has become as unstable as money, morals, or religion. To think that we once believed the last word had been spoken—or at any rate that we had only to advance along the lines laid down for us!"

"You exaggerate," I replied. "What you once taught remains, though new facts have come to light."

"No," he replied sadly, "the whole interpretation of nature —our conceptions of time, space, energy, the composition of matter, have altered. The result, according to the latest

197

theories, is that we should doubt whether the universe is substantial; the earth and the stars, the table at which we are sitting, our bodies—do they really exist? We have analyzed everything to the atom, and the atom is being dissolved. Physics and metaphysics have become the same subject. Everything is a mathematical formula, and we are only algebraic signs in the intangible mind of a Great Mathematician who has no corporeal being."

I have often thought of this disillusioned avowal of a physicist who thought he could not keep up with the pace of scientific progress. And he was speaking before the later experiments in the explosion of the atom which may eventually shatter the globe. He mournfully realized that morally, as well as materially, we were entering a new era. Already, one might foresee some of the effects of the ingenious use of antennae by Guglielmo Marconi, who, in 1896, found how the waves of Clerk Maxwell and Hertz might be utilized. In 1904, the transmission of sound over a considerable distance was made possible by the invention of the vacuum tube by James A. Fleming and the subsequent improvements of it by Lee De Forest. It will be noted that the physical basis for mass propaganda marched side by side, at the same epoch, with the emergence of the crowd, and he would be a bold man who would decide whether these material facilities were coincidental with the development of mass influence, or were one of the causes of it. What can safely be said is that the discovery of new physical laws, and the awakened consciousness of the peoples, far apart as they superficially appear, had a reciprocal effect one on the other.

In Chelmsford, England, and in Pittsburgh, Pennsylvania, almost simultaneously, in 1920, the broadcasting of speech and music became a reality. That is a memorable and epoch-making date, for better or for worse, in the history of mankind. During the next decade, radio was gradually changing its character: from a scientific toy it grew to be the most formidable instrument of propaganda humanity has ever known—at least prior to television which depends on radio. When almost morbid fear is expressed over the destructive potentialities of the atom-bomb—fear which is well founded, although the atom-bomb is no more than the multiplication by x of several other varieties of bombs—I marvel that no one has expressed comparable fear at the tremendous destructive potentialities of our broadcasting stations which can convey the shattering power of distorted and emotion-charged popular thought and sentiment to the ends of the earth.

Were I asked to name the true inventor of radio I should —after glancing at Maxwell, Hertz, Marconi, Fleming, De Forest and the rest—put my finger on Hitler. He was not, it is true, the material inventor of the instrument, but he was the "moral" and political inventor of the effective public use of the instrument to sway mass opinion on a national scale. Sometime in the 1930's he or his co-workers in evil realized that here was an extraordinary means of swelling the crowd from a few thousand to many millions. As the passions of the crowd rose, as their numbers increased, so that the whole nation listened, not as separate units but as a single mass, to the diatribes against all who could be accused of contributing to the plight of Germany: the foreign bankers, the signatories of the Versailles Treaty, the Jews, the Communists, and so on (for the speeches of Hitler, as I heard them, were frequently little more than a catalogue of culprits, a litany of hates), the prospect of the most devastating war loomed more and more darkly.

In comparison with this nation-wide manufacture and manipulation of the crowd, all other instruments of propaganda were relatively insignificant and impotent. Men might sit in their homes and read the newspapers without losing their individuality. They might be momentarily touched by a sense of injustice, or stirred to a sentiment of anger. But they were left in possession of their faculties, and they could still reason to some extent. There still remained, to some degree at least, Tarde's public, as contrasted with the crowd or mob of Le Bon. I do not underestimate the importance of the press, of which I was a small part for many years, often deploring its concealing of salient truths, often regretting its lack of insistence on constructive items, its mischievous vituperation, its nationalistic viewpoints, its readiness to think the worst and to overlook the best. But it is accurate to say that the printed word, for the most part, carries only an ephemeral poison. The good it may do, as well as the harm, is often forgotten the next day. When the newspaper is thrown aside, its contents are thrown away with it.

It is personal contact with a living leader, emotional reaction around a living leader, that most rapidly and completely converts the isolated elements of a nation into a unified mass with thoughts and feelings that are not the thoughts and feelings of the individual citizen. That is why the propaganda of the press, important as it may have been when judged by earlier standards, bears the same relation to the propaganda of the radio as the one-horse shay bears to the jet-airplane. Whether gathered together in a great open-air arena, in a huge hall, or in the privacy of the family sitting-room, the listeners to the radio become as one; they are subjected to the domination of the crowd. They are under the spell of a living voice. They are aware of the presence of the leader, and they are vicariously aware of the presence of their fellows. Television is making all this more true and effective.

That is why Hitler's appeal was stronger than the appeal of Roosevelt, potent as were the "fireside talks" of the American President. For, although Roosevelt's voice, warm and persuasive, penetrated into the sanctum of the hearer, it mainly conjured up a picture of one man, himself comfortably sitting with slippered feet in an arm-chair. So was it with Churchill and other statesmen who sought—more or less successfully, for they too managed to convey some sense of personal contact—to rally their compatriots to their views. They were, I repeat, fairly successful, since their hearers were already willing to share their opinions. But with Hitler and the sub-Fuhrers, there was something more —something that was absent from the "fireside talks" or even from Churchill's resounding and carefully rehearsed rhetoric. There was the crowd—the crowd whose emotional contagion we have stressed; the crowd with its spontaneous reactions, its cheers, its howls of rage, its enthusiasms. The crowd, as well as the orator, penetrated into the lighted room with the closed curtains. It came surging in, wild, in a sort of disciplined disorder, and who could resist it?

In the case of Roosevelt, ears were strained to listen to one man, he was the focus of many invisible mental eyes; but in the case of Hitler, eyes and ears converged not on a man but on a speaker who was the mouthpiece of an actual physical mass. Hitler roared, but the ten thousand, the hundred thousand, the seventy million, men and women who mentally and emotionally surrounded him, roared louder still. The listener could share their excitement, he could vibrate with their vibrations. The average listener could not fail to identify himself with the multitude. No private philosophy, no intellectual superiority, no personal conviction, is proof against the clamor of the crowd under these circumstances.

To discuss whether Hitler created the crowd or the crowd created Hitler, would be as irrelevant and inconclusive as to discuss whether the chicken or the egg comes first. They were part of each other and, in the technical conduct of the war, Hitler, reduced to the proportions of his own person, was as lonely and lost as any other man called upon to make momentous decisions. Any impartial historian will reveal him then as hesitating and fumbling, alternately headstrong and feeble, blustering and fearful, a poor fallible mortal, unable to make up his mind whether to stake everything on a desperate throw or to withdraw from impossible positions, whether to persevere in war or to sue for peace. This is the explanation of why Hitler lost the war with Russia. He fatally hesitated for a whole month in the summer of 1941 when vigorous advance would have assuredly meant the capture of Moscow long before cold weather set in. Again, his hesitancy in ordering a retreat from Stalingrad led to the loss of the great army of General von Paulus which was captured or massacred there.

Hitler was not Hitler except when he was incarnated in the crowd and the crowd was incarnated in him. His was not the cool directing brain of a Bismarck; he drew his strength, such as it was—and it was great in its maniacal way—from his contact with the crowd. I have seen him virtually alone, in his headquarters, under the portrait of Frederick the Great, and I have seen him on public platforms, borne up and inspired by the waves of popular acclaim—of adulation—and I was impressed by the strange contrast under the different conditions. The key to Hitler's character and to his temporary triumph lies here: without the legion of listeners of whom he was an integral part, he was puny; surrounded by the host which was consubstantial with him, he was of gigantic stature, for the stature was not his but that of the herd. I might add that, unlike Napoleon, who knew how to impose himself on the army, Hitler could not impose himself in any impressive way on the more disciplined body that is the army. Over the mob he was all-powerful; the soldiers he could command only because the army was necessarily composed in a considerable measure (and yet in different quality), of the crowd, already conditioned to Hitlerism. The genius which might have served him long in peace could not avail him in war, and he woefully misunderstood wherein lay his strength.

If I have dwelt upon the example of Hitler, it is because his sway over the masses, however acquired, was very real and he may properly be regarded as the inventor, in its present form, of the system of propaganda that now is an essential method of government. There is a lesson to be learned: it is that propaganda, whether by radio, by public speeches, by the press, which does not correspond to popular realities, is a hollow thing, and will ultimately and inevitably collapse like a pricked bubble when the test comes. It is one of the most potent weapons of popular diplomacy. As such, it is relied on by the statesmen of today who, in spite of the tragic consequences of the bluffing which is part of popular diplomacy, still trust it will conceal or compensate for the deficiencies of a policy that is not in consonance with underlying realities. There was in Hitler's method a large element of bluff, though this is not to discount the grim realities that underlaid it.

Are we sure that we are not substituting compensatory propaganda today for lack of real strength? Is there not much bluff, much wishful thinking, in our attitude toward the world situation? I am inclined to the belief that we, too, mistake advertisement and pretense for truth. In reading the newspapers with the trained eye of an old newspaper man, I am constantly struck by the palpable omissions, the obvious misrepresentations, the flagrant contradictions. We are less informed than we have ever been in my time with respect to what is actually going on in the world, and the public is thus encouraged in error at a most critical moment. About the stupendous events that are taking place on either side of the Iron Curtain, we know little or nothing. That is a grave statement, but it cannot be refuted. The public is bewildered. Are we about to be attacked, or are we not? If we are, why are we spending years in scraping up the miserably few divisions designed to defend us in Europe? If we are not, why these noisy and interminable wrangles about the size of the miniature army that is to "protect" us? It seems to me to make only palpable nonsense, it savors of the futility and folly of precisely that same popular diplomacy, self-stultifying and zigzagging, that has brought us to our present lamentable pass.

Let me give one trivial instance of the sort of reporting that would never have been tolerated in my day. I read in a reputable newspaper that, at the end of a broadcast in a foreign language from Prague, the speaker who had just been on the air calmly announced: "You have just been listening to another string of Communist lies." Just that: no more. Presumably the readers, like the editor, were satisfied with the story. I venture to say that a few years ago no self-respecting editor would have allowed such an item—perhaps meant as propaganda—to pass without some explanation. It may serve its purpose in deceiving the public, but it is to any expert eye utter nonsense. Either it is true or it is untrue, and in either case it should not have been printed in that form. What are the sources? Are they reliable? Has somebody really heard the statement? It should not be difficult to verify the news.

If it is true: the question then arises, was the speaker who behaved so strangely a vulgar *saboteur*, who would be hurried off to execution, as indeed he deserved to be, or, which is almost as incredible, a speaker who had suddenly gone mad? My own guess would be that, assuming the words actually to have been spoken, they were meant sarcastically —"You who doubt everything you hear that is favorable to Communism have just heard more indisputable facts. You will, of course, dismiss them in your blindness, as just another string of Communist lies." That, I say, is, without direct knowledge, my own interpretation; whatever is the explanation, hoax, sabotage, insanity, or sarcasm, it was the elementary duty of the editor not to print the story without full investigation, or, deciding to print it, to add a word of comment for the enlightenment of his readers. As it is, the item will doubtless be accepted by uncritical readers (who are the vast majority) as a faithful record which somehow redounds to the discredit of Czechoslovakia.

Is it good propaganda, in the sense we want it to be? Then, let it go in. Is it bad propaganda for our side? Then, let it be spiked. I am afraid that is the type of distortion the editorial mind has undergone after years of propaganda. Is there a capital penalty for a political offense in a country that is for us a potential ally? Then suppress it (I could give hundreds of cases). Did it happen in Spain (assuming that we are against Spain)? Then, play it up. Tito of Yugoslavia? A red-handed Communist tyrant? No, wait a minute, he may be induced to help us against Stalin. Forget about his prisons, his Communism, his past; set him up among the heroes of the Liberation. Korea? You think there are just Koreans, just as good or just as bad as the rest of the peoples of the Orient. That is where you are wrong; there is now a race of devils known as North Koreans, and a race of angels known as South Koreans. No diabolic deeds are ever perpetrated in the South—they occur only in the North. Peoples are divided into friends and foes by a simple and superficial dichotomy. Public morality has become a matter of geography and politics.

A few years ago, no praise was too high for Russia; now, no vilification is too strong. A few years ago, no imprecation was sufficiently harsh for Germany; now, no blandishment is sufficiently saccharine. Our appreciations and appraisals of countries are not absolute and unchanging; they can be radically reversed as opportunity and expediency dictates. Political morality is a matter of time as well as space. As in Dickens' story of Little Nell: Codlin's the friend, not Short—unless Short's the friend, not Codlin. It depends on circumstances.

Again, I search in vain in the newspapers for a fixed opinion about the prospect of war. One day, we are assured that there is no danger for many years; the next day, we are told that the worst may happen at any moment. The same men, the same newspapers! One day, I read that the French economy (for example) was never sounder; the next day, the French Prime Minister declares that France is experiencing an unprecedented crisis. Is it asking too much to call for honest statesmen, honest newspapers?

When Catherine the Great stirred from her palace, Prince Potemkin put up, we are told, like the most ingenious Hollywood producers, cardboard landscapes of smiling peace to hide the hideous villages filled with want and misery. I have always doubted the story, but there are plenty of Potemkins today—indeed, it is the first qualification for a "statesman," a radio operator, or a newspaper man, to be able to rig up *papier-maché* screens at a moment's notice. Be sure, however, that they will be blown down when the winds rage, and that the naked reality will be revealed.

Particularly in economic matters is the public deceived by the utterances of glib words and the omission of all serious facts and explanation. I turn the knob of the little magic box in my study and the room is filled with the voice of a far-off orator. I know in advance that he will make great verbal play with "democracy," but I know also that he will not define "democracy." I turn the button again, and another speaker in a distant land is using the same expression in his own tongue. Are all peoples then dominated by an identical ideal?

Not so; in America, as in the England of my youth, the word democracy (apart from party labels) has social rather than political connotations. In theory at least, every man should be free to live his own life, to pursue his own happiness. The state should not interfere in his private concerns. Above all, his private initiative in industry and commerce should be respected. Business should not be hampered by endless restrictions. That has been the American meaning of democracy.

But, as I listen to many a continental European radio, I find that democracy means exactly the contrary. Every enterprise should be nationalized—placed under the ownership of the state, run by functionaries, directed by a minister who may be entirely ignorant of the subject, careful not to make profits, assured that the taxpayer will take care of losses. One man should not try to outdo his fellows in production; to work harder than the others is a deadly sin; the pace must be measured by that of the lowest; no one should be handicapped because of his incapacity, his laziness, or his reluctance to give of his best; there must be a dead level of inefficiency.

It occurs to me that the two fiddles of democracy are not attuned. These are two entirely different conceptions—the conception of individual freedom and initiative through which a man may, by hard work and skill, rise above his fellows and attain success in his occupation, and the conception of state slavery, which is certainly not oppressive for the least competent, but is irksome for the ambitious, and inevitably lowers the economic standards of the community.

Nor is it only industrial enterprises which are kept in leading strings; mines, railroads, electricity and gas undertakings, which once paid handsome dividends, have now to be subsidized by the taxpayer to avoid bankruptcy. The personal profession of medicine is, likewise, taken over by the state in England and some continental countries; there are hospitals, dentists' parlors, clinics, which are now run by bureaucrats, for whom patients are matriculation numbers. Road haulage, since it might compete with the train service, is strictly supervised. Presently, we may all be ticketed, employees of the state, and the private person, pursuing his own trade, earning his own living, working as he pleases, will be as dead as the dodo.

Now it is impossible to reconcile such vastly dissimilar interpretations of economic democracy. Behind the Iron Curtain writers have already lost their independence, and must write as the state dictates. A musician, on pain of being refused a hearing, must take his inspiration from the powers-that-be. An artist must paint pictures that somehow praise and endorse the governmental system. On the other hand, behind the Iron Curtain, as I gather, strikes are forbidden, and prizes are awarded for efficient production. There is here, then, a third conception of economic democracy. It is qualified, pleonastically, popular democracy.

It is not for me to pronounce in favor of one or the other conception. There is doubtless much to be said for and against individual freedom, and much to be said for and against state ownership and control. Competition has a great deal to offer for the men and women who are prepared to take their chance, though the Devil may seize the hindmost. *Laisser-faire* is bad for the slackers, but good for the alert. As the majority are (if I may venture on a palpable truism) the mediocre, state control is excellent for the majority. We cannot all be champions in the race; it may be hard on the champions to be held back, but the large crowd of non-champions is contented.

When I remember the misery I have seen around me, the poverty in the midst of plenty, destitution amid extravagance, the willful destruction of the necessaries which millions lack in order to maintain high prices and large profits, when I remember the evils of trusts and monopolies, I cannot but rejoice in whatever offers an amelioration of the lot of the humble. What is questionable is whether the remedies applied are always in the true interest of the poorest, and in the interest of society in general. For example, in France, where there is an immense—almost tragic—shortage of houses, a shortage which must last for a very long time, relatively large premiums are offered for every birth, and family allowances (so considerable that they may permit a biologically prolific "bread-winner" to go fishing instead of working) are made in accordance with the number of children. That is surely putting the cart before the horse: houses first, children afterwards would make sense.

Am I digressing? In what way does the constant passing of demagogic measures which the state cannot afford—which must, since they inflate the currency, and are not provided for out of true national income, result in ruin to the nation, not to a class but to all classes—in what way does such economic and financial demagogy touch upon the subject of popular diplomacy? The two themes are intimately connected, and we must take a few pages to consider how the quest for voters, the appeal to the masses, has brought the crowd into every domain of public life.

"The greatest good for the greatest number"—certainly; but the greatest number will not necessarily bring the greatest good. It would be difficult, for example, to demonstrate how the taxation of incomes above a certain modest level at the rate of 19½ shillings out of 20, thus making it virtually impossible for any but a very privileged few in England to enjoy a net revenue of more than £5,000 a year, can help the community.[1] There is infinitely less capital available for industry, to say nothing of the encouragement of the fine arts and culture. The levelling down process, as distinct from a levelling up, must in the long run be harmful. But since the poor are voters, and since they are the majority, it is their opinion on the difficult and intricate matter of a fair distribution of wealth that mainly counts with the ambitious politicians of our day.

[1] An expert tells me that in England, in order to enjoy a net income of £15,000 a man must earn the preposterous sum of £1,000,000 per annum—£2,000,000 if he is a bachelor.

Higher wages? Certainly. America, first taught this by Henry Ford, has long ago realized that higher wages are better for industry, for the "capitalist" as well as for the worker who willingly gives of his best if properly remunerated. As production expands (in theory if not invariably in practice), wages expand. The contrary course has been taken in Europe, where the pay-packet is constantly being swelled without an equivalent increase of production—where, in fact, the worker is urged to go slowly.

Again it is the crowd—through the trade unions and syndicates, sometimes in the hands of the Communists—which decides. The trade unions, whose objective is perfectly legitimate, whose existence is necessary, have become in some countries not the defenders of the workers but rather the wreckers of the community.

How short-sighted is their policy—and the provocative policy of the employers had been no less short-sighted—may be seen by the perusal of some figures which I recently came across. A distinguished statistician told the British Association that, from 1900 (when the crowd began to enter the field) to 1918, there were no fewer than 2,536 stoppages of work by workers in England who hoped to better their position. The amount lost in wages by the miners alone through industrial disputes was sufficient to have enabled the miners to buy, lock, stock, and barrel, the whole of the collieries of Great Britain. In voluntary absenteeism a similar amount was lost. The country as a whole has lost, directly, without counting indirect losses, four times the present-day value of the collieries.

These are striking figures; whether they are strictly correct I will not attempt to ascertain; that they indicate the enormity of the sacrifice to both workers and owners and to the community is clear enough. Now the prosperity of England was built on its coal fields, and that no other method has been found of settling disputes than that which has such disastrous consequences is a sad reflection on human intelligence. No doubt later figures would confirm the conclusion to be drawn. We know that England, which exported coal before 1939 is now obliged, in spite of her penury of dollars, to import coal. "Bringing coal to Newcastle" was a proverbial expression of supreme folly; that, under the bad management of the private owners and the possibly worse management of the state owners, this very folly has been perpetrated, is a grave indictment of the crowd, to whom wiser men must bow.

Wiser men must bow, for there is no stemming the tide. But what are we to think of the political propagandists who have, to catch votes, persuaded the public that Poor Richard was wrong when he said that you cannot get a quart out of a pint pot? In economics, as in diplomacy, the whole effort is to please the crowd, whatever the consequences. It is probably true that, in economics as in diplomacy, there are not a hundred men in the world who are entitled by their knowledge and wisdom to make authoritative statements. Yet, on both these vital matters, there are tens of thousands of arrogant pretenders and cheap-jacks ready to offer their wares. Their dogmas are accepted by the uninstructed masses, who would hiss from the platform a real authority who told them the truth.

Nevertheless, every advertiser is aware, in this age of advertisement, that mere advertisement is not enough. He must be prepared to deliver the goods if he is to remain in business for long. The goods must be up to standard. He will not be saved from ignominious bankruptcy by taking more and more colored pages in the magazines to propagate his lies; a half-hour show on the radio or on television will not buttress up a shoddy product for very long.

Propaganda has its uses—on condition that it is propaganda for truth. When it is a substitute for truth, it is a pernicious expedient. "You can deceive some of the people all the time," said Abraham Lincoln, "you can deceive all of the people some of the time, but you cannot deceive all the people all the time." It is true that you cannot keep on deceiving any considerable number of the people long enough to build up a permanently paying business on the basis of defective merchandise. Alas, in politics and in economics and in diplomacy, however, you can continue deception long enough to ruin the buyers, while contriving to escape yourself, for, when disaster comes, the crowd forgets to inquire into the causes. They blame fatality.

Today, every nation in the world of combatants, with the doubtful exception of the United States and Russia—and of Russia we know little, and of the United States we know that it has had to support the burden of the bankruptcy of Asia and Europe—is impoverished, dependent on charity, unable to face with its own resources the menace of a coming war. But few persons stop to ask whether the nations are not the victims of their own impulses and of false propaganda. The past, for them, is the past. They have made no mistakes. Their leaders have made no mistakes. No postmortems! Things just happened like that. For my part, in glancing at the blunders of the past half century or so, my sole purpose is to issue a warning against similar blunders to come. It is the future that matters most now.

Let us look then at the present panaceas and see whether we have profited by the lessons of the past or are falling into exactly the same errors, in spite of the palpable bankruptcy of our popular diplomacy.

12

FALSE RHETORIC OF PEACE AND GRIM
REALITIES OF INTERNATIONAL TENSIONS

M Y PROPOSITION is that the methods of popular diplomacy today are chiefly based on the excitability of the masses, who are in the nature of things irrational, a mass of excitability exacerbated by the politicians. The latter, in their love of the limelight, prefer the easy short-sighted course of acquiescence to the more difficult task of moderating the instincts of the herd. These methods have completely failed and should be abandoned without delay if our civilization is to have any chance of survival.

War is too serious a business to be left to the soldiers, is a remark attributed to I forget what politician. But it would be far more true to say that both war and diplomacy are too serious a business to be left to the politicians, who represent the crowd and are guided by the emotions it stimulates, while sharing them. War throws into the balance the destiny of nations; as it is now pursued in these days of scientific mass destruction, it may throw in the balance the destiny of the world.

If, then, war is to be retained as the ultimate arbiter of international relations, it requires the brains of a superman to direct it to reasonable results. I purposely refrain from discussing the pacifist viewpoint, realizing that complete pacifism is best suited for a world in which there are no ambitions, no spirit of domination, no danger of attack on a "way of life" which is dearer than existence itself to us; a world in which mankind everywhere is peaceful and friendly. That is far from being the case, nor is it likely to be the case for many generations. Before we reach that ideal there must be a universal change of heart. Although I number myself among the peace-lovers, I cannot, as one who has spent his life in observing the character of men—not in one country but in a number of countries—be unrealistic enough to believe that wars will be banished from the earth in our time.

Indeed, one of the methods of popular diplomacy which I would definitely rule out is periodical proclamations of perpetual peace. I have noticed that whenever peace is loudly proclaimed, war is most imminent. One of my tasks as a diplomatic correspondent was to report the signing of the Briand-Kellogg Pact, outlawing war as an instrument of national policy. The extraordinary credulity of the peoples and of many leaders who should have known better on the occasion of this foolish ceremony, prompted me to utter the hope (which I now repeat) that, if pacts there must be, it would be especially desirable to have a pact outlawing *peace* as an instrument of national policy. For not only are these peace pledges as useless as New Year resolutions, proverbially made to be broken, but they are, even worse, mischievously misleading. They merely mean that, at a given moment, the crowd wants peace, but is already thinking about war. The peace promised is conditional on everybody being in accord on every subject for all time. While the Briand-Kellogg Pact was in process of elaboration everybody was busily quarreling with everybody else. Hence, any stiffening of opposition to any country's demands, or any insistence on those demands, was calculated to brand one or the other side as a warmonger.

Two clowns in a circus used to put on an act that has always seemed to me to be a perfect image of popular diplomacy: one professed to give the other a lesson in a peculiar kind of boxing: "When I say go—you strike. When I say stop—you stop hitting." The first delivered his blow while crying "stop"; and then while the other was again unprepared, lashed out with the word: "Go."

No wonder Hitler declared that, since everybody wanted peace, France could now disarm to the level of Germany. No wonder that France replied that, since everybody wanted peace, the post-war treaties need not be touched, for to revise them might provoke war. No wonder that England, perhaps more honestly, excluded from the Briand-Kellogg Pact "certain regions" in which her interests might be challenged. No wonder that Italy stipulated that her navy should obtain parity with that of France and that her influence in the Balkans should be recognized. No wonder that Russia hailed the Pact as consolidating the Communist régime. No wonder that the United States was content, for a brief spell, to repudiate any responsibilities in a world at last won to peace. No wonder that Hungary and other Balkan nations welcomed the Pact as a stepping-stone to revision of the treaties, while the "Little Entente," on the contrary, held that it signified the perpetuity of the *status quo*. In short, peace was a key that fitted all locks. By peace was intended both the satisfaction and the repudiation of all claims, and these contentions were contradictory.

The Briand-Kellogg Pact was not worth the paper it was written on; and I said so at the hour of its signing. It is not Germany alone which has regarded treaties as "scraps of paper." No close student of diplomacy can honestly deny that treaties are respected only so long as they suit both parties. The Russian sociologist and pacifist, Jacques Novicow, computed that more than 8,000 treaties of peace were signed between 1500 B.C. and A.D. 1860. Each was intended to remain in force forever, but the average time they operated was two years. A French publicist, Alcide Ebray, wrote a whole book, *Chiffons de Papier* (Scraps of Paper), devoted solely to the treaties violated since 1815. And pacts and proclamations couched in vague and general terms have no validity whatever. A politician like Briand managed to found his diplomatic fame on declarations and promises that were quite false.

The ink on the Briand-Kellogg Pact was hardly dry before the mood changed and world war loomed in sight. The American Secretary of State announced that the Pact did not imply the slightest restriction or impairment of the right of self-defense—and everybody knows that self-defense can be invoked in any war. A reference was made to the Pact when the Chinese Eastern Railway dispute broke out, but it was found that it was ineffective. A little later, it was again appealed to in the Chinese-Japanese conflict in Manchuria; it did not stop the fighting.

The unrepentant "peace-lovers," who believe that hostilities are regulated by treaties, bewailed the breakdown of the Briand-Kellogg "scrap of paper," but explained it on the ground that it had made no provision for "enforcement" of its terms. Is it possible to be more illogical? Enforcement means coercion, and coercion means (in some form or another) war. So, the argument was that Satan should be called upon to cast out sin, and war be resorted to in order to stop war. For my part, I was thankful that there was no means of enforcement; had there been, the prospect of a huge world war, in which two sides would line up according to their sympathies and interests would have been brought that much nearer. No, the issues of peace and war are not decided by "scraps of paper"; but by other more tangible considerations.

While such "scraps of paper" as the Geneva Protocol and the Briand-Kellogg Pact did not do anything to prevent war, they had disastrous effects in encouraging war and war-like attitudes. For example. Secretary of State Henry L. Stimson, either through naiveté or malice, assumed that the Pact had actually outlawed war and that any country which started warfare was an "aggressor" to be curbed by force. He wished to apply this silly notion to the Japanese in Manchuria, and there is a real possibility that a world war might have ensued then if Britain and President Hoover had backed up Stimson, but they did not. Indeed, Mr. Hoover put severe restraint on his bellicose Secretary. But, only a few months later, in January, 1933, Mr. Stimson sold his dangerous doctrine to President-elect Roosevelt, who followed it persistently right to Pearl Harbor, with the result of the bloody war with Japan and the conquest of much of the Far East by Russian and Chinese Communists.

The whole idea of the unique wickedness of "an aggressor" in warfare, which was one of the most widely promoted of the League myths, is, of course, sheer hypocrisy. It was invented chiefly by representatives of countries which had built up great nations or empires by aggression and wished to be secure in their conquests. The whole theory was not unlike the zeal of an ex-robber who develops an acute sense of the sanctity of private property after he has accumulated wealth by theft. As Harold Nicolson observed in his *Portrait of a Diplomatist:* "The Germans, during the period which I cover, were fired by exactly the same motives and energies which illumine what we still regard as one of the most noble passages of our [English]history. We, for our part, were protected against all imprudence by the repletion, passivity, and, I should add, the selfishness of old age."

Rather more legalistic was the earlier Locarno Pact which was generally accepted as a definite renouncement of war, so far as England, Germany, France, and Italy were concerned. It purported to range England and Italy automatically on the side of Germany were Germany attacked by France, or on the side of France were France attacked by Germany. There was, naturally, no truth or substance in this interpretation. In the first place, would such a French move (I take it as an example, though it occurred earlier) as the occupation of the Ruhr, which the British held to be illegal, be regarded as an act of war? In the second place, before there could be any intervention, the powers (i.e., England and Italy) had to be convinced that a violation of the Pact constituted an "unprovoked aggression" and that immediate action was necessary. Even so, they were *entitled* to act, they were not *obliged* to act. They could consult the Council of the League of Nations, which might recommend—but not command—action, should the vote be unanimous. Plenty of loopholes existed, it will be seen. There could be no preliminary military plans, for that would be prejudging a case that had not arisen. Nor would France be allowed to assist her ally Poland, except in certain conditions and, as we know, there was perhaps the most serious danger-spot in Europe.

All the contractual methods of preventing war are a delusion and a snare. There were several declarations by America about her willingness to "consult" with other nations in the event of a threat of war. But nations have always "consulted" each other on such matters, and the excitement that was created by those who wished to persuade themselves that at last peace was assured, as though the whole weight of America would be thrown into the scale and would thus give an "aggressor" food for thought, was uncommonly silly. I say that these "proclamations of peace" debase the currency; they are meaningless, but they tempt nations which consider themselves in the right (as do all nations) in a dispute, to assume an attitude of belligerency, assured, as they believe themselves to be, of assistance from abroad, instead of seeking a reasonable compromise. No one does more harm to the cause of real peace than the professional "peace-proclaimers."

I could multiply my illustrations, but perhaps the most striking paradox was the so-called "Peace Ballot" taken in Great Britain when Italy was contemplating her move in Ethiopia. Certainly I condemn the aggressive program of Mussolini, though it was less blameworthy than the British war on the Boers; but I am convinced now, as I was then, that a fair arrangement could have been reached had England, instead of using threats, used her good offices. But the hundreds of thousands of signatories to the "Peace Ballot" were voters and, in signing in favor of peace, they in reality declared a limited war on a country which did not accept the temporary British view of the deep iniquity of the very policies and acts which had built up the British Empire. When Stanley Baldwin went to the polls, he had no difficulty in rallying the electors, and although his own intention was to calm their ardor after the elections, popular diplomacy compelled him to go ahead with "sanctions" against Italy.

The result was a bloody war with Ethiopia, which, of course, the Italians won. In addition to the lives lost, the war cost Italy, and France, Britain and the other nations involved in the "sanctions" policy over $100 million in lost trade. After their victory the Italians blandly annexed the whole country of Ethiopia. Without "sanctions" there would have been no question of annexation. Italy would probably have assumed a rôle in Ethiopia not dissimilar from that of France in Tunisia or in Morocco, or (though Egypt is nominally independent) to that of England in Egypt. The "Peace Ballot" greatly harmed the cause of a free Ethiopia. For, be it noted, Italy, once installed in that country, would have remained there firmly and solidly established, had there not been the Second World War.

The Second World War, moreover, was a direct outcome of the "Peace Ballot," since it threw Italy into the arms of Germany and embittered her against England. Without the Italo-German "Axis," it is likely that there would have been no war in 1939, or at any rate not under the same conditions or arising from the same causes. The war, had one come, would probably have been one of Germany against Russia. Italy withdrew her guard on the Brenner Pass, and permitted Germany to annex Austria, an annexation she had vigorously opposed hitherto. She thus surrendered the key to Central

Europe, which began the series of operations that led straight to the Second World War. Moreover, the failure of the half-hearted "sanctions" discredited and broke up the League.

It is difficult to imagine a more catastrophic example of popular diplomacy than that which was expressed in the so-called "Peace Ballot." Every experienced diplomat whom I consulted foresaw what might happen, and deplored the folly of the unconsidered electoral campaign which ultimately placed England in her present unhappy situation. I myself wrote a long memorandum showing the menace of the "Peace Ballot," in an effort to bring home the danger; and I resigned various posts rather than be a party to so lunatic a policy.

It is poor consolation to the prophet to find his worst fears fulfilled. Whenever I now hear assurances that our preparations for war are proof of our desire for peace—and that is now the theme of innumerable discourses—I shudder. They have an ominously reminiscent sound.

As another futile example of ominous proclamations of peace, I will remind readers of the affirmation of Neville Chamberlain, on his return from Germany in 1938—a year before the war: "My good friends, this is the second time in our history that there has come back from Germany to Downing Street peace with honor . . . It is peace for our time." There had just been a naval treaty between England and Germany, and now there was a peace pact. The French, not to be outdone, immediately concluded a "good fellow-ship pact" with Germany, assuring the world that they would not again go to war with their "hereditary" enemy. This was indeed ominous: next year Hitler fell upon Poland, and France and England declared war on Germany. Beware, I say, when men talk of peace: many times did Franklin D. Roosevelt, like Woodrow Wilson, announce that American soldiers would not be sent to fight in foreign lands; today, in the face of unprecedentedly vast preparations for war, the magic word, most glibly and perhaps sincerely spoken, is peace.

I have put the constant mouthing of peace—which by antithesis suggests war—in the foremost place in this summing up of the lessons we should learn from contemporary history, because it overlaps many of the other lessons. No one who runs about announcing that he will not commit a murder can be sure that no one will murder him, except by antiphrasis—at least if he is sane. War, whether in its positive form or its negative form of peace, has become an obsession. In normal everyday life we take it for granted that no one has evil designs on us, and that we have no evil designs on others, and we do not talk about it.

In one respect there has recently been rather less hypocrisy than there was between the two World Wars. At least, we hear little now about disarmament. For years I paced the hall of the League of Nations in company with the kindhearted and sincere President of the Disarmament Conference, Uncle Arthur—for there were uncles before Uncle Joe of Russia—Arthur Henderson. He, too, was saddened at the lack of progress and, when I told him one day: "If the nations want to disarm, they can disarm; it is because they don't want to disarm that they call a conference," he shook his head dolefully, deprecating the epigram but recognizing its point. Now we are content with infrequent and perfunctory references to the mere possibility of disarming—provided Russia begins by disarming massively. The Russians retort in offering to reduce arms and armies by, let us say, a third all around, which would lighten the burden on us. But we reply: No, you would still be relatively stronger than us. And we set to work to bring up our level of armaments to the Russian level. When we have reached that level, then we and Russia can begin to discuss in what proportions we can reduce our arms and armies simultaneously. We can then "negotiate from strength." But Russia, too, prefers to "negotiate from strength," that is to say, with pistols on the table.

Now, between the two World Wars this particular form of reasoning was not logical, for the potential enemy, Germany, was in fact long disarmed. We could, then, have safely brought down the level of our armaments to the German level—at least so argued the Germans. We had promised to do so in the Versailles Treaty. But there were plenty of excuses for delay and evasions. We ingeniously invented the "hogs, bogs, fogs," theory. Have you forgotten it? It meant that, before disarming, we must take into consideration historical, geographical, metallurgical, demographic and other factors. We must know all about the shape of heads, the gastronomic habits, the educational methods, the disposition of the railroads, the size and number of the factories, and so forth, in the countries concerned, for these things were part of the *potentiél de guerre*. From a military viewpoint it makes a difference whether a country has a good supply of pigs to feed the army; whether there are marshes which will hinder or help maneuvers; whether there are mists which may cover advances; and so on *ad infinitum*. There could be no end to such discussions, and well did the delegates know it. They were at Geneva mainly to satisfy foolish popular diplomacy rather than push ahead to real disarmament.

It seemed odd that the first meeting of the Disarmament Conference in February, 1932, synchronized with renewed fighting in the Far East, although the Briand-Kellogg Pact had already been signed which outlawed all wars. We were solemnly gathered together to ascertain the quantity and the quality of the arms with which we should be allowed to wage the wars we had sworn never again to wage.

Germany, the future enemy, was then disarmed. We were heavily armed. This did not, however, prevent Germany, a few years later, from being more efficiently armed than we were, so that she was more than a match for England and France—not to speak of Belgium and Holland and Poland—

and, perhaps, even for an unaided Russia. The conclusion seems to be that safety lies not in theoretical strength, but in eternal vigilance—in keeping one's powder dry. All the rest is "eye-wash."

Now, the potential enemy is Russia, and Russia is said to be immeasurably stronger than we are. It would be particularly fatuous to try to persuade her to agree to a reduction in order to save us expense. But how has she got "like that"—supposing that she has? What has become of the immense stocks of arms we possessed in 1945? Are the Russians the wise virgins who kept oil in their lamps, and we foolish virgins who poured out the oil in ours? Admitting that arms grow obsolete, surely there was something to be salvaged from the great stocks which eventually overthrew the might of Germany? It is useless for me to quote figures which change every day, except by way of rough-and-ready indication; but we may well ask how the United States can afford to spend ten million dollars a day—or is it an hour?—and for how long? We may well ask how the United States can afford to subsidize Europe in order to save her from economic bankruptcy, and at the same time contribute two-thirds of the cost of rearming Europe. France, in 1939, could put five million men in the field adequately equipped; today, she talks of raising, after years of idle quibbling, a paltry ten to fifteen divisions, provided the money comes from America. Germany, of course, could do much more, but Germany, after being denounced as a militaristic nation a few years ago, her cities blasted to bits, her territory devastated, millions of her best soldiers killed, her generals in prison, may well reply that, for a change, she is pacific, and sees no reason to help the Allies against Russia who could doubtless overrun Germany in the first few weeks in spite of the most heroic resistance. Would it not be better to be neutral? Or perhaps to join hands with Russia? Besides, France, unable to forget her follies in the past, opposes German rearmament at every step. Almost it would appear that she would prefer to be occupied by Russia than be saved by Germany. So, while Russia is said (personally I am without knowledge on this matter) to have three hundred divisions ready for service, the whole of Western Europe and America contemplate the raising of around fifty divisions in two, three, or five years—perhaps never. I submit that all this does not make sense.

Ah, but you forget the atom-bomb, I am told. Churchill calls it an umbrella held over Europe. As Russia, too, has atom-bombs, it may turn out to be not an umbrella but a lightning-attractor. There is a difference between a shower of rain and a thunder-storm. If, however, we accept the simile, how nonsensical it was to have an Atomic Disarmament Commission headed by Bernard Baruch to discuss how we can throw away our umbrella. If I do not believe in the perfectibility of human nature, I am bound to believe (since our scientists tell us of it) in the perfectibility of human weapons of death and destruction. Yet, the scientists seem to have twinges of conscience; some of them shrink from the consequences of their discoveries; others, who sympathize with Russia and cannot accept the "unfair" position in which she may be placed, sell secrets to her or even run to help her to make bigger and better bombs.

For that matter, I wonder why quite so much excitement is raised concerning the atom-bomb. Was not the bombing of Hamburg with phosphorus bombs just as cruel and deadly as the bombing of Hiroshima? And cannot Dresden be set beside Nagasaki? At least three times as many persons were killed in the bombing of Dresden in mid-February 1945, as were blotted out by the atom-bombing of Nagasaki during the following August. Has anybody looked at Hamburg or Cologne? One is tempted to ask why the existence of the atom-bomb was ever revealed. Was the "experiment" on Japan really necessary? Had there not been definite Japanese offers of peace over six months before—offers about identical with those accepted in August, 1945?

These remarks lead me again irresistibly to my conclusion that, as in the 1930's, so in the 1950's, all this talk of armament and disarmament may amuse—or scare—the public, but it takes us nowhere, unless it be to the verge of doom. The root of the trouble lies in the conduct of the 1939–1945 war and the incredible misjudgments made by the men in command of world affairs since 1945. Not by putting up a compensatory barricade of words can we now conjure the peril brought upon us by their incompetence and rashness. "By their fruits shall ye know them," and the fruits of popular diplomacy are exceeding bitter and deadly.

Between the two World Wars there was a hurried making of alliances. The balance of power, which did help to preserve peace, was an accepted doctrine of the old-fashioned diplomats, and we may well keep it in mind that to be old-fashioned in diplomacy is not necessarily to be wrong. Each nation either tried to surround itself with a ring of friendly nations or to surround its presumed enemy by a ring of hostile nations, in order to oppose one set of forces against another set of forces. The equilibrium achieved was, however, precarious. Many of these alliances were of the feeblest kind. I have accompanied ministers on their tours of Europe in the quest for treaties of alliances and have marvelled at the fragility of the arrangements obtained.

It was plain that the combinations would not stand the least strain. Thus, the so-called Little Entente—Czechoslovakia, Yugoslavia and Rumania—were united in opposition to Austria and Hungary; they were not united in opposition to Germany. Their ministers told me many times: "If there is any attempt to bring back the Habsburgs we shall fight, but if there is an attempt to join Austria to Germany we shall not fight." When I protested that the Habsburgs at Vienna or Budapest would prevent the *Anschluss*, while the

Anschluss would give Germany the key to Central Europe, they gave no effective answer; they only repeated that the Habsburgs were their *bête noire*. Poland had a grudge against Czechoslovakia, but an alliance with France, while France had an alliance with the Little Entente. Germany and Italy were antagonistic—until they constructed the "Axis," which was shattered in the war that came later on. Russia made an alliance with Germany at Rapallo in 1922, and then an alliance with France in 1935, and the latter alliance was broken when Stalin made another alliance with Hitler in 1939.

To attempt to enumerate the alliances of Europe between the two World Wars would be wearisome and without point, since they were entirely dependent on conditions which rapidly changed. I note, nevertheless, since it is significant today when we are "fiddling" with the idea of a *European* army— as though nations are likely to give of their best unless they are fighting under their national flag, in defense of their national interests—that in 1933 a report of the Foreign Policy Association of New York estimated that France and her allies could put into the field, not half a million to a million men, as we hope for today, but "a total of eleven to twelve million men organized and for the most part well trained and equipped with the most recent inventions in modern warfare."

So much for the false expectations of a criss-cross of alliances. What became of the twelve million well-equipped men? What, we may ask, would become of the (put it as high as possible) one million men now promised? Yet every alliance was welcomed by the deluded peoples and their diplomatic stooges as a new victory for their diplomacy. Today, we are bidden to welcome an alliance—named the North Atlantic Treaty Organization—which would aim at raising a heterogeneous European army composed of soldiers from a reluctant France (where Communism is rife), Italy (where Communism is a very strong element), a few minor countries which could not long withstand a serious assault, an England which intends to retain her own autonomy, and perhaps from Spain and Germany who are, if not excluded, regarded as undesirable partners. None the less, there are great shouts of satisfaction every time the smallest advance is made, and years of quibbling debate are wasted on a costly scheme which cannot meet the emergency that is alleged to have arisen or will arise in the near future. If this be security, may God help us!

Again, between the World Wars, the public was lulled into a false sense of security by so-called guarantees. After the Versailles *Diktat*, England and the United States were to guarantee France against German aggression. But the American Senate refused to ratify the agreement, and England promptly released herself from any such engagement. Léon Bourgeois endeavored to wrest promises from the League by which the flags of many nations would be associated with that of France, in case of an attack on any of the members of the League. Here was the first serious suggestion of an international army. Now it was precisely the weakening of national sentiment, the reliance on other than one's own efforts, in a word, the internationalization of military forces, that brought about the collapse of France. Popular diplomacy in our day always looks for an easy way. It is bellicose—on condition that others will spill their blood for it. It will be defiant —as long as others will do the fighting. It is all for militaristic sanctions—provided they are backed up by troops from abroad.

There was a Treaty of Mutual Assistance, and there was a Geneva Protocol. Both of them came to naught; they were designed to place on other shoulders the burden which we each must bear, individuals and nations, in the defense of what we conceive to be our rights. Popular diplomacy, if bellicose at times, is lazy and evasive at others. Let some one else do the work. Incidentally, I would observe that the same tendency in economic and social life—of looking to the state instead of to ourselves in the struggle for existence—equally enfeebles the fibers of the European countries, and to a less extent of America. In spite of the indubitable lessons of the past decades, facility is still the cry. We want to be guaranteed against every evil. We must have many rights, but as few duties as possible.

Guarantees! Security! Whether in the social sphere or the international sphere, in these words is to be found the explanation of much of the miseries of our time. Surely a nation that is not determined to survive does not deserve to survive. An individual who weakly succumbs is worthless. I am not harsh enough to intimate that we should not render every assistance in our power to the poor and the weak; but I do suggest that they must, man or nation, first show their will to live, and not fall back on the soft pillow of assured outside aid. Incalculable harm has been done to Europe—to the world—by the preaching of the new gospel of internationalism, which means that safety must be found mainly from outside ourselves. God helps those who help themselves, wisely declared an old proverb, now generally ignored. I wish Europe would remind herself that she must help herself if she would be helped by America.

The moral texture of Europeans has been rent; the resolve of Europe to preserve the civilization that stemmed from ancient Greece, from Rome, from Palestine the cradle of our religion, has been perhaps irremediably softened by the habit of receiving charity and protection from America—or, as millions of fanatical devotees of Communism would prefer, from Russia. Great and proud nations, who once held to their freedom and independence as their most precious possession, who, while accepting aid from their friends, were convinced of their own ability to surmount adversity, to repel every foe, now offer the pitiful spectacle of becoming whining subordinate countries, unwilling to make sacrifices for their own future. I trust they will recover the sense of their heritage, their proud traditions, and will realize that they have a spiritual part to play in a world that is growing more and more materialistic. I trust that they will be duly grateful to America for her extensive assistance—but I am sure that they must first throw off the slothful wish to live in a state of mendicancy, afraid of war, ripe for the shameful position of poor kept relations, if they are to play any effective rôle in the defense of the community of free nations—or of themselves.

13

THE MENACE OF INTIMATE
TOP-LEVEL CONFERENCES

I⟨T WAS⟩ President Wilson who began the fatal practice of "Top-Level" conferences in diplomacy when he came over to Europe to take a personal part in the peace-making at Paris. He set a precedent that has been followed with increasingly dire effects on peace and human happiness. Thenceforth, presidents, prime ministers, secretaries of state, and foreign ministers thought it their business to enter into personal negotiations, take personal decisions, be guided by personal considerations—sometimes electoral, sometimes purely temperamental—in matters that far transcended their persons, in matters that should be approached in the most impersonal manner possible. In foreign affairs, in particular—I say nothing in this connection of domestic policies—a president, a prime minister, or any other high functionary of the state entrusted with the most vital responsibilities, should, first and last, make, as it were, an abstraction of himself. He should forget that he is Wilson or Roosevelt or Truman or Acheson, or Dulles or Churchill or Eden; he should remember only that he is a lofty and lonely figure, a final court of appeal placed by his office above the dusty arena of personal contacts, personal prepossessions, personal prejudices, personal sentiments of any kind.

The recent doctrine and practice of cultivating warm likes, and therefore extreme dislikes, for the representatives of other countries, is palpably wrong. The contrary doctrine of avoiding human relations in the course of one's duties, is the correct one. Let a president or prime minister fondle his children and grandchildren, let him cherish his wife, let him surround himself with personal friends—on condition that wife, children and friends refrain from influencing him in public concerns. He is a man and, therefore, entitled to his private life; but his private life should be quite distinct from his rôle as arbiter, as moderator, as supreme judge for the nation, or as supreme judge in his own department of the nation.

The old kings had their favorites, both men and women, but the best of them understood that these favorites belonged to an intimate circle from which affairs of state should be rigorously excluded. It sometimes happened, when the king was frivolous or old, that he forgot the golden rule of kingship, like Louis XIV in his declining years, when he allowed Madame de Maintenon to wrest from him the revocation of the Edict of Nantes. The results of such intervention were always disastrous. Moreover, when the kings of old received the emissaries of foreign countries, it was strictly in their regal rôle, and the ambassadors remained in their ambassadorial rôle—that is to say, impersonal. There was no back-slapping, vodka-drinking, toasts, no desire to charm, and no desire to be charmed; the issues at stake had nothing to do with the personal feelings of "Frankie" for "Joe" or "Joe" for "Frankie." There were no "Winnies" whom we loved and no Adolfs whom we detested; in this realm, the "Tonies" and "Deans" ceased from troubling and the Benitos were not present.

All this affectation of Christian names, of pet names, are part of the new popular diplomacy, and as such are abhorrent to sound diplomacy. Leave the business of pokes in the stomach to the local politicians, and embraces to the cinema stars and pin-up girls. I have written it before, but I must repeat it, that I first realized that a new era had dawned when I saw in an illustrated newspaper a photograph of the Lord Chancellor of England, who should be known to the public only in his gorgeous robes of ceremony, sprawling on the beach at Biarritz in a skimpy bathing suit. No doubt he had a right to sprawl on the beach in a skimpy pair of bathing drawers, but not for public exhibition. More recently President Truman was proudly exhibited wearing bizarre beach-combing raiment on his Florida vacation.

The dignity of office is not a vain thing. It is essential to the dignified and sensible conduct of the state. Far from these personal contacts, now deemed normal, now flaunted in the press, now followed with far more interest than the problems under discussion, helping towards an understanding and adjustment of foreign policy, they actually darken counsel by introducing distracting elements which are irrelevant to sober judgment. What does it matter, for example, whether Uncle Joe produces a good or bad impression on statesmen of the West? Is he a boon-fellow, or a sort of male courtesan, to whom may be given handsome rewards, great areas of territory that do not belong to the givers, millions of people who are not the subjects of the givers?

In entire opposition to the practice of my time, I assert that the habit of top-level meetings has brought untold harm to the world. It began at Versailles, and has continued in a countless series of top-level conferences, in which "top-levels" entertained each other in the most diverse surroundings, made themselves "feel good," and wrested mutual concessions from each other. Probably never before in world history was as much damage done to international well-being, peace and decency as at the wartime top-level conferences, running through Casablanca, Cairo, Teheran, Quebec, Yalta, and Potsdam. The top-level leaders had plenty of trained official agents. What were those agents for, if not to transmit to their chiefs, who should carefully study the facts in the quiet of their official studies, thinking only of their nation's present and future welfare, without paying the slightest heed either to the clamors of the crowd or to the "charm" of host or hostess?

If I remain the last of my opinion, a despised relic of a more dignified and sensible age, I will continue to assert that, much, perhaps most, of our misgovernment in world affairs and its hideous consequences have had their origins in the modern conviction that top-level talks will magically solve all international problems. It is not so. It is demonstrably not so. It is demonstrably the opposite of the truth. The personal equation in diplomacy—at least on top-levels—can bring only false judgments founded on the mood of the moment, the sort of dinner that has been eaten, the number of glasses drunk, the spirit of comradeship aroused. In an atmosphere of momentary geniality, contentment, or alcoholic exaltation, the highest personages, with the most overwhelming responsibilities, are inclined to yield on points that are of the utmost weight, as they would never do in the calm deliberation of their study.

It is now generally conceded that the decision taken at Casablanca at the beginning of 1943, for example, was highly regrettable, since it needlessly prolonged the war for more than a year, and brought complete chaos to Europe. That decision, it willl be remembered, was to insist on "unconditional surrender." Now Wilson had been wiser for, at the time of framing the Fourteen Points, he had not stirred from the White House. The trouble was that he afterwards betrayed most of them through his disastrous personal contacts with European statesmen as a result of his combination of a top-level diplomatic conference with a belated honeymoon. Those Fourteen Points, in large measure, induced Germany to surrender. But, after Casablanca, in spite of the growing antagonism to Hitler in the German army, the generals and the German people were informed that there was no hope for them. They could do nothing but fight while any fight was left in them.

It is not a sane objective of a responsible leader of nations at war to force the enemy to fight to the last man. We are told that the idea came to Roosevelt in a sudden flash, that he remembered that General Grant (who, nevertheless, treated his vanquished foe, General Lee, with fine soldierly respect) had pronounced the words "unconditional surrender." Without more thought, he threw out the suggestion, and we are told that Churchill reluctantly adopted it. No doubt it suited the temper of the Allied peoples at the moment; no doubt it was popular diplomacy; but it had fatal results for us all. Roosevelt was even sloppy on his history: it was at Fort Donelson in 1862, not at Appomattox in 1865, that General Grant had demanded "unconditional surrender." By leading to the total destruction of Germany and the enthronement of Soviet Russia as the dominant power in the Old World, the Casablanca Conference can very accurately be regarded as one of the most disastrous turning-points in world history.

Later, at Teheran, Russia, the United States and Britain, represented by their top-levels, took decisions amid Levantine festivities that sealed the fate of Europe, of the East, perhaps of America. The reactionary doctrine of "spheres of influence"—in other words the domination of Great Powers over weaker powers—was revived, to the advantage of Stalin. It was a joyous occasion, but it was the parent of endless misery, confusion, and difficulties, from which we now suffer and are likely to suffer for generations. Does anyone imagine that Churchill or Roosevelt would have given so much away —in contradiction to the Atlantic Charter—had the proposals been submitted to them in the privacy of their closets? Yet at Yalta and Potsdam, the conquests of Stalin were confirmed and augmented. Also at Teheran, Stalin, Roosevelt and Churchill laid the basis for the notorious war-crimes trials at Nuremberg, Tokyo, and elsewhere. These assured that future wars will be waged with unprecedented ferocity, since leaders must spare nothing to prevent a defeat which would mean their immediate liquidation, at the best only delayed by the duration of a mock-trial. Stalin made this proposal for the mass-murder of 50,000 German generals and technicians at Teheran in the same spirit in which he had already murdered 15,000 Polish officers, political leaders and technicians, in the Katyn Forest and elsewhere. The Stalin-White-Morgenthau Plan, adopted at Quebec in September, 1944, assured the completion of the destruction of Germany after hostilities had ceased. It later cost the United States many billions of dollars even partly to undo the damage wrought by this idiotic scheme and to help to restore Germany as a bulwark against Soviet Russia.

In my view, a similar desire to please Stalin, who had become a world hero in the struggle against "Fasnazism"—and also a whim to do the spectacular thing rather than the wise thing—dictated the choice of the "Second Front" in France, rather than in the Balkans. This choice left Eastern Europe at the mercy of Stalin. Had the Allies pushed up from Italy and the Balkans through the Central European countries, the Germans would have been obliged to abandon France. As the Allies forced them back from the Balkans, the Allies, and not the Russians, would have penetrated into these countries. The Russians would, therefore, have been "contained" in the specifically Russian lands. There was no need whatever to facilitate the Russification of the Balkans, no need whatever to have permitted the Russian troops to occupy half of Austria, no need whatever to have waited for them to take possession of Berlin and a large part of Germany. Problems which have now become all but insoluble were then gratuitously created.

The Slavilization of much of Europe and a considerable part of Asia was due to the impulsiveness of statesmen who did not understand that, whenever grave decisions are to be made, no one, however able he may think himself to be, and however able he may actually be in his sober moments, has a right to act according to his temporary personal feelings, or the excited momentary feelings of the public. He must not be hasty in his judgments; he must make them, so far as possible, in seclusion, after careful consideration of the immediate and subsequent consequences. He must listen to all, but he must not be unduly influenced by any. It would seem that Churchill was not wholly blind to the possible results of hysterical popular policy, but he was overawed or overruled. Churchill was something less than enthusiastic over the "unconditional surrender" plank at Casablanca, and was outraged by Stalin's suggestion at Teheran that 50,000 generals and technicians be murdered after hostilities. But he gave way on both of these disastrous proposals. "He thinks too much of the post-war situation," Roosevelt is reported to have said of Churchill; "He fears that Russia will become too strong. Would a strong Russia be a bad thing? Anyhow, Stalin merely wants security for Russia." And on the assumption that "noblesse oblige," that Stalin would be touched by the generosity of the Allies and would show himself equally generous, the irreparable damage was accomplished.

It is not my purpose to criticize Roosevelt; he was a sick man in the later stages of the war; but it is incumbent on me to condemn the method of personal contacts at top levels. It was there that the mischief was done. That Uncle Joe appeared to be an amiable and decent sort of chap in these meetings was not a sufficient reason for taking an immense gamble with human lives and the very destiny of the human race. To imagine that an appeal to Stalin's moral sense would alter the fate of Poland or the Baltic States was disastrous folly. Indeed, from the Russian viewpoint, Stalin would have been blameworthy had he surrendered to any such personal persuasion. He was well within his rôle in obtaining all he could, and of sticking to what was given to him. He would have been a poor leader had he relinquished an inch of territory offered to him or won by him, except on grounds of national prudence. He, at least, was not susceptible to flattery or to mere sentiment. And to talk about his moral sense is not merely absurd, it ignores and obscures the immorality of his interlocutors in bartering away the liberties of innocent and helpless peoples. Ingenuousness has never been pushed farther in international dealings.

Had America stood up to Russia at Teheran and Yalta, she would have saved herself billions of dollars, and she would have spared Europe the horrors of enslavement. For, if Stalin was not amenable to flattery or to sentiment, he would have been amenable to force and firmness in 1945. I certainly have no excessive sympathy for Germany, but the most elementary knowledge of Europe—or even of physics—would have indicated that you cannot create a void in the heart of Europe without inviting another power—in this case Russia —to fill the vacuum. And what a void is a defeated and unarmed Germany in Europe! What a void are the Balkans, emptied of their German occupants! These voids it was our duty to fill before others could do so. To grant in principle to Russia at Teheran a zone of influence without effective guarantees, to consent to the new partition of Poland and of Germany, to permit the deportation of ten to fifteen million Germans from lands their ancestors had occupied for centuries, was to stultify the Atlantic Charter which proclaimed that there should be no change of territory, no exchange of peoples, without their formal consent. To concur at Yalta, on the last-minute promise of Russia to help America against Japan (help even then known to be quite unnecessary), in the Russian occupation of the Kuriles, of Sakhalin, and in the Russian domination of Port Arthur, of Darien, of Manchuria, of part of Korea, was to ignore the possibilities of later Russian expansion throughout the whole of Asia, and the tragic possibilities of the bloody fighting which has already come in Korea. The effect of these wartime top-level conferences were fully as disastrous as those of that first ominous top-level conference at Paris in 1919. They were so bad that they even prevented any general peace conference after the war.

Perhaps it will be objected that these arrangements were no part of popular diplomacy. Certainly, the peoples were not asked their advice—they would have had none to give. It is true that spectacular top-level conferences pass above the heads of the peoples, who see only general results. Indeed, there has never been so much really "secret diplomacy" as since Woodrow Wilson declared that open covenants should be openly arrived at. Open diplomacy is by no means incompatible with a mystification of the masses. It would not be exaggerating to say that it leaves the ordinary man more in the dark than did the old diplomacy. The atmosphere is all that counts in popular diplomacy, and the atmosphere from, let us roughly put it, 1942 to 1945 or 1946, was enthusiastically pro-Russian. Anything accorded to Russia was cheered without reflection, and anything refused to Russia would have been condemned by the masses. Russia was our "loyal ally."

Were I inclined to cynicism, I would say that there are in reality no "loyal allies." There are allies whose interests momentarily coincide with ours, there are allies whose fugitive sentiments resemble our own, but there are no allies whom we should trust when these interests and sentiments change— as they almost invariably do. For the astute diplomat, "loyal allies" do not exist. He knows too much history to stake the fortunes of his country on their absolute and enduring loyalty.

If, then, we try to put ourselves back in the atmosphere of 1942–1945, we shall recall that Joseph Davies, Harry Hopkins, Thomas Lamont, and many others were convinced that nothing was too good for Russia. Organizations like "America First" were dissolved. Special numbers of popular magazines devoted their pages to eulogies of Russia. Top Communist leaders like William Z. Foster addressed great war bond rallies. The Communist Party endorsed Roosevelt for the presidency in 1944. To be sure, Russian supporters were not then necessarily Communists, though it was not looked upon as a crime to be Communist at that period and many misguided persons have since suffered the loss of their posts and have been imprisoned because they then had Communist leanings or were members of pro-Communist organizations. Even in England, pro-Communist sentiment was almost as strong as in the United States. Mr. Churchill rather rashly requested everybody "to do everything possible to help Russia." Literally interpreted, this would have justified Communists in attempts to overthrow capitalist governments by force and the betrayal of atomic secrets to Russia by Dr. Fuchs, the Rosenbergs, and the like.

Now it is precisely because we expect a statesman to rise above the mood of the moment, because we expect him to think seriously of the future, that we place him in office. It was perfectly proper to make temporary military use of this pro-Russian feeling, it was perfectly proper to make whatever temporary compromise was needed to gain our ends without jeopardizing the future, but it was not proper to mortgage our hopes of a better world to gain the momentary favor of Stalin. Francis I, in France, was clever enough to make an ally of the Turks—the "infidels"—without becoming an "infidel" himself or proselytizing for Mahomet. Richelieu, hard pressed by rivals, was astute enough to join hands with the Protestants, without converting himself or his country to Protestantism. After the war, General De Gaulle flew to Moscow to sign a pact of alliance with Stalin which, incidentally, is presumably still binding, without professing Communism—on the contrary, he is perhaps the most outstanding anti-Communist in France. A diplomat is always ready to appear a "fellow-traveller," but, in so far as he is a diplomat, he takes care not to travel too far with his companion.

President Truman, after his unfortunate lapse at Potsdam, when he was new to office, rightly declined to lend his countenance to top-level talks. One would have thought that every sensible man would have looked askance on a system that has been so tragically discredited in our time, but it would seem that Churchill has continued to hanker after top-level talks. So, seemingly, has Stalin and his successors. In the light of his vast gains from the top-level talks of wartime, one could hardly blame Stalin for wishing to perpetuate them. Surely, the only safe guide for the head of a state is to demand that any propositions shall be put in writing, examined impartially by experts, and submitted to him without the pernicious and debilitating influence of personal contacts. He must beware of his own weaknesses, his spells of weariness and inattention, and the "charm" of those whose natural and legitimate design is to betray him into errors and concessions that cannot be undone.

Though this is not the place to deal with the matter at length, I cannot altogether omit the results of another top-level decision of which I was an eye-witness in France—happenings which had their counterpart in other European countries. Encouraged and helped by parachuted arms and money, there was created, in France, by England and America a form of "resistance" which had no military value, but started a civil war and permanently injured unfortunate France morally and materially. What romantic ideas were in the heads of Churchill and Roosevelt I do not know, but I suppose the propagandist value of internal "resistance" outweighed other considerations. The "partisans" were mainly Communists who took the opportunity of training themselves, under the cover of patriotism, in the use of light weapons particularly suitable for insurrection. They did not, except spasmodically, attack the German army; their attentions were chiefly directed to the "liquidation" of anti-Communists in France—and wherever else they operated. No clear-headed statesman could have failed to see that the moral unity of France—or any other defeated nation—was of supreme importance at the moment. In the plight in which France found herself, passive resistance—moral opposition to the invader—was far more valuable than the development of a sort of political banditry under Communist leadership.

Guerrilla warfare—real guerrilla warfare—might be an effective method in Arabian countries, where mobility is assured in the desert spaces. In France, it could be translated only into assassination and pillage of the peaceful population. If a few German soldiers were killed, the vengeance of the Germans fell many-fold on the innocent civilians. There were, of course, other "partisans" whose intentions were honest; but the Communists were the principal beneficiaries of the breakdown of law and order. In what has since been the tragic history of France, the British and Americans thus have a heavy responsibility.

You cannot teach that it is a virtue to disobey, to ignore the legal authority, to commit crimes under the cover of "patriotism," without demoralizing a community for a long time, perhaps for ever. The formation of schools of rebels, where the young men were trained to rob and slay, with a view of seizing of power at the Liberation, followed as it was by a vast "purging" of political adversaries, has weakened France in every way. While the French Communists openly affirm their resolve to fight not for France but for Russia in the event of another war, many other citizens, genuinely patriotic, hesitate to take sides in the struggle between East and West, afraid of what will be their fate should France be overrun by Russia, or if Communism is later established in France by a "putsch."

In Italy, the situation is substantially the same. In Germany, disabled, there is strong opposition to any participation in a new war. For Germany is divided into two parts and, therefore, Germans will be pitted, doubtless contrary to their will, against Germans. Whichever side wins, the other side will be "traitors." And, as the European nations, previously respected in the Near East and in North Africa, are manifestly shadows of their former selves, as guerrilla warfare has been taught and encouraged, as agitation for full independence has been promoted, as nationalism has reached the height of paroxysm among the native races, our difficulties, both in peace and in war ("cold" or "hot") have been multiplied a hundredfold. Could not these results have been foreseen?

Yes, on condition that the responsible Allied leaders remained at home, directing from their studies, with unimpassioned wisdom, the tempest they had provoked. No, if they cast aside their intelligence and leaped forth into the dusty arena. Leaders in time of war—and indeed in time of peace—should possess a sort of Olympian aloofness. Unhappily, they prefer to join the crowd.

If one excludes Russia from Europe—and Russia is defined as the most Eastern of Western countries and the most Western of Eastern countries—then the situation of Europe today, after the smashing of Germany and the bedevilment of France, corresponds closely to that described in a brilliant epigram by Pope:

> "Now Europe's balanced; neither side prevails,
> For nothing's left in either of the scales."

Now what is true of presidents and prime ministers and other heads of state, whose place is in their official executive offices, applies almost equally to their principal ministers. Surely, they have plenty to occupy their attention in collecting and appraising the information that comes from their agents in the field? Surely they have not too much time left to think out the problems? Surely, the management of their department and the issuing of well-pondered directions to

their subordinates is a full-time job? Why this craze for passing the bulk of their days in airplanes, in trains, or in steam-
ships? What is the purpose of rushing personally from land
to land, shaking hands with other foreign ministers, exchanging hasty words, many of them imprudent, and hurrying
back home in the belief that they have settled something?
Surely, it cannot be to excite the press, to find themselves the
center of acrimonious debate and endless interpretation? Or
is it?

I have protested against lack of sobriety, of seriousness, in
diplomacy as it was practiced between the two World Wars.
But I find that, in defiance of the lesson which should by this
time have been learned, nothing has been changed. Spectacular trips, resounding expressions of optimism, a few days'
gloom, an indecisive communiqué, immense agitation, mis-
understandings, misrepresentations, and confusion worse confounded—these are the usual upshot of the flying visits: much
hot air which resolves itself into a whirling wind-storm.

Is it argued here that foreign ministers should get to know
each other? I say that they cannot get to know each other
under these conditions and, moreover, that they should not
try to get to know each other; their job is to know themselves, their own minds. Have they no trusty servants to tell
them all that they need know about the policy and diplomatic personnel of foreign countries? But, it may be said,
they should learn something about the temper, the imponder-
ables, of foreign peoples. Is it to be supposed that they return
home from these brief and flying visits with the slightest increase of their knowledge of foreign peoples? They have
never seen them, except from their airplanes, train windows
and automobiles. And the knowledge, assuming that it can be
obtained, should already have been theirs. It should be one
of the qualifications for their post that they have a certain
experience of the manner in which foreign peoples react.

They should not have to begin to instruct themselves in the rudiments of their task, at our expense, after they have taken office.

I am a truly modest man, without the slightest personal ambition, but I am bound to say that, in literal fact, I know far more about a number of important countries than any foreign minister I have ever known—and I have known many. Nor am I sure that such personal knowledge, coming before or after the acceptance of an important post, knowledge of the people as well as of a diplomatic "opposite number," is really indispensable. The secretary of state or the foreign minister should be dealing with facts—which can be conveyed—and not with feelings; his business is to know his own country and, for the rest, to play the difficult game, after a close examination of the facts (and not of the falsehoods which will be presented to him abroad) with an inflexible purpose and a cool head.

If I had seen any good come from the modern mania for traveling ministers, I would join in the praise for the superhuman beings who can be in Washington, Paris and London, and heaven knows where, in a single week, and at the same time can conduct efficiently the affairs of their charge at home. For the most part, I have seen no such good arising; I have seen mainly complications and heard only interminable wranglings. I have read only a great splutter of erroneous comment in the newspapers lightened up by the printing of menus of the luxurious repasts of the distinguished visiting statesmen and their hosts. Indeed, when one comes to think about it, what sort of a foreign minister is he who can be persuaded, by an hour's talk with another foreign minister, that he has been wrong, or who imagines that he can speedily convince the other foreign minister of the latter's mistakes? I assume, of course, that both of them have fully informed themselves of their case and of the possibilities of agreement beforehand and that, at the best, they accomplish no more than any sensible man could have accomplished, much more clearly, by an exchange of memoranda, without the hubbub of publicity and speculation.

There is another type of conference, frequent enough before the last war, but still more frequent today, when its futility has been proved. I refer to the protracted conferences in which secondary personages, without authority, without the power to come to any final settlement of anything—except perhaps their agenda, and that too may take months of useless discussion—meet in this or that capital, and behave in a manner similar to the famous Alexandrine which "like a wounded snake drags its slow length along."

There was one of them held in Paris after the war, ostensibly to prepare a later top-level meeting; it went on and on, making a little stir now and again, its members sometimes getting together for five minutes or so in the day, and in the end, after alternately raising and dashing the hopes of naïve readers of the newspapers, abandoning the proceedings altogether. Even the most hardened delegate must eventually reach the limits of his patience, or perhaps it would be more correct to say that the public becomes exhausted and will not read any more about the abortive quarrels. There was such a conference in Korea, presumably to fix an armistice which apparently nobody wanted, for a solution that could be obtained in a few hours if there was a real desire for an armistice.

There are plenty of other conferences which it would be wearisome to enumerate—life today sometimes seems to be just one conference after another; but what sticks in my mind most of all are the conferences—or congresses—which profess to be "remaking Europe." There are several of them, indeed, so many that it is permissible to affirm that, while a few years ago Russian troops would have encountered no opposition in advancing westward, now they will find a hostile committee, commission, congress, or conference for

European unity at every street corner. It often happens that those who are loudest in their demand for European unity are those who are most embittered against other nations—for instance against Germany or Spain—and have done the most to wreck the unity of their own country.

Let us not linger too long on this theme of conferences and congresses and meetings of ministers; it is impossible for any normally intelligent person, who does not earn a living or gratify a love for the limelight in such public parades, not to recognize that, for the most part, they arrive nowhere and, in the nature of things, cannot arrive anywhere.

What is infinitely worse than their futility is the impression they make on a troubled world of perpetual international crisis. Undoubtedly, we are living in an epoch of institutional upheaval and of constant political and military danger; but I have been present in countries where even revolutions were in actual progress, and I have observed that the average man, just outside the range of shooting, not directly affected by the disorder, is inclined to continue his occupation, to go on living as though nothing was happening; he is barely conscious that great things are in progress, and he is glad to be unconscious of a situation he cannot alter.

The vast majority, if not stirred up by leaders and propaganda, are ready to accept changes that do not touch them immediately. I think it is well that this should be so. Today, in our European countries, there would be few, not professionally engaged, who would be seriously disturbed by world tension, were it not for the constant comings-and-goings, the unceasing clamor of the press and radio that accompanies the delegates and ministers as they journey from New York to Lisbon, to Rome, to Bonn, to Berlin, to San Francisco. The natural apathy of the populace is constantly undermined. Their brains are in a whirl. They fear the worst, and they believe that at any moment catastrophe will overtake them.

This is not a healthy state of mind for the populations of

any country. It is bad for their work, it is bad for their home life; it destroys the very mainspring of action; it demoralizes them; they dare not look ahead; "eat, drink, and be merry, for tomorrow we die" becomes their attitude. Thrift is useless; to raise a family is folly; to behave decently in accordance with ancient precepts is old-fashioned, all very well for our fathers, but not in tune with the modern world. The sense of existing on the rim of a volcano which may at any moment be covered with flames and lava is fatal for a healthy community. Most communities in Europe (to a lesser degree in America) are, in consequence of the unceasing prophecies of imminent disaster, increased by the vociferations of the crisis-conferences, afflicted by a feeling of uncertainty and impending calamity. Statesmen cannot proclaim a state of emergency every five minutes, and then expect the masses to pursue their daily tasks in peace and calm. It is the bounden duty of public servants, while warding off the blows of fate, to conduct their deliberations without alarming the public.

Of the U.N., the United Nations Organization, what is there to say, except that it is worse than the League? The League, at any rate, did arouse hopes, it did hold up an ideal. But no one believes today that the U.N. can keep peace. It appears, on the contrary, to be an instrument of war. Its title is ludicrously false. United Nations? What nations are united? In what are they united? They are notoriously at loggerheads. On one side, are the nations of the North Atlantic Treaty Organization who are bidden to rearm; on the other side, are the nations of the Russian group; and, in between, are the nations who demand independence for their fellows of the same or similar complexion, and another body of nations who remain indifferent.

Does the U.N. bring them into harmony? No, for it provides a platform on which the antagonists can noisily air their grievances, launch their propaganda, declare their implacable hostility. The League was subject to criticism, which I have not spared in these pages, but it did discuss problems with some decorum and dignity. Now, decorum is thrown to the winds. Silence were far better than the noisy exchange of vituperation, stiffening every quarrel, rendering compromise more difficult, perhaps impossible, ranging the world into hate-camps.

I watched with amazement the Sixth Session of the U.N. in Paris. Even the record of the preceding sessions at Lake Success, with the steady flow of insults, the litany of "Niet," the inability to agree on anything substantial whatever, did not prepare me for the torrent of abuse that flowed from the French session prepared at such expense. The delegates devoted their time to accusing each other of terrible crimes against humanity. To be sure, the Soviet Union was the master in the art of obloquy and the Western nations were beaten out of the field at this ghastly game.

If the U.N. is to meet only to exchange charges of barbarity, would it not be better to shut up the shop at once? Millions of displaced persons, as the refugees are euphemistically called, millions more in concentration camps or deported to inaccessible regions, many millions more living in utter misery, tortures, assassinations, oppressions of every kind, shame our humanity. I do not doubt where the balance of guilt lies, I do not doubt that for one iniquity of the Western nations there are five iniquities on the Russian side. But I do not doubt that we have some complicity in iniquities such as the obliteration of once-happy countries. But the striking of the balance of right and wrong is not the task of U.N.; its task is to soothe animosities, to repair evils, not to exacerbate angry sentiments by repeated loud fulminations heard around the globe. I can think of many better ways of ameliorating conditions; I can think of none worse than the international vilifications of which the U.N. is the sounding-board. The Nazis and the Russians made long and extensive use of diplomatic billingsgate for purposes of propaganda for home consumption. They hoped in this way to strengthen their hold on their peoples. There was no thought of promoting or attaining peace. This dangerous precedent has become all but universally accepted in the procedure of the United Nations.

Let me make it plain that I admire the work of various departments of U.N., and particularly of U.N.E.S.C.O., in bringing educational facilities, medical care, the spread of civilization in the world. But this is not the point. However excellent may be some of the specialized activities of a world organization, its principal task, without whose fulfillment all the rest is as nothing, is to bring peace to the nations. Not only is the U.N., divided as it is, as it must be, unable to bring peace; it definitely brings war nearer by permitting these violent imprecations to be hurled from its rostrum. Had there been no U.N., we should have heard a great deal less of the cleavage between East and West.

But the cleavage would still have existed, you may remark; and it is perhaps preferable that it should be brought into the open. I do not agree. The gulf is widened between East and West as it would never have been had not this public platform been provided for a flood of invective. It may be that the gap could not have been filled, but it is certain that the gap will not be filled while a constant stream of minatory and scurrilous speeches ascend to heaven.

As for the war in Korea, which was not a minor war but a war, which, a half century ago, would have been regarded as a major conflict, I am told that it could never have taken place except for the possibly accidental absence of the Russian group from the U.N. when authority was given America to intervene between North and South Koreans. Russia might have vetoed the war. If this be true, is it not incredibly ironic? The war is America's war, primarily, but it is also the U.N.'s war—a strange function for an organization whose objective is peace. Yet, only by a technical lapse in its operations, was it possible for North Koreans (who presumably are much the same as South Koreans) to become our foes, and South Koreans (who belong to the same country that we artificially divided) to become our protégés.

Later commentators have suggested that, perhaps, Russian absence from the Security Council when the decision was taken to intervene in Korea was not accidental at all, but the result of shrewd foresight. This interpretation rests upon the assumption that Stalin and his advisers already saw in 1950 how a long and indecisive Korean war would favor the Soviet interests and weaken and discredit the United States and its supporters in the U.N. It would help unite Communist China and train her soldiers and air men. It would constitute a frightful economic and financial drain on the United States. The failure to conquer the North Koreans and Chinese Reds after years of war would destroy the legend of American omnipotence among the peoples of Asia and it would cost Russia nothing. Mr. Truman provided indirect confirmation of this interpretation when he charged in late December, 1952, that it had been the main purpose of Russia to get and keep the United States bogged down in a long and indecisive Asiatic war.

"And what if the League's army is beaten?" once asked Jacques Bainville. The U.N. army—since the American army is regarded as the army of U.N.—came near to be beaten. If it had been thrown off the peninsula in the first days of the struggle, it is unthinkable that the United States would have accepted the defeat, and a World War might easily have arisen from the technical lapse. As the war went on, the prospect of a clean-cut victory receded; if something like the *status quo* is finally obtained, the power of the U.N. to stop aggression remains doubtful. What is hardly in doubt is the possibility that the U.N., like the League, may lead us some day into an all-out world conflict.

Somewhere on my desk are statistics telling how many

million words were spoken at the Sixth Session of the U.N. in Paris. Forty million "handouts," 10,720,000 words, enough to fill twelve Bibles—a queer new Bible of Humanity, bigger if not better than the original one. The compiler seemed to be proud of the record. They were so many million words too many. It would have been more interesting and relevant to tell us what permanent good works the U.N. has accomplished at Paris or since in promoting durable world peace.

14
EXPERT DIPLOMACY VERSUS
POPULAR DIPLOMACY

As we approach the close of our survey of the rise, decline and fall of popular diplomacy, an interested and discerning reader might make some such observation as this: All this may be true, but it is only negative. What positive proposals do you have to put forward? What, in your opinion, are the proper, or possible, solutions for the serious public problems which have been produced by the defects and evils of popular diplomacy and have been detailed in the preceding pages?

Let me say, in the first place, that I have not committed myself to any responsibility to provide positive and infallible solutions for the public ills of our time, which have been created by an undisciplined and untrained democracy and its projection into world affairs under the guise of popular diplomacy. My main task and theme have been to show how this new pattern of diplomatic ideals and practices has arisen, and how its operations have brought untold disasters to the world in the first half of the present century—disasters which the old diplomacy would probably have prevented, provided it could have functioned at all, in a world dominated by contemporary agencies of communication, which may be sheer and unsupported assumption.

There may, indeed, be no solution for the problems. The biological episode of the domination of the planet by the human race may be a temporary matter. Other species have lorded it over creation for long periods, and have disappeared in the struggle for existence. Popular diplomacy may well be the method whereby the species known as *homo sapiens* will commit racial suicide and be eliminated from its reigning position. Such a thought represents no cheap cynicism or semantic rashness. The follies of popular diplomacy have already brought us close to oblivion and have placed us on the verge of a third World War, which is very likely to obliterate such of the race and its civilization as have survived the first two world conflicts. Any final mopping-up can await the fourth World War.

The limitless idiocies of popular diplomacy, taken in conjunction with the unprecedented revolution in our capacity for dealing out death and destroying material culture in the atomic age, present unparalleled opportunity for winding up the human experiment, and there is an uncomfortable prospect that we may exploit that possibility. At least, we may say with confidence that all the really cogent and relevant summonses to a return to sanity pass utterly unheeded by those in control of public affairs in the main countries on the globe. Even those rulers of powerful states who call attention to the current realities in the way of facilities for mass-murder and global destruction do no more than to threaten their enemies with these new and more deadly agencies, while continuing precisely the same methods of popular diplomacy which make it almost certain that, sooner or later, the lethal explosion of a third World War will take place. They do not seem to reckon with what the enemy may also possess in the way of retaliation in kind with respect to the new technology of devastation. Of one thing we may be certain: there is no hope unless popular diplomacy can be shelved or abandoned in favor of diplomatic ideals and methods which are governed by disciplined rationality and are administered by trained experts who can carry out their responsibilities free from the hysterical tyranny of the crowd and its short-sighted leaders.

Anyone who looks at the problem objectively and seriously must quickly recognize that it will take something very close to a miracle to accomplish any such transformation of diplomacy. In the first place, any suggestion along the line of introducing expertness and rationality into any department of government runs up against the democratic bogey and is at once branded as totalitarian or "Fascist," even though the author of the suggestion may have been a lifelong democrat and libertarian. This is especially true of any proposal to make diplomacy expert and confidential. The public will permit a certain amount of expertness to prevail in quiet, drab and technical phases of government, such as administering the national budget, and we can here install trained administrative commissions which can operate without interference by the crowd. Their activities are rarely exciting "news." But it is a different matter with diplomacy, for, in our day, world affairs have come to have greater news value than anything else save physical violence and sexual irregularity.

This has been brought about in part by the sensational methods which popular diplomacy has introduced and which lend themselves admirably to publicity in newspapers, movies, radio, television. This development has, in turn, given the above agencies of communication a powerful vested interest in perpetuating the diplomatic practices which have come to have such great financial value to them. These agencies, which exert so tremendous a power and influence in popular government, would battle to the death against diplomatic reforms that would eliminate most of the current sensational publicity from international relations. This they would do, even though they recognized that the reforms might be the only way of preserving the human race from mass destruction, and that the continuance of popular diplomacy inevitably doomed humanity to extinction.

Since world affairs have not tended to push domestic political and economic problems into the background, the politicians in a democracy have also come to have a predominant vested interest in making international relations the most sensational football of partisan politics. The politicians would resent any proposal to take the political appeal out of diplomacy and have our foreign affairs conducted by trained, appointive experts, operating quietly in their official quarters, without issuing frequent striking news releases or dramatic trips and conferences, top-level or other. Our political leaders have become the victims—the addicts—of popular diplomacy, its spirit and techniques, at least in the countries still outside the Iron Curtain. The politicians, to protect their vested interest in popular diplomacy, would raise a great outcry that democracy was being threatened by any effective reforms in diplomacy, though it is obvious that it would be no more "undemocratic" to operate the state department quietly and efficiently than it is to conduct the treasury department or the department of interior with skill and dignity—which we now do and accept as a matter of course. The naïve democratic dogmas and partisan advantages would be immediately enlisted in the struggle to prevent any rational reform of diplomacy in the direction of expertness, dignity, and confidential operations.

Any proposal to take diplomacy out of the realm of sensational news would meet with special difficulty today, in the period of cold war and hysterical excitement about the loyalty of those in the diplomatic service. No other group of public servants possesses the same news value as diplomats today. Even one disloyal clerk in the foreign office or the state department will get more attention in the news than a loyal foreign minister or secretary of state would normally have received fifty years ago. Rational reforms in diplomacy, which might have been accorded some respectful consideration, even in the press, fifty years ago, would now be assailed with violence and vituperation and probably be smeared as some underhanded trick of Communist origin, even though the main aim of such reforms might be to enable the so-called Free Nations to conduct a more competent diplomatic campaign against any Communist threat to the Free World.

The above brief and restrained statement of the facts of life in our political era today makes it clear why we could state earlier that nothing short of a miracle will enable us to bring about those reforms in diplomatic practice which might prevent popular diplomacy from continuing its fatal trend toward world ruin. But there are other obstacles to rational diplomatic reforms in our age of popular diplomacy and cold war, especially a movement away from anything which can rightfully be called diplomacy at all, and toward an era in which such international relations as exist are limited to ruthless propaganda and hate campaigns, conducted within the borders of great blocs or coalitions of nations, which have no formal diplomatic relations whatever with each other.

There are definite trends in this direction in the actual state of world relationships today, with the increasing hostility between the so-called Free Nations and those behind the Iron Curtain, and the gradual withering away of normal diplomatic contacts between these two great political divisions of humanity. As we have pointed out in earlier pages, the give-and-take procedure in international relations, which was the whole sum and substance of the older diplomacy, has now been all but smeared out of existence as wicked "appeasement," first of the Nazis and now of the Communists. Hence, such of the slight diplomatic relationships as still persist between the two main political groupings of mankind are, in practice, a farce and a hollow sham, since neither side can make any concessions without being charged with moral weakness, and being in danger of losing "face." The forms of diplomacy may still survive, but the reality has all but disappeared among the great political groups, between whom amity must be restored by diplomacy, if there is to be any hope of averting the third World War.

Such are the obvious facts of the world around us. The trends lend all too much support to the prediction of worse things to come in the book by George Orwell, *Nineteen Eighty-four*, to which reference has been made several times previously in the course of this volume. He predicts a world in which diplomacy will be ruled out altogether. There will be three great groups or coalitions of powers: Oceania (the Americas and the British Commonwealth of Nations); Eurasia (the U.S.S.R., Continental Europe, and the Middle East), and Eastasia (China, India, and Malaysia). The three great groups of powers have no diplomatic relations whatever with each other. They are in a state of perpetual phony or cold war with each other: Oceania warring first against Eurasia and then against Eastasia. There is no desire to achieve peace, and the phony war, since the latter is the only way in which the economic order, devoted to depriving the masses of the fruits of our ever more efficient technology, can be maintained. The only attitude cultivated toward other countries is one of intense and unrelieved hatred, developed and maintained by a vast system of propaganda carried on by every known agency of communication, all rigorously controlled by the state. It will be admitted by most candid observers of the world today that there are more symptoms of the onset of a "Nineteen Eighty-four" régime than there are discernible trends toward the rational reform of diplomacy.

Such are the obstacles to the elimination of those diplomatic abuses and defects that have already brought man to the brink of destruction. Some may throw up their hands and protest the utter hopelessness of the situation. A logical response to this might well be that the sooner we recognize the desperate need of reforms and the difficulties in the way of achieving them, the speedier and more determined should be our positive reaction to the challenge to do something while any time still remains.

Since it is expected that criticism be "constructive," I will offer some suggestions along this line of thought. First, however, let me deny the assumption that one cannot render needed and constructive service by merely exposing fatal errors and abuses. That, quite conceivably, may be the most important service of all, even though, by a curious quirk, it has now become the fashion to protest whenever the evils of any system are pointed out. But, what have you to put in its place? is always asked. It may not be necessary to put anything in the place of bad practices. It may be sufficient to abandon them. If a dipsomaniac is urged to stop drinking to save his life or preserve his sanity, it is rather fatuous to tell him to try taking narcotics, chewing gum, or eating candies. He can, if he pleases, take drugs, chew gum or eat candies; it is possible that this substitution of one habit for another will help; but it is no part of the business of the person who warns him of the consequences of his dangerous addiction to teach him how to contract other habits. He must stop drinking—that is the first step.

Now, to be sure, there are drugs that a doctor may recommend to destroy the taste for intoxicants, but they must not be taken as substitutes—they are meant to aid the defective will. The real and only cure is to cease poisoning the body. So with the system of popular diplomacy, whose ravages I have described briefly in these pages. If we are, as nations, to recover from the serious public illness into which we have fallen, the first and last recipe is to stop further indulgence in at least the grosser and more fatal phases of popular diplomacy. Cut out the much advertised conferences, the top-level meetings, the bitter public discussions, the perpetual agitation, the interminable speeches about foreign affairs, the inflammatory newspaper comments, the incessant comings-

and-goings of politicians, the working up of crises. More discretion, decent silence, these are "negative" remedies; but the result will be a "positive" gain in diplomatic health.

Yet, for those who find this a lame conclusion in these days of public excitement, I will indeed venture on some suggestions before I close. They will not be startling but they will, I trust, be sound. For those who insist on "something to put in its place," perhaps I should recommend going to the "pictures," provided the cinema, in its turn, refrains from ministering to the morbid passion of the public for "political" themes. For the rest, who are prepared to consider seriously the follies into which we have fallen, I would once more endeavor to persuade them, for example, that nothing could be more childish than the daily announcements of our military and moral weaknesses—or strength.

On the one hand, we have the Soviet Union, which never tells us how strong or weak it is; it quietly prepares for a possible clash, without frequently informing the world of what it is doing. By accident, we learned that it was making experiments with the atom-bomb, but we know little about its progress in atomic research and armament. By espionage and deduction, we think we know something about the size of the Russian armies, and the armies of its satellites, but the figures given vary greatly. By mere guesswork, we fix dates for the next war, but we are really quite in the dark as to whether Russia really means to launch a new war or not. There are rumors of enormous industrial cities somewhere behind the Urals, but we are ignorant of the capacity and the efficiency of the Soviet factories. Russia does not tell us. Russia may have deliberately led us in error, in order that we may spend more money than we can afford on armament, undermine our economy, lower our standards of living, and thus clear the way for Communism in Western lands. The Russian delegates to U.N. and other assemblies make much hubbub and provoke us into wild retorts, but we cannot be sure whether their only design may be to create a sort of fog-screen, behind which Russia pursues her inscrutable purposes.

On the other hand, we never fail to inform Russia, in parliamentary discourses, in Atlantic Treaty Conferences, in top-level disclosures, precisely what we are doing, how many divisions we shall have ready at a problematic date in the rather distant future. Russia is kept *au courant* of our development of the jet-fighter, of our discoveries of uranium, of the hydrogen plants, and of the progress of our rocket warfare—and I recently read that a detailed map of the atomic stations in the United States was being freely circulated.

The world was told of the consultations of General Eisenhower in Europe, of the decisions that were reached, of the secrets that were no longer secrets. What do we intend to do next? Somebody is always ready to call for full revelations. The U. S. House of Representatives, for example, demanded that President Truman should "tell all" of his conversations with Premier Churchill, after the latter's visit to the United States in 1952. While I deprecate the top-level conversations, which could not possibly accomplish anything that could not have been achieved by less spectacular methods, surely it has come to a pretty pass when private conversations between heads of states must be carried out before a microphone and transmitted by loud-speaker.

I do not pretend to know whether there were important decisions taken, whether the State Department was "vague and evasive" in its communiqués, but it is surely a pity that, as a result of earlier meetings, there should be suspicion of "the shocking kind of agreements reached at Yalta and Potsdam." "Peoples have a right to know what went on behind their backs," cried one Congressman. There are, happily, others who realize that it is crazy, if, for example, uranium deposits were discussed, "to release that kind of information for the benefit of Stalin." "We might as well blazon every understanding on the walls of the world," argued a more sensible Congressman, "and send Stalin a full report. We shall rue the day if we do so. It will come to haunt us later on. We shall be sorry if we establish this precedent."

But we have already, on too many occasions, established the precedent, and we have released all too much information for the benefit of Stalin, with no reciprocation on his part. In recent years we have told our enemies all we are doing. Is this one-sided revelation of "secrets" not lamentable? Is it not partly due to the advertised and belauded perigrinations of peripatetic statesmen? Has there not arisen a paradoxical situation in which, taught by experience, we demand that there should nowadays be no traditional diplomacy at all? Since secret diplomacy becomes open diplomacy, and open diplomacy does not escape the suspicion of secrecy—this is, I repeat, a situation in which there can be no diplomacy at all.

As for the demand that, if I criticize the methods, I should provide the solutions, this confounds two entirely dissimilar subjects. I suggest that there is a better method than that which we have adopted to our grievous damage and that it is by this method that we may arrive at solutions. My contribution is in regard to methods. Not possessing divine wisdom, I have no offer of cut-and-dried solutions of deep-seated problems that have been complicated by the bungling and amateurish improvisations of many years of popular diplomacy.

We must return to the more discreet and competent methods of professional diplomacy. *This is my basic contention.* There should be appropriate privacy and no misleading and mischievous publicity. There should be patient negotiations by competent trained men, who have no need to hurry, no need to achieve striking popular results, no eye fixed on the voters or their electoral bodies, no need to "make the front page."

The close reader will, naturally, remember my seventh chapter, in which I pointed out the defects of professional diplomats. I stand by my description of their inadequacy. But, in large part, their present inadequacy arises from the fact that for many years they have been relegated to the background; they have been handicapped or discouraged in the execution of their tasks by the politician-diplomats. Their functional activities have been repressed; and there has been an atrophy of the diplomatic corps through disuse. Responsibility and initiative have been taken from them, as we have pointed out in an earlier chapter. They have been superseded by presidents, and prime ministers, and secretaries of state, and foreign ministers, all in a hurry. They have become little more than social ornaments and glorified messengers. It is, therefore, not enough merely to restore to them their more important duties. There must be a thorough reform of the diplomatic corps.

Nevertheless, it is in the direction of returning diplomacy to the trained diplomats that we must move. Oddly enough, it was President Franklin D. Roosevelt, unfortunate though his experiments were, who supplied what might develop into a valuable idea. He surrounded himself with a number of "personal representatives," of whom Harry Hopkins was the most conspicuous—in other words, with a body of super-ambassadors. They turned out badly. They were not coördinated with the regular diplomatic corps. They often operated at cross-purposes with it, or they took over the jobs that ought to have been left to the "career-men." The "career-men" counted for less than ever; they became the office-boys of the "personal representatives." At the same time, the regular ambassadorial posts were usually given to men who had no knowledge or training—they were reserved for party followers, as rewards for services rendered in another field, gifts to men who had still an axe to grind on the political grindstone. They had preconceived views, if any at all, and were not trained observers. I have mentioned Joseph Davies who exemplified some of these faults. It would be possible to mention others, but my object is not to discuss persons.

I will, however, recall the World Economic Conference in 1933, from which we expected the most comprehensive arrangements. The regular American representative, Secretary of State Cordell Hull, was in London, where scores of delegates from the principal nations were gathered. Then there came suddenly on the scene the "personal representative" of President Roosevelt. His instructions were quite different from those of the State Department. There was a deadlock. It was essential to the success of the Conference that the real policy of America should be ascertained. The matter was referred back to the President, but the President was out fishing and could not be found. In the end, the Conference broke up, unable to settle anything. A serious step was then taken by default toward the second World War.

These examples would seem to show the undesirable character of the idea of Mr. Roosevelt, and yet it struck me then, as it strikes me now, as containing the germs of a diplomatic system more in consonance with our age. Mr. Roosevelt, for reasons which I need not elaborate here, was not a suitable person to work out the implications of a diplomatic hierarchy. It is a condemnation of the Roosevelt system merely to point out that the title was that of "personal representative"; for it is precisely in order to help remove diplomacy from the "personal" domain that I have written this book.

There have, however, been diplomats, whether called "roving ambassadors" or (rather too grandiloquently) "Wise Men," such as Norman Davis and Hugh Gibson, who have done good work unostentatiously, without undue publicity, whose missions are not synonymous with crises, whose conversations are not recorded, who supplement rather than supersede the routine work of the fixed ambassadors. Their timely intervention, almost unnoticed, has often greased the wheels of international relations.

There is here matter for careful reflection. No experienced diplomat would disagree with me when I observe that, today, diplomacy is not merely an affair between two nations, between the home office and the country to which a representative is assigned. It is more often an affair among five or ten or twenty nations, whose interests are interlocked, or, at any rate, cross at given points. Therefore, the functions of an ambassador sent to a given country are too limited. He should be expected to fulfill them, limited as they are, with far more initiative and responsibility than have lately been accorded him. But, when he has done his utmost, he cannot, in the present system, be more than a go-between of (let us say) Paris and Washington, or Paris and London. He has, so to speak, little personal cognizance of what is going on in Brussels, or Bonn, or Rome. He is accredited to one country, and to one only. Hence has arisen the pretext for the meetings of the foreign ministers which I have deplored on, I think, substantial grounds.

It is clear, if my reasoning is correct, that a super-ambassador, linking up the activities of a number of capitals, having the task of coördinating these activities and shaping multilateral policy in permanent consultation, quite unpublicized, with the ambassadors to a number of nations, is a fatal missing link that should now be supplied. Confidential conferences of expert diplomats would then become a normal method of diplomacy, without the futilities and inconveniences of the transient, sporadic, spectacular, and necessarily inconclusive affairs to which the attention of the newspapers and the public is now fiercely directed.

I do no more than throw out what I consider to be an important suggestion—so important that it would be a pity to spoil it by entering into controversial detail. I especially commend it to the notice of Mr. Eden and Mr. Dulles, or whoever may yet occupy their posts, in order that it may be worked out on practical lines. I think I discern the beginnings of such a coördinating and hierarchical system, but it is as yet only spasmodic and haphazard. No one should be better pleased to escape the constant trips and conferences by the heads of foreign offices than serious foreign ministers who have something more to do than seek the limelight and are well aware of the sometimes disastrous results of snap meetings and snatch declarations.

In broad outline, my proposal is that, in addition to the embassies and legations which now exist, there should be a series of super-embassies, which would interrelate and coördinate the embassies in a certain region, conduct multilateral negotiations in that region, be kept informed of relevant facts in each country and keep the various ambassadors well acquainted with all of these in the region which may modify the purely national viewpoint. These super-embassies should, of course, not overlap or supersede the functions of the ordinary ambassador—on the contrary, I believe they would keep the embassies on their tiptoes, and stimulate their activities. The embassies should be in constant touch with each other through the intermediary of the super-ambassador, and present collective reports, thus simplifying the work of the national foreign office. It would be the duty of the super-ambassador to keep in the closest agreement with his chief, and, when a problem concerned a number of countries, to conduct the multilateral negotiations (accompanied by the various ambassadors) with the heads of the countries concerned.

Is it not strange that, in an age when the interdependence of the world is recognized as a physical and moral fact, an obsolete type of diplomatic organization and administration dating from the Renaissance, continues to operate? There are, indeed, in the Foreign Office, departments and sections concerned with this or that region of the world, but representation abroad is confined to countries regarded as separate entities, virtually without connection with the rest of the region. The need of a wider scope for ambassadorial duties is surely self-evident, but the machinery remains unchanged from the epoch in which a nation could deal one by one with foreign nations. Moreover, the service has been weakened by the ill-advised substitution of ministerial conferences for the true functions of the ambassadors, and the ambassadors, relieved from their real responsibilities, have now become the bed-makers and chambermaids of ministers.

In every other branch of human effort, notably in industry, there have been radical reforms, and there is not a large business concern with international ramifications that has not a network of intertwining representatives, not merely connected with the head office, but through a whole hierarchy of regional representatives joined one with another. No agent works in isolation. Only diplomacy remains with a machine obviously outmoded. The improvisations such as "special" or "personal" or "traveling" ambassadors, on the one hand, and the frequent conversations of two or three or ten foreign ministers, on the other hand, not only fail to remedy the defects; they discourage whatever remains of the better aspects of the spirit of the old diplomacy, while producing on the public mind the regrettable impression of ever recurring crises.

If it is urged that the U.N. provides the proper meeting-ground, I deny the contention. In so far as the U.N. provides machinery for world organization of indispensable global services, it is admirable; but, in so far as it provides a talking-platform on world policy for vituperation by disputatious diplomats it is detestable. No matter how much improved, it cannot ever take the place of the well organized and closely interrelated diplomatic system, which is now lacking. The

U.N., as it is today, is the negation of diplomacy; diplomacy implies quiet and careful study of problems which interest two or twenty nations, by authorized representatives in unobtrusive conclave or, better still, in *tête-à-tête* talks, without attracting the attention of the public, without loud launching of defiances, without arousing antagonistic national sentiments which are fatal to any agreement. The U.N., in its controversial and political aspect, is precisely the opposite of a diplomatic organization. So long as it promotes billingsgate in international discussions, it will infallibly wreck the efforts of diplomacy to arrive at an accord on any matter on which there is a serious difference of opinion.

I would lay it down as axiomatic that the best foreign minister or secretary of state, is he who is least heard, and that the worst is he who "makes the headlines" most often. I would lay it down as axiomatic that the best foreign policy is that which is most inconspicuous, and the worst is that which allows itself to be subjected daily to violent debate.

It follows that the best foreign minister is he who aims not at the public and noisy arraignment of countries other than his own, but at the tranquil and untroubled adjustment of rival claims; and, accordingly, he who has at his disposal the most appropriate machinery to achieve this end. The foreign minister who would make it his first task to reform those aspects of his diplomatic services which are not well conceived in the present condition of international relations, is he who would deserve the highest praise. He might not immediately reap such praise—it is far easier to go abroad, make inconsiderate speeches on some international forum, or encounter his "opposite number" in a foreign capital, and then return home with a triumphant *communiqué*, directed against a third party. It is easier for him, if he desires immediate applause, to do these fatuous things than to reorganize the machinery upon which he must depend if he is to work effectively. Reorganization on the lines I have suggested is, one must admit, utterly opposed to the current of popular thinking, to popular diplomacy; and for this task a bold man is required, who is not content to float with the stream to our final destruction.

It should not be impossible to find such a man. He would earn the gratitude of unborn generations. He would have rendered services to mankind incomparably greater than those he now tries to render in flying hither and thither in a vain attempt, either by public discussion or secret debate, to force the hands of his adversaries.

The restoration of the individual ambassadors and their staffs, which have, in my own time sadly degenerated, to their rightful rank, their proper importance, is part of the task of such a foreign minister. A diplomatic writer, Delisle Burns, declared many years ago, as I have pointed out in this book, that "the telegraph and the telephone [he might have added, the constant personal interference of ministers and international assemblies] have reduced Embassies to post-offices. An Ambassador . . . has not the responsibility or power of a diplomat in former days."

Burns notes, too, that the training of diplomats is defective. They are mostly men who belong to a certain class, often without knowledge of industry or commerce, who do not understand the life of the common people of even their own country, and certainly do not trouble to learn the life of the common people of the country to which they are accredited. They have not made the vital distinction between the "legal" and the "real" nation, which is often immense. They gravitate in official and social circles, with occasional visits to fashionable cabarets or state theaters. They have been taught the smallest of small talk. They are good diners-out. Now, assuredly, these are not adequate qualifications for the successful diplomat. If he is to be the vital cog in the international machine that he should be, the whole conditions of his recruitment must be altered, and more suitable types of men chosen. It has happened in my experience that the principal ambition of many "career-men" has been to accumulate as many decorations as possible from foreign governments and to measure their success by these marks of appreciation.[1] I do not demur; their job is to be on good terms with the government; but diplomacy is something more than the possession of excellent manners and good social qualities.

Let us then strive to reverse the movement that has diminished the rôle of the diplomat. Let us try to give him his essential place. We can help in this by the simple process of reducing the rovings of ministers, by abolishing public platforms for delegates to denounce each other, and so rid ourselves of the acrimony that has poisoned public life and made international problems all but insoluble. The diplomat may still come into his own: *first* by a better choice of men destined for the diplomatic service, *second* by the appointment of regional ambassadors, *third* by the thorough overhauling of the diplomatic branch of the public service on which the issues of peace and war may depend, and *fourth* by the refusal of the top-levels to stir, for the sake of a little dangerous applause, from the desks where their real work must be done. We have had more than enough of popular diplomacy; it is time we had sound diplomacy.

I would quote here the words of Harold Nicolson, whose experience of diplomacy is unquestionable. In his book *Peacemaking*, he says:

---

[1] In this connection, I am bound to say that journalists are equally to blame. In my day as a diplomatic correspondent in France, many newspaper men considered that they were honored by the acceptance of decorations. Few of us—I can think only of two or three besides myself—refused the Legion of Honor; most were proud of the "ribbon to stick in their coat." It has always seemed to me incompatible with the functions of a correspondent to be under any kind of obligation to a foreign government.

The main problem is that of adjusting the emotions of the masses to the thoughts of the rulers. [He assumes that the rulers have thoughts, and that they are right thoughts.] What the statesman thinks today the masses will feel tomorrow. Yet the time-lag between the emotions of the masses and the thoughts of the statesman is a most disadvantageous factor. The attempt to bridge the gulf between mass emotion and expert reason leads, at its worst, to actual falsity, and, at its best, to grave imprecision. The essential to good diplomacy is precision. The main enemy of good diplomacy is imprecision. The old diplomacy may have possessed grave faults, but they were venial in comparison with the menaces which confront democratic diplomacy. Amateurishness leads to imprecision. No statesman, in advance, and in the open, is prepared to bind himself to a particular policy. [Though this is generally true, the tendency is to throw discretion to the winds and to bind policy to the emotions of the masses.] An imprecise policy means no policy at all. It means aspiration only. [And often vituperation.]

The relinquishment of the methods that have failed, the abandonment of the public international platforms that have been so plentifully provided for electioneering and propagandist discourses, a self-denying ordinance for politicians and for the press, prone to "make capital" out of the tragedy of the universe, and the rehabilitation of the old professional diplomacy, though with a *complete* reorganization of its *personnel* and machinery—in these things and in these things alone lies our hope of salvation, in handling problems of world affairs.

Accompanying the sordid abuse of each other by political parties within each nation, and of foreign countries by other foreign countries, there has been a nauseating employment of pious hopes, of vague ideals, of sonorous pronouncement of empty words. Scurrility and idealism will not mix. Neither will ignorant idealism and informal realism blend. There is nothing that popular diplomacy likes more than to be served with indigestible dishes of scurrility and idealism, nothing that it dislikes more than a healthy dose of realism. But realism we must have, and not superficial sentiments served up with a sauce of hatred.

The old virtues of the diplomat were his rejection of personal prejudices, his aloofness from political parties, his suavity, his resolve not to create unnecessary incidents or to provoke needless crises, his horror of vehemence, his unsusceptibility to considerations of *amour-propre*, and his ability to carry on conversations as long as necessary to arrive at a compromise, without interrupting them to hold up the half-achieved results prematurely to the public for mass approbation or disapprobation.

The diplomatic machinery is now antiquated; it relies on the mere outward forms of a dead tradition; it has been emptied of its contents by tub-thumpers. But it can be revived, it can be modernized to meet the needs of the modern world. Many of our troubles would vanish overnight if we ceased to talk of them constantly; and it is the business of sound diplomacy to talk as little as possible of our troubles. Can we not safely place our problems of foreign policy in expert hands without thereby foregoing the ultimate popular control of international affairs.

We are none the less democrats because we do not perpetually interfere with the captain to whom we have entrusted the ship. We recognize the simple truth that any technical operation must be confided to tried and trained men. It is only in regard to matters of which we can know little or nothing, but on which may turn our whole destiny, the destiny of our generation, of generations unborn, of our country, of the world, that we ourselves propose, by our absurd pretense to popular diplomacy, to take charge of the machinery, amid contradictory clamors.

Back, then, to real diplomacy, with modern methods, with a modernized diplomatic corps, in the world of grim reality, if we would not be involved, with all our fortunes, in the fall of all diplomacy and with it of orderly civilization.

INDEX

CPSIA information can be obtained
at www.ICGtesting.com
Printed in the USA
LVHW082228111219
639936LV00041B/771/P